James B. Angell
From his Friend,
R. P. Dunn
April 9th 188

Germany;

ITS

UNIVERSITIES, THEOLOGY, AND RELIGION.

Dr. Neander

Page 270.

GERMANY;

ITS

Universities, Theology, and Religion;

WITH SKETCHES OF

NEANDER, THOLUCK, OLSHAUSEN, HENGSTENBERG, TWESTEN,
NITZSCH, MULLER, ULLMANN, ROTHE, DORNER,
LANGE, EBRARD, WICHERN,

AND OTHER

DISTINGUISHED GERMAN DIVINES OF THE AGE.

BY

PHILIP SCHAFF, D. D.,

PROFESSOR IN THE THEOLOGICAL SEMINARY, MERCERSBURG, PENNSYLVANIA.

PHILADELPHIA:
LINDSAY AND BLAKISTON.
NEW YORK:
SHELDON, BLAKEMAN & CO.
1857.

HENRY B. ASHMEAD, BOOK AND JOB PRINTER,
George Street above Eleventh.

TO THE ALUMNI

OF

FRANKLIN AND MARSHALL COLLEGE,

AND OF

The Theological Seminary at Mercersburg,

THIS BOOK IS AFFECTIONATELY DEDICATED, IN REMEMBRANCE OF TWELVE YEARS OF PLEASANT AND PROFITABLE INTERCOURSE DURING THE MOST INTERESTING PERIOD IN THE HISTORY OF THEIR LITERARY AND THEOLOGICAL ALMA MATER,

BY

THEIR TEACHER AND FRIEND,

P. S.

PREFACE.

"Providence has given to the French the empire of the land; to the English, that of the sea; to the Germans, that of the air." By this famous saying, Jean Paul, himself a denizen of the air, intended to proclaim the strength, as well as the weakness, of his native country; and those critics who, in good or ill humor, quote it to the disparagement of the Germans, seem to forget that the air is the habitation of the warbling nightingale, and the soaring eagle, and is as necessary and useful to man, as the land, and the sea.

Defined neither by political nor natural boundaries; divided into thirty-eight sovereign kingdoms, grand duchies, duchies, electorates, principalities, and free cities; including all forms of government from the absolute monarchy of Austria, to the republicanism of Hamburg and Bremen; embracing a still greater variety of tribes, dialects, customs, and opinions; and almost equally balanced between the conflicting interests of Romanism and Protestantism: Germany, with all her numerical strength, is destitute of that compact national unity and imposing political power, which characterizes France and Great Britain. But, situated as she is, in the heart of Europe, she furnishes, at least to a great extent, the heart's blood, the ideas and principles, of modern history, and takes the lead in the intellectual mastery of the world. As, in times past, she invented the printing-press, and produced the Reformation, the two principal levers of modern civilization and Christianity, so she excels, at the present day, in every department of science and art; and these are, after all, next to virtue and religion, the noblest pursuits, and the highest ornaments, of immortal man.

The Universities of Germany are regarded by competent judges, as the first among the learned institutions of the world. The modern literature of that country hardly yields to any other in depth, variety, and interest. It cannot be denied that in its original form as well as in multiplying translations, imitations, and more independent works, it has become already a power for both good and evil in England, and the United States, as irresistible as the current of a mighty river. The German theology of the last thirty or forty years, whatever be its errors and defects, its extravagances and follies, which we would be among the last to deny, or to defend, is, upon the whole, the most learned, original, fertile, and progressive theology of the age, and no active branch of Protestantism can keep entirely aloof from its contact without injuring its own interests.

America will no doubt produce, in due time, a classical theology of its own, that shall rise superior to the sectional and denominational schools, which so far have mostly prevailed amongst us, and be truly catholic in spirit, and influence. That theology, if we are to judge from the extensive preparations now going on, among Congregationalists, Presbyterians, Episcopalians, Methodists, Baptists, Lutherans, German Reformed, and other denominations of the land, will not be simply a continuation of either the English, or the German alone, but the result of the combined action and reaction of both, as applied to the peculiar wants and condition of American Christianity and society.

But in order that the modern evangelical theology of Germany may become properly available for the benefit of the cognate Anglo-Saxon race, it must first be better and more generally understood, and placed in its proper light against both ignorant and malevolent censure, and indiscriminate praise. The growing interest in it seems to call for a work, which should furnish reliable and satisfactory information of its origin, history, connections and bearings, and thus serve as a guide to the English and American student through the luxuriant forest of Teutonic systems and opinions.

To such a task the writer brings the advantages of a regular German university education, some experience as a university teacher, and an American residence, sufficiently long to enable him to understand the relations of German and Anglo-Saxon Christianity and literature, and to view the old world from the standpoint of the new. With all the divines described, in the third part of this book, except the late Dr. Olshausen, he is acquainted not only through their works, but also by more or less intimate personal intercourse, lately renewed, during a protracted and delightful visit to Germany. Some of them were his honored teachers at Tübingen, Halle, and Berlin; others his fellow-students, or colleagues; and with many of them he still keeps up a familiar correspondence. In occasionally introducing personal incidents, and harmless traits of character, not before made known to the reading public, he hopes he has in no case violated the strictest laws of propriety and delicacy, which are doubly binding when we treat of persons still living. He could easily have increased the number of sketches from personal knowledge; but he preferred to dwell more at length on the most worthy, characteristic, and influential representatives of the evangelical theology and Christianity of modern Protestant Germany.

The writer has endeavored to make his book both instructive, and interesting to the general, as well as the learned reader. But he must ask the kind indulgence of English scholars for the unconscious Germanisms, and other defects of style, as this is the first time that he ventures before the public, in a work of such size, without the aid of a translator.

That this volume may contribute its humble share, toward bringing the German and American mind into closer union and friendly coöperation for the advancement of sound Christian literature, theology, and religion, is the hope, and will be the best reward, of

THE AUTHOR.

Mercersburg, *Pennsylvania*, *Feb.* 26, 1857.

TABLE OF CONTENTS.

FIRST PART.

GERMAN UNIVERSITIES.

CHAPTER I.

THE UNIVERSITIES OF GERMANY.

CHAPTER II.

THE FACULTIES.

CHAPTER III.

THE PROFESSORS.

CHAPTER IV.

THE STUDENTS.

CHAPTER V.

UNIVERSITY REFORM.

CHAPTER VI.

BERLIN.

CHAPTER VII.

HALLE AND BONN.

CHAPTER VIII.

GOTTINGEN AND LEIPSIC.

CHAPTER IX.

JENA AND THE BURSCHENSCHAFT.

CHAPTER X.

HEIDELBERG AND TUBINGEN.

SECOND PART.

GERMAN THEOLOGY AND RELIGION.

CHAPTER XI.

CHURCH AND STATE IN GERMANY.

CHAPTER XII.

THE CONFLICT FOR RELIGIOUS FREEDOM.

CHAPTER XIII.

THE ESTABLISHED CHURCHES.

CHAPTER XIV.

THE DISSENTING SECTS.

CHAPTER XV.

THE SKEPTICAL ERA OF GERMANY.

CHAPTER XVI.

THE REVIVAL OF EVANGELICAL THEOLOGY AND PIETY.

CHAPTER XVII.

THE CONFLICT OF CHRISTIANITY WITH THE LATEST FORMS OF INFIDELITY.

CHAPTER XXII.

HISTORY AND RESULTS OF THE CHURCH DIET.

CHAPTER XXIII.

THEOLOGICAL SCHOOLS AND CHURCH PARTIES.

CHAPTER XXIV.

THEOLOGICAL SCHOOLS AND CHURCH PARTIES, CONCLUDED.

THIRD PART.

SKETCHES OF GERMAN DIVINES.

CHAPTER XXV.

NEANDER.

CHAPTER XXVI.

THOLUCK.

CHAPTER XXVII.

OLSHAUSEN.

CHAPTER XXVIII.

HENGSTENBERG.

CHAPTER XXIX.

TWESTEN.

CHAPTER XXX.

NITZSCH.

CHAPTER XXXI.

JULIUS MULLER.

CHAPTER XXXII.

ULLMANN.

CHAPTER XXXIII.

ROTHE.

CHAPTER XXXIV.

DORNER.

CHAPTER XXXV.

LANGE.

CHAPTER XXXVI.

EBRARD.

CHAPTER XXXVII.

HUNDESHAGEN, SCHENKEL, HAGENBACH, HERZOG.

CHAPTER XXXVIII.

WICHERN.

FIRST PART.

GERMAN UNIVERSITIES.

CHAPTER I.

THE UNIVERSITIES OF GERMANY.

Their General Character and Importance—Judgment of Sir William Hamilton and Dr. Tappan—List of the German Universities—Their Denominational Character—Their Founders—Their Support.

THE Universities are the pride and glory of Germany. They exert more influence there than similar institutions in any other country. They are the centres of the higher intellectual and literary life of the nation, and the laboratories of new systems of thought and theories of action. They reflect a picture of the whole world of nature and of mind under its ideal form. They develop the talents and form the principles of nearly all who fill the places of power and influence in church and state, from the village pastor to the "Oberconsistorialrath"—from the advocate at the bar to the head of the cabinet. They receive the best minds, from the lowest as well as the highest ranks, to mould them for the learned professions, and fit them for public usefulness. From them emanate principally the ideas and maxims which rule the land, either in the service of the existing order of things, or in the interest of progress. It is characteristic that the Reformation in Germany proceeded, not from princes and bishops, as in England, but from theological professors. The great philosophical and theological revolution of the last century, and the counter revolution of the present century, have likewise proceeded mainly from the studies and lecture rooms of academic teachers.

Such a supremacy of literary institutions and literary men has its disadvantages as well as its advantages, and would not be possible in a country like England or the United States, where politics and commerce occupy so important a position, and engage in their service a large proportion of the best talent and energy of the nation. But in Germany it is closely connected with the genius, history and condition of the people, and no one can form a correct idea of its higher and deeper life without a knowledge of its universities. Each nation has its peculiar mission and excellency. Ancient Israel was elected to prepare the true religion for the world; Greece had to develop the principles of science and art; Rome was chosen to actualize the idea of law and civil government. So in our times the chief significance of Germany lies neither in politics, nor in war, nor in commerce, but in science and literature.

The German universities exert also a powerful influence upon other countries. Situated in the heart of Europe, and visited by strangers from all quarters of the globe, they are the firmest anchors of general learning and literature, and amongst the principal strongholds of modern European and American culture under its highest aspect.

The late Sir William Hamilton, in his review of Cousin's celebrated report on the Prussian system of education, truly remarks: "The institutions of Germany for public instruction we have long known and admired. We saw these institutions accomplishing their end to an extent and in a degree elsewhere unexampled; and were convinced that if other nations attempted an improvement of their educational policy, this could only be accomplished rapidly, surely and effectually, by adopting, as far as circumstances would permit, a system thus improved by an extensive experience and the most memorable success." Dr. Tappan, Chancellor of the University of Michigan, responds to this favorable judgment of the distinguished French, and the equally distinguished Scotch philosopher, and holds up especially the universities of Germany as the most perfect educational establishments in the world.

The following is a list of all the German universities in the chronological order of their foundation. We exclude those of German Switzerland, (Basel, Zürich, Berne;) the Alsace of France, (Strasburg;) and the Baltic provinces of Russia, (Dorpat,) which are likewise German in language and spirit, but not in a political or geographical sense:

(A.) *From the Fourteenth Century.*

1. Prague, founded A. D. 1348, Roman Catholic.
2. Vienna, 1365, Roman Catholic, (but including now also a Protestant Theological Faculty.)
3. Heidelberg, 1386, Protestant, (Evangelical.)
4. Cologne, 1388, Roman Catholic, (abolished.)
5. Erfurt, 1392, Mixed, (abolished in 1816.)

(B.) *From the Fifteenth Century.*

6. Leipsic, founded 1409, Protestant, (Lutheran.)

7. Rostock, 1419, Protestant, (Lutheran.)
8. Greifswalde, 1456, Protestant, (Evangelical.)
9. Freiburg, 1457, Roman Catholic.
10. Ingolstadt, 1472 Roman Catholic, (transferred to Landshut in 1802, and from thence to Munich in 1826.)
11. Tübingen, 1477, Mixed.
12. Mayence, 1477, Roman Catholic, (now reduced to a Theological Seminary.)

(C.) *From the Sixteenth Century.*

13. Wittenberg, founded 1502, Protestant, (Lutheran, transferred to Halle in 1817, and now reduced to an Evangelical Seminary for candidates of the ministry, who have finished their University course.)
14. Frankfort-on-the-Oder, 1506, (transferred to Breslau in 1811,) Mixed.
15. Marburg, 1527, Protestant, (Evangelical.)
16. Königsberg, 1544, Protestant, (Evangelical.)
17. Dillingin, 1549, Roman Catholic, abolished in 1802.
18. Jena, 1558, Protestant, (Lutheran.)
19. Helmstädt, 1576, Protestant, (abolished in 1809.)
20. Altdorf, 1578, Protestant, (abolished in 1807.)
21. Olmütz, 1581, Roman Catholic.
22. Würzburg, 1582, Roman Catholic.
23. Gratz, 1586, Roman Catholic.

(D.) *From the Seventeenth Century.*

24. Giessen, founded 1607, Mixed.
25. Paderborn, 1615, Roman Catholic, (reduced to a Seminary.)

26. Rinteln, 1621, Protestant, (abolished 1809.)
27. Salzburg, 1623, Roman Catholic.
28. Osnabrück, 1630, (abolished.)
29. Linz, 1636, Roman Catholic, (reduced to a College and Seminary.)
30. Bamberg, 1648, Roman Catholic, (reduced to a College in 1803.)
31. Herborn, 1654, Protestant, (reduced to a Theological Seminary.)
32. Duisburg, 1655, Reformed, (abolished in 1804.)
33. Kiel, 1665, Protestant, (Lutheran.)
34. Innsbruck, 1672, Roman Catholic.
35. Halle, 1694, Protestant, (Evangelical.)

(E.) *From the Eighteenth Century.*

36. Breslau, founded 1702, Mixed.
37. Göttingen, 1737, Protestant, (Lutheran.)
38. Erlangen, 1743, Protestant, (Lutheran and Reformed.)

(F.) *From the Nineteenth Century.*

39. Berlin, founded 1810, Protestant, (Evangelical.)
40. Bonn, 1818, Mixed.
41. Munich, 1826, Roman Catholic.

Deducting those institutions which have been either entirely abolished or reduced to mere Colleges and Theological Seminaries, we have twenty-six Universities left for the entire German Confederation. Of these six belong to the Kingdom of Prussia, (Berlin, Halle, Bonn, Königsberg, Greifswalde, to which may be added the Roman Catholic High School of Münster;) six to the

Empire of Austria, (Vienna, Prague, Olmütz, Gratz, Salzburg, Innsbruck;) three to the Kingdom of Bavaria, (Munich, Erlangen, Würzburg;) two to the Grand Duchy of Baden, (Heidelberg and Freiburg;) one to the Kingdom of Würtemberg, (Tübingen;) one to the Kingdom of Saxony, (Leipsic;) the rest to the smaller principalities.

As regards religion, eight are exclusively under the influence of the Roman Catholic Church, thirteeen belong to the Protestant Church, and five to both denominations, having a double theological faculty. The Roman Catholic Universities, especially those of Austria, are greatly behind the Protestant in learning and efficiency. Olmütz, Salzburg and Innsbruck are incomplete.

The Protestant Universities, are again, either Lutheran, or Evangelical, *i. e.*, devoted to the union of the Reformed and Lutheran Churches. All the Prussian Universities, except Münster, which is not complete, belong to the latter description. Exclusively Reformed Universities there are none in Germany proper. But the Swiss Universities of Basel, Zürich and Berne, are all German Reformed. The Dutch Universities of Utrecht, Leyden and Groningen, which differ little from the German, are likewise Reformed.

The German Universities were founded by emperors, princes, or ecclesiastical dignitaries; in a few cases, as in Cologne, Erfurt and Strasburg, by the magistrates of the cities. The motives which prompted these great establishments, were without exception, pure and elevated, and generally pious and Christian. The founders wished to promote thereby science and virtue, knowledge and wisdom, the glory of God and the happiness of man.

In the middle ages, the Pope as the spiritual head of the Christian nations of Europe, gave the charter and conferred the academic privileges upon the new institution. He also elected the first chancellor. Since the Reformation, of course, the papal sanction is confined to strictly Roman Catholic institutions, or has ceased entirely. The Protestant Universities, which date from the sixteenth and seventeenth centuries, were founded by the authority of the emperor; but since the dissolution of the German Empire, every sovereign can establish such an institution in his own name. Berlin, Bonn, and Munich, have neither papal nor imperial sanction, but owe their origin simply to the kings of Prussia and Bavaria, and yet they stand in the foremost rank of universities.

The support of these institutions is derived from princely, or private donations in money, or real estate, from tithes, and from annual appropriations of the government. The Popes frequently transferred to them the proceeds of a part of the church property. At the time of the Reformation, the wealth of the secularized abbeys, and since 1773, the funds of the Order of Jesuits, were to a considerable extent devoted to the same purpose. Besides, the universities are generally exempted from taxation, and enjoy other temporal advantages. The tuition forms the least source of income. The students have to pay, besides the matriculation fee, a certain sum (from $2 to $10,) for each course of lectures, to the treasurer, for the benefit of the teachers; but the latter receive their principal support from a fixed salary paid by the state. This varies from a few hundred to several thousand dollars, according to the age, merit and reputation of the professor.

CHAPTER II.

THE FOUR FACULTIES.

General Organization of the German Universities—Difference from the American Colleges, and the English Universities—The Theological Faculty—The Philosophical Faculty—The Faculty of Jurisprudence—The Faculty of Medicine—The Academic Degrees.

THE organization of the European universities is derived from that of Paris, the oldest among them (founded in the twelfth century,) and was originally of a double kind; national and literary. They were divided into four, or as many more nations, as were represented in the body of teachers and pupils; and into four faculties, a term which signifies both the professors devoted to a particular science, and the sciences themselves.

The former division has been long since abolished; the latter remains. Each faculty has its dean, who is elected annually from the professors, who constitute it. At the head of the whole academic body stands the rector, or the chancellor, who is likewise chosen for one year, from the regular professors of the various faculties in turn, and entrusted with the care of government and administration, according to the statutes or constitution. The legislative power resides in the academical senate, which is composed of all or a delegated part of the ordinary professors of the four faculties.

A university is thus a complete republic of letters, with an organization of its own, and enjoys, with the exception of Austria, a high degree of independence upon the church and the state, although it serves the interests of both by furnishing to them ministers, lawyers, physicians, and all the higher officers.

The academic liberty both intellectual, moral, and personal, the liberty of the professors to teach, and of the students to learn, without any restraint from without, is regarded as one of the highest privileges of a German University.

The four faculties embrace all the divine and human sciences, and make up the idea of a university; a term which as Savigny has shown, was first applied to the body of teachers and pupils, (*Universitas Scholarium,*) but is now understood mainly of the totality of letters, (*Universitas Literarum,*) and the completeness of the system of instruction.

Hence such an institution is something very different from an American College. Our colleges claim and exercise, indeed, the academic privilege of conferring all the literary degrees; but in their studies and organization they correspond rather to the German Gymnasia, or Lycea, which are simply preparatory schools for the professional studies of the University. The institutions of Cambridge, New Haven, and Charlottesville approach nearer the European idea, since they have a legal, medical, and, with the exception of Charlottesville, also a theological school in addition to the literary or classical department. But the latter forms the proper body of these institutions, and the law school and medical school—the philosophical faculty is wanting altogether—are simply an appendage to it; while on the Continent of Europe the professional studies constitute the university education, and are pursued on a far more extensive scale, and on the basis of an already finished college course. Our colleges are built upon the English plan, which differs considerably from the Scotch and the Continental. For Oxford and Cambridge are simply a confederation of colleges, in which the tutorial system rules, and the lecture system with the professional studies is made subordinate, although the recent reforms have given them a little more prominence.

We now proceed to a separate notice of the four professional schools, which belong to a German university.

1. The *theological* faculty still has the supremacy of honor, since at the time when the most of the universities were founded, theology was emphatically the queen of sciences, to which all the others were contributary. The great institution of Paris was at first simply a theological and philosophical school; the philosophical studies served as a preparation to scholastic divinity, and the philosophical professors were all divines and ecclesiastics.

In the middle ages theology was confined to the interpretation of the Latin Bible on the basis of the *Catenæ Patrum*, and to scholastic dogmatics and ethics, under the guidance of the Sentences of Peter the Lombard, called the "*Magister Sententiarum.*"

In modern times, the field has been greatly enlarged by the addition of oriental philology, biblical criticism, hermeneutics, antiquities, church history and doctrine history, homiletics, catechetics, liturgics, pastoral theology and theory of church government. No theological faculty is considered complete now, which has not separate teachers for the exegetical, historical, systematic, and practical branches of divinity. The German professors, however, are not confined to their respective departments, as is the case in our American seminaries, but may deliver lectures on any other branch, as far as it does not interfere with their immediate duties. Schleiermacher, for instance, taught at different times almost every branch of theology and philosophy.

2. The *philosophical* faculty is by far the most comprehensive as to the number of teachers and the subjects of instruction, and embraces many branches, which have nothing or very little to do with philosophy proper, as history, ancient and modern languages, mathematics, belles letters. It was formerly called the faculty of arts, (*facultas artium liberalium,*) hence the terms, Bachelor and Master of Arts, still in use in England and America. In the middle ages all human sciences as distinct from theology, were divided into seven *artes liberales*, viz., grammar, rhetoric, dialectic, arithmetic, music, geometry and astronomy, and expressed by the following versus memorialis:

"Lingua, tropus, ratio, numerus, tenor, angulus, astra."

The first three constituted the *Trivium*, the remaining four the *Quadrivium* of the academical course. The principal text-books in these departments were the dialectical, ethical and physical works of Aristotle, until the Reformation, and the philosophy of Bacon and Cartesius deposed the great Stagirite from his long reign in the temple of science.

Since that time the historical, philological, and natural sciences have made such immense progress, that the philosophical department might easily be divided into three or four separate faculties. This would be done, too, no doubt, if the universities were organized now in keeping with the actual state of science. The University of Paris has five faculties, the philosophical department being divided into the *faculté des sciences*, and the *faculté des lettres*.

The philosophical study, properly so called, includes logic, metaphysics, philosophy of nature, anthropology and psychology, philosophy of law or political ethics, philosophy of history, philosophy of art or æsthetics, moral philosophy, philosophy of religion, and history of philosophy.

3. The faculty of *law*, (*facultas juris canonici et civilis*) embraces in Germany a greater variety of studies, especially also the history of civil, criminal, and common law, the exposition of the ancient Roman code, and the Canon law, than our law schools which are almost exclusively concerned with the common law of England and the laws of our own country, but which are perhaps better calculated on the other hand, in connection with the many opportunities for public speaking, and our republican institutions, to prepare for the exercise of the profession at the bar, and for practical statesmanship. The oldest law school was founded at Bologna and served as a model for the others.

4. The faculty of *medicine* comprehends chemistry,

physiology, anatomy, phrenology, pathology, and similar sciences, which are taught also in all our regular medical colleges. The universities of Berlin, Munich and Vienna enjoy, next to Paris, the greatest reputation in this line, since they have all those facilities of large hospitals and extensive collections, which can only be found in populous cities.

The academical *degrees* originated likewise in the middle ages. They seem to have been used first in the law school of Bologna towards the end of the twelfth century, and were then further developed in Paris. The title Doctor appears already before that time, as also that of Magister and Dominus, to signify the office of teacher, but not a special dignity. It was then probably applied in an emphatic sense to the most eminent professors, and so passed over into its technical meaning. There were formerly three academic degrees for each faculty, that of the bachelor, (*baccalaureus*, or *baccalareus*, of doubtful origin, either from *bacca laurea*, or from the *baculus*, which the graduate received as a sign of honor, or from the French *bachelier*,) licentiate, and doctor. They looked originally to public teaching and marked as many steps in the promotion to this office.

In England the bachelor's degree is still retained for the liberal arts, the law and divinity. In Germany the lower degrees have gone out of use, except for divinity, but the doctorship remains for each faculty. It may be acquired after the completion of the prescribed course of professional studies, by a special examination, printed dissertation or book, and public disputation conducted in Latin, and connected with considerable expense.

The diploma of Doctor of Philosophy, however, which corresponds somewhat to our Master of Arts, and also that of Doctor of Medicine, can be more easily secured at least from several smaller universities.

Some years ago complaint was entered at the Diet of Frankfort, against the traffic with the lower diplomas, which brings them into disrepute, and effectual measures were taken to compel the governments of the lesser German States to check it. The Prussian Universities adhere very scrupulously to the condition of a rigorous examination, and public disputation, and never bestow a degree *honoris causa,* without sufficient reason.

In theology there are still two degrees, that of the Licentiate (corresponding to the English Bachelor of Divinity,) which confers the right of public teaching in the university, and that of D. D. The latter is considered the highest academic honor, and hence much rarer than the doctor's diploma of any other faculty. It may be acquired by the regular process of a written work and Latin debate, in which every member of the university can enter the lists against the published theses of the candidate; but it is now generally given *honoris causa* as an acknowledgment of distinguished literary merit, or eminent usefulness in the church.

4*

CHAPTER III.

THE GERMAN PROFESSORS.

Ordinary Professors—Extraordinary Professors—Privat-docenten—Mode of Instruction—The Lecture System, its Merits and Defects—The True System.

WE must now introduce the reader into the active operation and life of the German universities, and point out their peculiar excellences and defects. We commence with the professors who direct and animate these institutions.

There are three classes of teachers in the universities of Germany.

1. The *ordinary* professors, who are regular members of the faculty, receive a full support from the State independent of the proceeds of their lectures, and can be elected to the academical senate and the rectorship.

2. The *extraordinary* professors have no seat in the faculty, nor in the senate, and a smaller income, but are generally promoted to a regular professorship, when a vacancy occurs. Not a few, however, remain in this subordinate condition for life.

3. The *private lecturers*, (*privatim docentes*,) who have passed through the *examen rigorosum*, deliver lectures like the regular professors, but are without

appointment, and receive, with a few exceptions, no salary from the State. They depend, therefore, for their support upon the lecture-fees of their hearers, or upon private tuition, or extra literary labor. Unless they have means of their own, or eminent popular talents, which attract the students by crowds, and which secure to them sometimes a special appropriation from the Minister of Public Instruction, they drag out a very hard and unenviable existence. I know of *Privat-docenten*, who spent ten and fifteen years in this literary purgatory, anxiously waiting for a call, laboring day and night, and forced to resort to proof-reading and other mechanical work, to keep themselves from literal starvation. The difficulty is increased in larger universities, where they have to compete with the most celebrated names in all departments of science. Not a few, with all their talents, learning and industry, are compelled at last, to quit the academical career in despair, while others are so fortunate as to be promoted to a professorship after only one or two years' probation.

Most of the professors have to pass through these preparatory stages, until they reach the honor and benefit of a regular or ordinary professorship. Some few, however, are called directly from the ranks of the ministry, or practising lawyers and physicians, if they distinguish themselves by learned contributions to the science of their profession.

The number of teachers varies from thirty to a hundred and fifty, or more, according to the wealth and extent of the institution. Thus in the year 1853, the university of Berlin numbered no less than 168 teachers, (52 ordinary, 41 extraordinary, 7 honorary professors, 60 privatim docentes, and 8 teachers of languages,) the university of Vienna 116, Göttingen 109, Leipsic 109, Munich 94, Bonn 91, Heidelberg 91, Halle 71, &c.

One of the most important characteristics of the German universities, is the *professorial* or *lecture*-system, as distinct from the *tutorial* system, which prevails in England. Instead of a number of colleges as in Oxford and Cambridge, where the students live together under the moral supervision as well as intellectual instruction of tutors and fellows, we have in a German university simply one large building with a number of halls (Hörsäle,) where the students spend a part of the day to attend the lectures, if they choose. For there is no compulsion at all. The student is entirely left to his own sense of duty and enjoys more freedom than he ever can enjoy afterwards in any walk of life. Industrious and conscientious students are, of course, always on the spot, and hear sometimes as many as four or five lectures a day. When the clock strikes, they take their seat in their respective Hörsaal, unfold their portfolios and fix their ink horn, armed below with a sharp iron spike, into the wooden desk, waiting for the learned oracle. After an intermission of ten or fifteen minutes, the professor leaves the conservatorium, ascends the rostrum and with the familiar address, "Meine Herren!" begins his lecture either standing, or sitting, either reading in full or in part, or speaking extempore. Some of the hearers take down in short-hand every word that drops from the mouth of living wisdom, thinking with the freshman in Göethe's Faust:

"Denn was man schwarz auf weiss besitzt,
Kann man getrost nach Hause tragen.

Or to quote another verse equally illustrative of the difference between writing, and knowing a lecture:

"Der Studio muss in's Collegium,
Dass er die Wissenschaft allda erschnappe,
Und ist der Weg zur Weisheit noch so krumm,
Er trägt sie fort in seiner Mappe."

(For lectures sound the student's bound,
Deep wisdom not to catch ill,
And when it's caught, his head knows naught,
It only fills his satchel.)

Others show their independence and their contempt for goose-quill-learning by simply listening, or noting merely the general heads as a guide for the memory. The most judicious appropriate the lecture to their mind as it goes on, and reproduce it in a condensed form. If the professor speaks indistinctly, some show their interest by giving him a hint with a motion of their feet to repeat the sentence. But not all professors pay attention to this *lingua pedestris*.

Each lecture lasts about three-quarters of an hour, till the clock gives its accustomed sound, when the professor shuts his manuscript, and the students wipe their pens, shut their inkhorn, take their hat or bonnet and portfolio, and crowd to the door, to return either to their lodgings, or to attend another lecture.

This is generally all the instruction in these institutions. In some of them, however, for instance in Berlin and Halle, there are what are called *Seminare*, i. e., meetings in the professor's house, for the explanation and discussion on biblical, and patristic, or classical authors, and the composition of Latin prize essays. Thus Neander used to read in this more familiar way Tertullian's *Apolegeticus*, Origen's Commentaries, and *De Principiis*, Augustine's *Confessiones*, Chrysostom *De Sacerdotio*, etc. But these meetings which are conducted in Latin, are attended only by a few. In Tübingen the lecture-system is supplied by weekly *repetitoria* and *examinatoria* conducted by the *Repententen*, who may be compared to the tutors or teaching Fellows of the British universities.

Until the middle of the eighteenth century the university-lectures were all delivered in Latin, a method, which was very injurious to the cultivation of the German language. The scholars of the seventeenth century wrote and spoke the classical, or scholastic Latin better than their mother tongue. It is the merit of Thomasius, professor in Halle, to have broken the way for the gradual abolition of this learned pedantry, and the cultivation of the national language as a medium of academic instruction. At present very few lectures in the German universities are delivered in Latin, while this language is still used, very properly, in academic dissertations, the conferring of degrees, and other public solemnities.

Text-books are very rarely used, except in the universities of Austria, where a despotic and pedantic government prescribes them at the expense of the free development of thought.

It is easy to see that the lecture-system has great advantages both for the professor and the student. It imposes a much greater amount of labor upon the teacher than the use of text-books. Only think of the trouble of writing one or more learned lectures every day, at least in the beginning of the professorial career. But it draws out, at the same time, all his mental powers, and in this way benefits the science. Hence the high standard of scholarship and the marvellous amount of literary fertility, by which the university professors of Protestant Germany surpass their colleagues in other countries. Most of the classical and other scientific text-books used in England and in this country, are directly or indirectly of German origin.

To the student, this system is generally the most interesting and impressive, and best calculated to arouse him to a consciousness of his own individuality and originality. For a professor is more master of a subject if he has wrought it out in his own mind, given it a peculiar shape and form, and reduced it to writing, and will deliver and explain his own production with greater animation and enthusiasm, than the production of another mind. The great advantage of oral instruction, and the power of the living word, as compared with the dead letter, is generally admitted, and shows itself to its fullest extent in the lecture-system, when a science proceeds in bodily form and clothed in living flesh and blood from the mind of the professor, as the goddess of Wisdom from the head of Jupiter. But the writing of the student also, although by no means absolutely essential, is yet a considerable help. Those who ridicule the mechanical use of the pen, forget that the very process of writing, if accompanied by thought, as it always should be, is generally speaking the best method of mental appropriation and digestion.

But on the other side, it must be admitted that the German universities promote individuality of intellect and fertility of opinions to an excess, which forms just the opposite extreme to the almost stagnant steadiness, uniformity and traditionalism of Oxford and Cambridge. If the German governments allow too little political liberty to their subjects, the German universities afford an unbounded freedom of thought and doctrine to the professors and students. With a rare amount of invaluable learning and useful theories, they have brought forth also many fantastic, absurd, and revolutionary views and systems. They have been the hot-houses of rationalism, skepticism, and pantheism, and all sorts of dangerous novelties.

The truth seems to lie here, as elsewhere, in the middle, or rather in the deep between two extremes, although it may be very difficult to fix the exact line of demarcation. A model university while affording the widest field for the cultivation of all sciences, ought never to lose sight of the great aim to benefit society, and to train the rising intellects of a nation for practical usefulness in church and state. They should reconcile the claims of authority and freedom, and guard the unity and harmony of truth as well as the diversity and universality of science. The lecture-system can be and ought to be combined with the catechetical mode of instruction, by which the progress of the student may be ascertained, and the subject of the lecture be more fully explained and applied with special regard to his peculiar wants and his future discharge of the active duties of life.

CHAPTER IV.

THE GERMAN STUDENTS.

Necessary Preparation—The Gymnasial Course—The Examen Maturitatis—The Academic Freedom—Life, Manners and Habits of the Students—Recent Improvements.

THE students of the university must have passed through a regular preparatory course of nine or ten years in a gymnasium, which is generally divided into nine or ten classes, and corresponds to our academies and colleges, comprising a methodical tutorial instruction in ancient and modern languages, mathematics, natural sciences, geography, history and philosophy.

Almost every large city has one or more such classical schools. Berlin alone numbers six gymnasia, besides what are called Real, or Polytechnic institutions, schools of artillery, military engineering, architecture, sculpture, painting, and music, and the Academy of Sciences. The gymnasia confer no degrees, like the colleges of England and America, which have retained the scholastic number of four and seven years for the attainment of the bachelor's and master's diploma. But the gymnastic course terminates with the *examen maturitatis*, without which no one can be admitted as a regular student to the university.

Other tests do not exist. The German universities

maintain the principle of universal admissibility, both for those who wish to teach, and for those who wish to learn, on the sole condition of intellectual capacity. There are no sectarian or religious disabilities as at Oxford and Cambridge, except for the professorships of the theological faculty. Thus you may find Lutherans, Reformed, Roman Catholics, Greeks, and even Jews, and many foreigners from all countries of Europe and America, amongst the students. There they enter upon an unlimited field of independent study, where they may for four or more years carry on and complete their education for a profession, or for a particular science, or for a professorship in any of the faculties, and acquire, on examination, an academic degree from a body of masters in their department, who alone are competent to confer them upon real merit.

The students have generally passed the eighteenth or twentieth year, when they leave the gymnasium and the hackneyed machinery of school tuition. Their final examination and matriculation in the university, is a complete emancipation from intellectual guardianship, and the commencement of an era of perfect freedom, such as they never enjoy again in subsequent life. They choose the profession, the professors, and the lectures; they may attend them with scrupulous regularity, or waste their precious time in idleness and dissipation. They are supposed to have attained such a degree of intellectual and moral maturity as to be fully able to take care of themselves, except in political matters, in which the German governments are as illiberal and intolerant, as they are liberal in allowing an almost unbounded freedom of thought and speech on every other subject. The only indirect compulsion to study are the requisite examinations for the attainment of the doctor's diploma, or for the active service of church and state. But the strongest stimulus to industry is supposed to be a disinterested, enthusiastic love for science, and the highest culture of the mind.

The German universities are not training schools, like the gymnasia, and our American colleges, but represent the unity and universality of scientific knowledge, the arena for the investigation and spread of truth; and afford the students the best possible opportunity for prosecuting their studies by their own self-educating abilities, with perfect freedom, for any number of years, and to an almost unbounded extent. To many a youth this academical freedom proves disastrous; but as a general rule, the German student is proverbial for his plodding disposition, and his toilsome, unwearied patience in the pursuit of knowledge.

The number of students in the different universities varies from three or four hundred to two or three thousand. Those who can at all afford it, visit two or more universities, and thus come in living contact with the most distinguished scholars of the age, and acquire a more universal culture.

The peculiar dress, terminology, manners and habits by which the German students used to be distinguished from every other class of society, are disappearing more and more, especially in the larger cities, as Berlin, Munich and Vienna, where they are lost in the mass of the population. The "Burschenschaften" have been mostly dissolved, as hotbeds of political agitation and revolution. Still there remains a great deal of originality and peculiar attraction about the German university life. Some English travellers, such as Russell, Laing, and Talfourd, were rather repulsed by it, while William Howitt, and others, from longer observation, have described it favorably.

It must be confessed, that drinking, duel fighting, (although the latter is strictly prohibited by the authorities,) and other lawless and vulgar habits still disgrace several of these learned institutions, especially in smaller towns, as Jena and Giessen, where the students have the citizens, or "Philistines," as they call them, under their control. But if we make proper allowance for the difference of national genius and taste, they lose nothing by a comparison with the students of Oxford and Cambridge, while in industry they generally surpass them.

"A German student," says a recent English writer in the *Dublin University Magazine*, "does not feather his oar in a university boat on regatta day; he does not kick the foot-ball on Parker's piece; he does not skilfully take the balls at a cricket match. These gentle pastimes would not satisfy his bolder and noisier disposition. His thoughts are more excitable and somewhat enthusiastic. His manners are more cordial and unreserved. His appearance and demeanor are less aristocratic. Yet he is well bred, spirited and high-minded; he is frank and open; a faithful friend, and an eccentric lover of his *Vaterland*. He is a sworn enemy to all falsehood and all deceit. Peculiar notions of honor, and a deep love of independence and liberty, belong to his most deep-rooted principles. Song and music, social parties, convivial fetes, a martial, undaunted spirit, and excitement of the patriotic feelings, throw over his life an enchantment which gilds it yet in all his later recollections."

The students live not in one building, as is generally the case in our colleges, but scattered through the town. They spend from two to five hours every day in the lecture rooms of the university hall, and the rest of the time in reading and writing at home, or in intercourse with their fellow students. The majority, especially the "foxes," as the freshmen are called, join one of the clubs, or associations for social enjoyment after true student's fashion. The members generally wear, or used to wear, peculiar colors on their caps, flags, and breast-bands, are regularly organized, and meet on special days at a particular inn, or private room. There they sit around oblong tables, in the best of humor, drinking, smoking and singing, at the top of their clear, strong voices, "Gaudeamus igitur," or "Was ist des Deutschen Vaterland," or "Wir hatten gebauet," or, "Stimmt an mit hellem hohem Klang," or "Freiheit, die ich meine," or "Es zogen drei Bursche wohl über den Rhein," or "Wohlauf noch getrunken den funkelnden Wein." They discuss the merits of their professors, and sweet-hearts; they consult about a serenade to a favorite teacher, or about a joke to be practised upon some sordid "Philister" or landlord; they make patriotic speeches on the prospects of the German fatherland; they pour out their heart in an unbroken succession of affection and merriment, pathos and humor, wit and sarcasm, pun and taunt; they smoke and puff, they sing and laugh and talk till midnight, and feel as happy as the fellows in Auerbach's cellar in Göthe's Faust.

I wish the great temperance apostle, John B. Gough, would go to Germany and convince these merry students that the beer and wine goblets are by no means essential to a feast of reason and flow of soul, and that their absence would save them the "Katzenjammer" on the next day, and a heap of trouble beside. But they would probably meet him with the authority of the great Reformer, who, among many other unguarded things, said:

"Who does not love wife, wine and song,
Remains a fool his whole life long."

It must not be supposed, however, that all German students take part in these noisy enjoyments. The more serious amongst them live either in almost ascetic retirement, or confine themselves to friends of strict morality, literary taste and close application.

We must also add that the noisy, boisterous and semi-savage spirit of the old *Landsmannschaften*, and more recent *Burschenschaft* is fast dying away. Not only have the governments dissolved the political clubs, which drew the students from their proper avocation into the whirlpool of political agitation and revolution, but the traditional *Burschen-comment*, with all its ludicrous appendages, is beginning to fall into disrepute among the students themselves. The present generation of Burschen is a more refined class of men; they have exchanged the gauntlet for a pair of kids, the sword or rapier for a riding-whip or walking-stick, and it is no more an honor to besot one's self with beer and tobacco, and to provoke duels. The students of Berlin, Bonn and other universities have taken effectual measures to eradicate the barbarous custom of duelling, by establishing *Ehrengerichte*, or a student's jury, before which quarrels may be peacefully settled.

CHAPTER V.

UNIVERSITY REFORM.

Object of Proposed Reforms—Restriction of the Liberty of Teaching—Closer Union with the Church—The claims of the Lutheran Party—Advantages of the Academic Liberty—The Inner Mission in the Universities—Hundeshagen's View on the Subject—A word on American Universities.

As in England, so also in Germany, the subject of University reform has been agitated with a good deal of interest for the last few years. But while in the former country the object of the reformers is to liberalize the constitution of Oxford and Cambridge, to throw them open to dissenters as well as churchmen, and to engraft upon them the professorial system of the German universities, we perceive in Germany the opposite tendency, to make them more directly subservient to the practical interests of the church and the state. This is especially the case since the Revolutions of 1848, in which the students of Berlin, Vienna, etc., took a prominent part as champions of democracy and red republicanism. The modern reaction in politics and religion looks with a jealous eye upon the almost unbounded freedom of the German university system.

Thus the strict Lutheran party, headed by Dr. Petri, in the kingdom of Hanover, is at present engaged in a war with the excellent theological faculty of Göttingen, and charge them with a want of confessional orthodoxy. They insist upon the election of such professors which are acceptable to the church as represented by the clergy, which is becoming more and more exclusively Lutheran, Dr. Kliefoth, of Mecklenburg, has fallen in with this movement. Dr. Hengstenberg and the present minister of public worship in Prussia, Herr von Raumer, seem to sympathize with it likewise, and show a disposition to restrain the academic liberty of teaching.

To an American, nothing seems to be more natural and just, than that the church should have a vote in the election of the theological professors, who are to train ministers. It seems a perfect monstrosity that such thorough rationalists, as Paulus and Wegscheider, or a pantheist as Baur, should hold a place in a theological faculty of the Evangelical Church.

But on the other side, the liberty of teaching is one of the chief excellences of the German universities, and accounts for their extraordinary literary and scientific fertility. It must be borne in mind that the theological faculties of that country have after all a more comprehensive vocation, than a mere seminary for the training of preachers. They ought to cultivate and promote the sacred sciences in the most thorough and liberal manner, but of course for the edification, and not for the destruction of the church. In proportion as the religious life gains ground, such anomalies as we alluded to above, will disappear, as has been the case already to a great extent within the last twenty years; and the theological faculties will assume their normal relation to the church. The state authorities, too, will naturally, or ought certainly to respect public opinion, and elect men who enjoy the confidence of the religious community.

From a different point of view Dr. Hundeshagen, himself a theological professor, of Heidelberg, has treated the question of university reform in a very interesting paper on "Inner mission in the university," read, by appointment, in a special conference of the Seventh German Evangelical Church Diet at Frankfort-on-the-Maine, in 1854. He proposes no alteration in the constitution of these great establishments, and no restriction of their free action, but the infusion of a decidedly Christian spirit into their officers and operation. He charges the average culture of the educated classes in Germany with a sort of Rousseauism, or a false humanitarianism, which makes man, instead of God, the centre and chief object of study and pursuit; loses sight of the supernatural and eternal order of things, and ends at last in a refined materialism. Another charge is, the frequent separation of the *scientia* from the *conscientia*, and the over estimation of the intellectual powers of man to the neglect of his moral and practical interests. Hence the reproachful terms, professor's wisdom, book-learning, unpractical speculation, so often applied to German scholars. There are not a few, who will take the deepest interest in the most trifling scientific question, and write large volumes on the difference between two Greek particles, and be perfectly indifferent to the national welfare and the great social problems of the age.

Hundeshagen quotes with approbation a sentence of the late Dr. Thomas Arnold, who knew how to appreciate German learning: "The German scholars present us many examples of a one-sided literary industry, which transcends the proper limits, without real universality and thorough training to a truly manly, national and Christian character." He concludes his excellent suggestions with the words: "Let us not be ashamed, respected colleagues, of our title, Professors. There is in it a significant admonition. *Professores dicimur a profitendo.* Let us beware, lest it may be said of us: *Lucus a non lucendo, professor a non profitendo!* But *profiteri*, you all know, does not mean to make profit, nor to make an empty profession, but to profess the truth under all circumstances, to be faithful to the truth, and to suffer for it, if it be God's will. Hence let our motto be: *Profiteri, veritatem profiteri, Christum profiteri!*"

If this spirit should pervade all the professors of the German universities, they would soon be reformed without any organic changes of their constitution.

In this connection we may say a few words on the transfer of the German university system to American soil, which has been recently advocated by some of our most distinguished scholars.

It needs no argument to show that our college system is incomplete, and that we ought to have institutions of the first order which deserve the name of universities in the full and proper sense of the term. I have no doubt, that the time is not distant, when this great country will be able to compete with any country on the globe in every branch of education.

As regards the organization of these universities, however, we would by no means advocate a slavish copy of the German institutions, but such a modification and adaptation of them to the peculiar genius of our country, as to give them a truly national American character, and to mark a real progress in the history of university education.

It has been proposed already to establish such an institution in the city of New York. But one would, of course, not be sufficient for such an immense country as this. It seems to me that we need at least as many as we have states and territories. Let each respectable city have one or more academies and colleges, and let each state found a university, to which the colleges will be preparatory schools like the German gymnasia. These universities ought to be laid out on the largest scale, liberally endowed and supported by annual grants of the states, and be accessible to all denominations. Thus our national education system, which has made such rapid progress of late, would find its natural and necessary completion.

If the state legislatures are unwilling to do this work, the leading churches, or private individuals should take it in hand. This would, perhaps, be more in keeping with the genius of our country, where individual energy and enterprise have such a prominence and unbounded field of action, and would infuse at the same time a religious spirit into those institutions, without which, they cannot be expected permanently to flourish and to accomplish much good for the highest interests of society.

We have princely, or rather republican munificence enough to carry out such noble projects. James Smithson, an Englishman, bequeathed the bulk of his large fortune to the United States, for the establishment of an institution at Washington, " for the increase and diffusion of knowledge among men." John Jacob Astor, who came a poor boy from Germany, and died the richest man in America, devoted in his will half a million of dollars to the founding of a library in the city of New York, which is an ornament to that city. Stephen Girard, a native of France, left two millions for a college of poor boys in Philadelphia, and thus immortalized his name. Peter Cooper, a native American merchant, is now erecting, in New York, an institution for the promotion of the arts, sciences, literature and general knowledge among both sexes, at an expense of not less than half a million, which he gives in the vigor of life, and not with the stiffened hand of bequest. "An act like this," says the distinguished Dr. Francis Lieber, in his Lecture on Athenæums, "is an event and belongs to history; otherwise it might be indelicate to state that the mentioned sum is not the tithe, but the third or fourth part of the wealth which the generous donor's own industry has accumulated with the blessings of Providence. Nor are to him the words of wife and children mere terms, without the thrilling directness of reality."

Should not wealthy American Christians, native, or foreign born, animated by a higher principle than mere natural philanthropy and noble ambition, regard it a privilege to imitate, or rather to excel such liberality, by founding universities, not only for the cultivation of all human sciences and arts, but at the same time for a still greater and more enduring end, the promotion of the glory of God?

CHAPTER VI.

BERLIN.

The Prussian Universities—Berlin—Its Distinguished Professors, and other Literary Celebrities—Alexander Von Humboldt—The New Museum—The Egyptian Antiquities—Kaulbach's Historical Pictures—The Destruction of Jerusalem—The Pulpit and Christianity in Berlin—The Religious Destitution compared with America—Recent Improvement and Progress.

To this general description of the character, organization and active operation of the academic institutions of Germany, we must add sketches of those universities which enjoy the widest reputation and have most attraction for the theological student, or suggest such other literary and religious information as may be interesting to our readers.

To an American, who wishes to complete his liberal and professional education in Germany, we would recommend to devote the winter to Berlin, and to divide the summer between Bonn and Heidelberg. If he has another year to spare, he may profitably spend the cold season at Halle, Leipzic, Munich, or Vienna, and the warm season at Göttingen, Tübingen and Zürich.

We commence with Prussia, which embodies more scientific and general literary intelligence than any monarchy in Europe, France or England not excepted, and takes the lead in almost every department of mental culture. Of the six Prussian universities, Berlin, Halle and Bonn stand highest, and deserve a special notice in this place.

The university of Berlin, although one of the youngest, occupies the first rank of all similar institutions in Germany not only, but in the world. It numbers generally from 160 to 180 professors and teachers, from 1800 to 2200 students, and its semi-annual *Index Lectionum* fills from 40 to 50 quarto pages. The professors are selected from all parts of Germany, and a considerable number of the students belong to foreign nations and countries, as Switzerland, France, Russia, Greece, Great Britain, and America.

This great institution was founded in 1810, at the time of the deepest humiliation of Prussia, and became one of the means of her intellectual, moral and national regeneration, which resulted in the victorious emancipation from the yoke of the French conqueror. Enlightened statesmen like Freiherr von Stein, and Wilhelm von Humboldt, and distinguished scholars like Wolf, Fichte, Schleiermacher, took part in its first organization. King Frederick William III., assigned for its use an extensive and magnificent building in the finest and most interesting portion of the city, on the broad and imposing promenade *Unter-den-Linden*, which leads to the large park, and in the immediate neighborhood of the royal palaces, the old and new museum, the public library of 600,000 volumes, the academy of sciences and arts, the arsenal and the dome. He favored it with rich endowments and many privileges, which his successor, Frederick William IV., an enthusiastic patron of literature, art, and religion, greatly increased. From the advantages of its location in the capital of Prussia and northern Germany, from the large number of literary institutions, libraries, museums and societies of every description which are collected there, and above all from a rare union of the highest talents in all the faculties, it soon became the metropolis of German science and learning.

The very first masters in almost every department of literature have taught in the university of Berlin either together, or in succession from its beginning to the present time, and form a more brilliant galaxy of names than ever adorned any similar institution during the same period of years.

Schleiermacher, unquestionably the most gifted divine of modern Protestanism, Neander, the "father of Church History," Tholuck, Hengstenberg, Marheineke, De Wette, Twesten, Nitzsch, Theremin, Strauss, filled at one time, or are still filling the theological chairs. Fichte, Hegel, and Schelling, the three greatest metaphysicians of the century, unfolded their new systems of thought to admiring audiences, while the equally genial Steffens introduced the students into the mysteries of nature, and the beautiful harmony of philosophy and poetry. Savigny, the head of the historical school of jurisprudence, Heffter, Puchta, Keller, Richter, Stahl, excel as teachers and writers on the various branches of law. Lachmann, of honored memory, Bœckh, and Bekker, the eminent classical philologists and critics; the brothers Grimm, who are regarded as the first authorities in ancient Teutonic learning; Bopp, the best Sanscrit scholar; Lepsius, the Egyptian traveller and antiquarian, expound the stores of heathen literature and antiquities. Raumer, and Ranke, both well known beyond the limits of Germany and Europe, teach ancient and modern history. Carl Ritter, the founder of historical and philosophical geography, and at the same time a venerable Christian gentleman, explains the surface of the globe in its relation to the character and condition of its inhabitants, and to the progress of civil and religious society. Encke measures the course of the wandering stars, one of which bears his name. Müller, Ehrenberg, Dove, Rose, Weiss, Schönlein, adorn with their distinguished reputation the various branches of natural and medical sciences.

Besides the regular members of the university, there are in Berlin quite a number of celebrated scholars and authors, who move in the professorial circles, and belong to the Academy of Sciences which adjoins the university buildings.

Of these, I need only mention Alexander von Humboldt, the world-renowned patriarch of natural sciences, the intellectual mirror of the physical cosmos, the living wonder of the age. In his eighty-seventh year—for he was born in 1769, the same year with Napoleon and Wellington, and within a few months of the elder Schleiermacher, and the younger Hegel—he still speaks and writes with the freshness of youth and the vigor of manhood, and seems to defy the wasting power of time upon the mortal frame. He never was married but to science. He talks with the same rapidity and fullness of information as ever, reads and answers some four thousand letters annually; dines almost daily with the King of Prussia, and performs, contrary to the wishes of his royal friend, the duties of chamberlain in his turn, refusing the indulgence of a chair; he is incessant in polite attention to friends and distinguished strangers during the day, and spends the half of the night in severe scientific labor, allowing his body only a few hours of rest.

What a melancholy reflection that such a master of all the mysteries of nature, the daily companion of a pious king, and in a moral point of view, a kind-hearted, benevolent and amiable gentleman of the highest finish, should like Germany's greatest poet, Göthe, content himself with the wonders of nature without rising to nature's God, and remain indifferent to the greater mysteries of grace. I may do him injustice, but I cannot remember now to have read even the *name* of God—not to speak of Christ—in the three volumes so far published of his Cosmos, except in an approving quotation from a lost work of the heathen Aristotle, as preserved by the heathen Cicero, (*de natura Deorum*, ii. 37.) We mean the sublime passage that puts to shame many a nominally Christian philosopher: "Nobly does Aristotle observe, that if there were beings who had always lived under ground, in convenient, nay, magnificent dwellings, adorned with statues and pictures and everything which belongs to prosperous life; if, then, these beings should be told of the being and power of the gods, and should come up through open fissures from their secret abodes to the places which we inhabit; if they should suddenly behold the starry heavens, the changing moon, the rising and setting of the stars, and their eternally ordained and unchangeable courses; they would exclaim with truth: There are gods, and such great things are their works."

How much is it to be desired that this truly remarkable man, before closing his unrivalled scientific career, should bow down in child-like adoration and faith before that one and true God whose living presence alone gives strength, order and beauty to the works of his hand, and whose glory shines from the starry heavens above us, from the solid earth beneath us, and from the rational will within us, from the book of nature, and the book of history, but brightest of all from the book of books, and the face of his only begotten Son, full of grace and of truth.

It would lead us too far from our immediate purpose to enter into a detailed account of the other literary institutions, collections and curiosities, which give additional interest to Berlin and make it one of the most instructive residences to the scholar. We will only direct attention to the New Museum, erected by the present king, which, when completed, will even surpass in interest the far-famed Pinacotheca and Glyptotheca of Munich, the German Rome both in point of art and religion. It contains among other curiosities, one of the richest collections of Egyptian antiquities, arranged in the very best order under the direction of Lepsius and Erbkam, the celebrated Egyptian travellers, and furnishing, in connection with architectural imitations, hieroglyphics and frescoes on the wall, the most graphic and instructive picture of the social, religious, and political life of that land of mysteries. There you may find also copies of the master-pieces of sculpture of all ages in chronological order, so as to give you a complete view of the history of this art. But the chief attraction of the New Museum are the magnificent stereochromic frescoes of the living painter, Wilhelm von Kaulbach, representing the great epochs of the history of mankind, the Fall of Babel, the Spring of Greece, the Destruction of Jerusalem, the Battle of the Huns, the Conversion of the Saxon Duke Wittekind, the Crusades, etc., several of which are not yet finished. These compositions, in our humble judgment, are unrivalled among the creations of modern art, and hardly surpassed by the master-pieces of Michael Angelo and Raphael.

Kaulbach's Destruction of Jerusalem especially, is conceived and executed in the grandest style, and makes an overpowering impression, like a tragic poem, or a solemn sermon on the judgment day. It is fully as sublime and terrific, as Michael Angelo's famous "Last Judgment," in the Sistine chapel of the Vatican, without being overcharged, or offending in the least against refined taste. The central group presents the Jewish high priest before the altar, thrusting the dagger through the golden breastplate, and supporting with the other arm his dying children; his wife imploring him to point the deadly weapon to her own heart; while around him the Levites mourn, or destroy themselves amid the scattered treasures of the burning temple, and men, women and children, frantic with hunger, eating their own flesh, furious, scornful, cursing, praying, desponding, despairing, are flying and lying about in wildest confusion. Above this fearful tragedy of agony, famine and despair, sit the four great prophets upon the clouds of heaven, in silent adoration of God's righteous judgment so long foretold in their books of prophecy, but disregarded by the wicked race that nailed the Saviour to the shameful cross. In the right corner above, the Roman Titus with his heathen soldiers, is seen victoriously approaching as the unconscious instrument for the execution of Jehovah's wrath. The left group below, exhibits the impersonation of unbelieving Judaism in the revolting figure of the Wandering Jew, lacerating his naked breast, driven on by three demons into the dark future, wishing to die, but never dying till Christ shall return to the final judgment, of which this destruction of Jerusalem is the type. The right group below forms a most beautiful contrast to this awful scene, by presenting a happy Christian family, who, in obedience to a divine monition, depart with hymns of praise, the open Bible, the cup of salvation, the palm of peace, from the devoted city, under the direction of three guardian angels, to the safe refuge beyond the Jordan.

Berlin is the centre of the government, and the ecclesiastical movements of the Evangelical Church of Prussia. Of these I will have more to say hereafter. I will only remark here, that the city presents the dark as well as the bright sight of German Christianity. It is true, large cities all over the world combine the very worst with the best elements of the country they represent, and even of London and New York, with all their churches, may be literally said what Tacitus charges upon ancient Rome, "quo cuncta undique atrocia aut pudenda confluunt celebranturque." But the religious statistics of Berlin are especially humiliating even if compared with other German cities, as Elberfeld, or Stuttgart, not to speak of London, Edinburgh, Boston, New York and Philadelphia. The American reader will be surprised to learn that the Prussian capital contains only about forty churches for a population of nearly half a million, that of this half a million not more than 30 or 40,000 are supposed to be regular attendants on public worship; though *all* children *must* be baptized and confirmed by order of the State; and that God's holy Sabbath, that "pearl of days," that "emblem of eternal rest," is almost as much disregarded and desecrated there as in Paris. In view of these painful facts, Prussian Christians may well cover their face, while American Christians may learn to prize, in profound gratitude to God, their glorious privilege of a quiet Sabbath, with its solemn services in thousands of well attended churches, erected and supported not by the cold step-motherly arm of a nominally Christian State, but by the voluntary contributions of a free Christian people. Although I knew these facts long since, I felt them more sensibly than ever, when, two or three years ago, I visited Berlin again, and could compare it in this respect, from personal observation, with our American cities.

But on the other side we must remember, that Berlin with the neighboring Potsdam, the Prussian Versailles, was once the residence of the all-powerful Frederick II., and the fiendish scoffer, Voltaire; that it became the stronghold of German infidelity; and that only fifty years ago hardly an evangelical sermon was heard from its pulpits.

Compared with this state of things a great and surprising change has taken place in Berlin, althongh it has not yet penetrated the mass of the population. The present king, whatever may be his defects as a political ruler, is as decided a believer in Christianity, as Frederick II. was an unbeliever, and encourages every Christian enterprise. Many of the first noblemen, statesmen, members of the Chambers, and of the Cabinet, are as devotedly pious as our best men in similar stations. A general respect for religion characterizes the highest society of Berlin, where it was formerly treated with ridicule and contempt. The main current of the university looks towards the harmony of science and faith, of literature and Christianity. In nearly all the churches the Gospel is at present proclaimed with more or less purity and power, and many of the ministers, a Hoffman, an Arndt, a Souchon, a Büchsel, a Krummacher, (now transferred to Potsdam) are among the most fearless, pungent, heart-piercing preachers of the age, and attract the largest crowds of devout hearers, often bathed in tears of repentance and gratitude to the infinite mercy of God in Christ.

CHAPTER VII.

HALLE AND BONN.

The City and University of Halle—The Theological Department, and the Changes and Revolutions it has passed through—The University of Bonn, and its Peculiar Attractions—The Rhine.

WHILE Berlin, though lying on a monotonous sandy plain, has, by industry and art, been converted into one of the finest and most pleasant residences of Europe, Halle on the Saale in the Saxon province of Prussia, though surrounded by some picturesque scenery at Giebichenstein and on the Petersberg, is one of the ugliest and most repulsive cities of Germany, full of old-fashioned uncomfortable dwellings, narrow, crooked streets, wretched muddy pavements, gloomy air, and intolerable smell arising from peat bogs, and salt springs, which yield from 225,000 to 300,000 hundreds-weight of salt annually. But in addition to its historical associations with the history of the Saxon Reformation, it has two great attractions for the scholar and Christian philanthropist, viz., the University and the Orphan House of Augustus Hermann Franke, that noble monument of faith in God and charity to man.

The University of Halle was founded in 1694, and was enlarged and enriched by the union with that of Wittenberg, which was merged into it in 1816, after the annexation of the Saxon province to Prussia. Formerly each professor lectured in his own house; but, in 1834, the government built an imposing edifice for that purpose, in the new part of the city. A large library, various museums, an anatomical theatre, chemical laboratory, botanic garden, and observatory, complete the literary apparatus. Some of the lectures are still delivered in Latin, according to old fashion. The late Professor Weber felt himself greatly insulted when once a dog sneaked into his lecture room while he learnedly discoursed *de statu integritatis*, and commanded the strange student, with much gravity and authority, "*Abi, canis, ubi loquuntur vernacule.*"

The theological department was always the most prominent in Halle, and numbers more professorships and students, (sometimes as many as 8 and 900,) than any other university. In 1848 the number declined, but is now again on the increase. In the winter session of 1854 to '55, the whole number of students was 660, of whom 378 were preparing for the ministry. The theological faculty of Halle has passed through all the recent revolutions of German Protestantism. During the former half of the last century, it was the literary stronghold of the pietistic school of Spener, and Franke who was himself one of the professors, and trained a number of missionaries for heathen lands, and the German Lutherans in Pennsylvania. But from the time of Semler, the father of German neology, it fell into the hands of rationalism, as represented by the celebrated Hebrew scholar, Gesenius, and the didactic divine, Wegscheider, who gave tone and character to the university for more than twenty years. During this period the venerable Knapp was the only evangelical professor there, and he, with all his learning and zeal, could not turn the current of the age. But, since the arrival of Tholuck, in 1827, a gradual change has taken place, so that the present faculty is composed of sound Christian teachers. The former rude habits of the students have likewise improved, although there is room yet for considerable progress in refinement.

Bonn, in Rhenish Prussia, the former residence of the electors and archbishops of Cologne, and the birthplace of Beethoven, was selected for a university, in 1818, and the extensive castle of the electors assigned for the lectures, the library, and the museum. Here most of the professional men are trained for the two western provinces of the Prussian monarchy. The young Prince of Prussia, and Prince Albert, of England, studied there. The theological department embraces two faculties, one for the Roman Catholic church, to which the majority of the population of Bonn and the surrounding country belong, especially Cologne, with its vast and wondrous dome; and another for the Evangelical church, which prevails on the lower Rhine, and in the Wupperthal, the most flourishing part of Prussian Protestantism, and the stronghold of the Reformed Confession in Germany. The Evangelical faculty has, within the last few years, sustained considerable loss by the removal of Nitzsch to Berlin (1847,) of Rothe to Heidelberg, and of Dorner to Göttingen (1853.) But it is still one of the best, and Bleek, Lange, Hasse, etc., fill their respective chairs very creditably. The other faculties embrace likewise a number of distinguished names, of whom I would especially mention Clemens Th. Perthes, professor of law, a son of the well-known publisher, and grandson of the poet Claudius. He is one of the finest specimens of a German gentleman and Christian, I became acquainted with.

Bonn is a favorite resort for students from foreign countries, especially in the summer season, when it offers peculiar attractions. I know of no university which is more advantageously located, if the educational influences of nature and historical associations are taken into account. For Bonn lies on the banks of the Rhine, a short distance from the most interesting and celebrated spots on that river, and in full view of the Drachenfels (Dragon's Rock,) whose summit, crowned by the ruins of a feudal castle, commands the finest prospect over a region equally famous for the beauties of nature and the charms of romance. There are, no doubt, grander, sublimer, and more overpowering views from the Alps of Switzerland, that rise, like cathedrals of God's own workmanship, from earth to heaven ; but none, perhaps, which blend in harmony such a variety of scenery with the ruins of the past and the busy life of the present.

> More mighty spots may rise, more glaring shine
> Than on the lovely banks of father Rhine ;
> But none unite in one attaching maze,
> The brilliant, fair, and soft,—the glories of old days ;
>
> The negligently grand, the fruitful bloom
> Of coming ripeness, the white city's sheen,
> The rolling stream, the precipice's gloom,
> The forest's growth, and Gothic walls between,

The wild rocks, shaped as they had turrets been
In mockery of man's art; and these withal
A race of faces happy as the scene,
Whose fertile bounties here extend to all,
Still springing o'er the banks, though empires near them fall.

The river nobly foams and flows,
The charm of this enchanted ground,
And all its thousand turns disclose
Some fresher beauty varying round;
The haughtiest breast its wish might bound
Through life to dwell delighted here;
Nor could on earth a spot be found
To nature, and to me so dear,
Could thy dear eyes, in following mine,
Still sweeten more these banks of Rhine.

CHAPTER VIII.

GÖTTINGEN AND LEIPSIC.

Gottingen—Its Former Fame—Its Recent Decline and Gradual Recovery—Leipsic—Its Literary and Theological Character—The Attractions of the City.

GÖTTINGEN, on the Leine, is the seat of the celebrated *Academia Georgia Augusta*, founded in 1734 by George II., King of England, and elector of Hanover. The cynical H. Heine, who was once expelled from it, pours, in his *Reisebilder*, the full vial of his sarcasm upon that city, "which, he says, is famous for its sausages and its university, belongs to the King of Hanover, and has four classes of inhabitants, differing but little from each other, viz: students, professors, philistines, and cattle, the last being the most important." But Göttingen took its place formerly amongst the very first literary institutions of Europe. Ever since the middle of the last century it was favored with professors of great learning and wide fame. We may mention Mosheim, Walch, Planck, and Gieseler, in church history; Spittler, and Heeren in secular history; Michaelis, Eichhorn, and Ewald in oriental literature; Heyne, and Ottfried Müller in classical learning; the brothers Grimm, and Gervinus in Germanic antiquities; Hugo in jurisprudence; Blumenbach in natural science; Gauss in mathematics; Herbart in metaphysics. Owing to the connection of the crown of Hanover with that of England, before the accession of Queen Victoria, the university attracted also a number of English students, and two of our most eloquent writers, Bancroft and E. Everett, graduated at Göttingen. The public library is one of the largest, best selected and arranged, in the world, and is especially rich in foreign literature.

But, since 1831, Göttingen has greatly suffered, first by a political disturbance which broke out after the July revolution of France, and resulted in severe reactionary measures; and then by the arbitrary overthrow of the constitution of the kingdom, in 1837. In consequence of this high-handed measure of the energetic despot, Ernest Augustus, formerly Duke of Cumberland, seven liberal professors, Dahlmann (now at Bonn,) Wilhelm and Jacob Grimm (now at Berlin,) Gervinus (residing at Heidelberg,) Ewald (who was called to Tübingen, but returned again to Göttingen,) Weber, and Albrecht, were deposed and expatriated, but met with an enthusiastic sympathy all over Germany, and received honorable calls to other universities. The number of students also declined rapidly, and scarcely reaches 700 now, while before 1831 it averaged, for several years, over 1400 annually. From these severe shocks the university will not fully recover for a long time to come, although it is now in a more flourishing condition than it was ten years ago.

The theological faculty sustained a great loss by the death of Gieseler, in 1854, and of Lücke, in 1855; but their places were filled with able successors. Dorner and Ehrenfeuchter are now its chief ornaments.

The university of Leipsic, founded in 1409, numbers as many ordinary, extraordinary, and private professors as Göttingen, viz: 109, and about 800 students, with a library of 110,000 volumes. It is highly distinguished for a large amount of philological and antiquarian learning, and immense literary industry, while in the speculative sciences it occupies only a secondary place, and rarely gives rise to new ideas and systems of thought. The Saxon schools generally turn out the best classical scholars, and make the language of Cicero, in the higher classes of the gymnasia, not only the object, but also the living medium of a thorough instruction.

In a theological point of view, this university resisted, at first, the reformation, and claimed the victory over Wittenberg, in the famous disputation which was held between Luther and Eck, in 1519, on the Pleissenburg, the old castle of Leipsic, now used as a barrack, and an observatory. But soon afterwards it embraced the new faith, and remained for a long time a nursery of orthodox Lutheranism, even after the royal house of Saxony, prompted by unworthy secular motives, apostatized from the Protestant to the Roman Catholic Church. Since the end of the last century, however, the old foundations gradually gave way, and Leipsic, together with Halle and Jena, became the chief patron of neology in northern and central Germany, and cursed Saxony, both the kingdom and the duchies, with a rationalistic clergy. It long resisted the revival of evangelical religion in the present century, and was less affected than most of the other universities by the theology of Schleiermacher and Neander, and the philosophy of Schelling and Hegel, which destroyed the power of the older deistic rationalism. But more recently a decided change has taken place in favor of Lutheran orthodoxy, and that mostly in its rigid confessional form. One of the strongest champions of this school, Dr. Harless, was called there in 1847, but remained only a few years. Dr. Kahnis and Lindner, two divines of the younger generation, labor in the same spirit as theological professors, and are greatly assisted by Dr. Ahlfeld, who is one of the most eloquent and pious German pulpit orators of the age. Dr. Liebner, a highly-gifted speculative divine, and excellent preacher, belongs to a milder form of a Lutheranism, and falls in more with the evangelical school of Nitzsch, Müller, and Dorner; but he was recently removed to the presidency of the consistory at Dresden.

The University of Leipsic enjoys many local advantages, more or less educational in their bearing. For Leipsic, the second city in the kingdom of Saxony, with about 70,000 inhabitants, has a large number of literary institutions, societies, and valuable libraries, and is the most extensive book market on the continent of Europe. It numbers 130 publishers and booksellers, and 31 printing establishments, which issue, it is estimated, 50 millions of printed sheets annually. At its noted fairs, especially at Easter, goods to the amount of 60 millions of Prussian thalers are sold or exchanged, of which 8 millions are for books. On these occasions the strangers from all quarters of the old world, especially the East, outnumber sometimes the inhabitants; and Turks, Greeks, Persians, Armenians, Polish Jews, and Hungarians, are seen walking about in their picturesque oriental costumes. The city lies in a fertile plain, at the confluence of the Elster, Pleisse, and Parthe, and is surrounded by rapidly growing suburbs and numerous gardens. The old fortifications have been converted into beautiful promenades, with trees and shrubberies. But the most pleasant walk is to the *Rosenthal*, where Schiller composed the poem, "*Freude, schöner Götterfunke*," while *Auerbach's Cellar*, in the centre of the city proper, reminds the lover of poetry of the famous drinking scene in Göthe's Faust. The citizens of Leipsic are generally intelligent, courteous, and polite to a degree which makes them strongly resemble the French.

The mass of the population is Lutheran, but there is also a Reformed, and a Roman Catholic Church there, and a Jewish synagogue. The memorable *Völkerschlacht* (battle of nations,) which was fought around and in Leipsic, Oct. 16–19, 1813, and which decided the defeat of Napoleon by the Allies, and the emancipation of Europe from the French yoke, gives the place an additional historical importance. Those were most glorious days for Germany, but mixed with a deep feeling of regret and humiliation for the Saxons, whose fathers, in blind obedience to their misguided King, fought under the banners of Napoleon against their own countrymen and fatherland.

CHAPTER IX.

JENA AND THE BURSCHENSCHAFT.

The University of Jena—Its Former Celebrity—Weimar and the German Classics—Origin of the Burschenschaft—The Wartburg Festival—The Sand Tragedy—Dissolution of the Burschenschaft—Distinguished German Refugees to America—Follen, Lieber, and Rauch.

JENA is a little town in the little grand duchy of Saxe-Weimar. But its university, which dates from the age of the Reformation, acquired great celebrity at the end of the last and the early part of the present century by a rare collection of profound philosophers, as Fries, Fichte, Schelling, Hegel, and genial poets and critics, as Schiller (for some time professor of history,) Schlegel, Tieck, Novalis, who resided there either as professors, or as private gentlemen, and prepared an intellectual reformation of Germany at the period of its deepest political degradation. Schelling's lectures had an electrifying effect upon the students, and opened to them new paths of speculation, as may be seen from the autobiographies of his admiring disciples, Steffens and Schubert. Hegel, who was far inferior to him as a lecturer, wrote the last pages of his first great philosophical work, the *Phaenomenologie*, under the cannon roar of the disastrous battle of 1806, which resulted in the annihilation of the Prussian forces at the hands of Napoleon. Fichte soon afterwards took a most active part in rousing the slumbering patriotism and indignation of the Germans against the French. These three philosophers moved ultimately to Berlin, while Fries continued in Jena, and figured prominently in the creation of the Burschenschaft, and the Wartburg celebration.

During the same period, Weimar, the capital of the grand-duchy, which is only 15 miles distant from Jena, deserved in an eminent sense the name of the German Athens, as the residence of the immortal heroes of German poetry. Göthe (died 1832,) Schiller (1805,) Herder (1803,) and Wieland (1813,) resided there till their deaths, attracted the most distinguished men of their age, as occasional visitors, to Weimar, and cast the lustre of their literary glory also upon the neighboring university. Unfortunately the cause of Christianity and the church, which, after all, far outweighs the highest creations of genius, and the richest flowers of art, received no encouragement whatever from these worshippers of beauty, except Herder. He was, indeed, an enthusiastic admirer of the poetry and religion of the Bible ; but could not arrest the flood of elegantly varnished infidelity and demoralizing worldliness which inundated that country, and which has hardly begun to recede.

Subsequently the university of Jena became the birthplace of the ill-fated *Burschenschaft.* It was organized in 1816, under a local character, and spread soon over Germany, taking the place of the old rotten *Landsmannschaften.* As it fills an interesting and characteristic chapter in the modern history of the German universities, we may here briefly refer to the principal facts.

The Burschenschaft was a voluntary association of German students for the purpose of realizing the patriotic ideals which had been awakened in the German nation by the successful war of independence. It was animated by a noble, though unripe and confused religious patriotic enthusiasm. It lacked, it is true, a solid basis, and a clearly-defined practical end. Still it might have accomplished an important work for Germany, if it had been wisely controlled, instead of being violently suppressed by the governments.

The first important act of the Burschenschaft of Jena was an invitation, drawn up by Robert Wesselhöft, to the students of the German universities, to assemble on the Wartburg, Oct. 18th, 1817, for the purpose of celebrating the approaching third centennial jubilee of the Reformation, and more particularly the recent liberation of Germany from French tyranny.

Accordingly about 500 students, representing 12 universities, many of whom had fought as volunteers a few years before on the battle fields of Leipsic and Waterloo, for the freedom of their fatherland, together with several professors, Dr. Fries, Kieser, Schweizer, and others, met on the market of Eisenach in the morning of the appointed day, made memorable by the decisive victory of Leipsic, and marched in solemn procession, with banners, and under the sound of festive music and all the bells of the city, to the famous castle where Luther, in involuntary confinement, three hundred years before, had translated the New Testament, and cast his inkstand at the devil. There, in the Minnesängersaal, they sung the warlike psalm of the reformer, "*Ein' feste Burg ist unser Gott;*" listened to a patriotic sermon and prayer of Mr. Riemann, a theological student of Jena, and Knight of the Iron Cross, which he had acquired in the bloody action of Waterloo; concluded the religious services with the German Te Deum, "*Nun danket alle Gott;*" and then, at 12 o'clock, partook of a common meal, highly seasoned by enthusiastic toasts upon German freedom, "the jewel of life," on Dr. Martin Luther, "the man of God," on the grand duke of Saxe-Weimar, "the patron of the day," on the victors of Leipsic, the volunteers of 1813, the German universities, and the Burschenschaft. After this feast of reason and flow of soul, they returned, at 2 o'clock, to the city to attend divine services in the church, reassembled on the market-place, in connection with the *Eisenacher Landsturm*, spent the evening in singing and gymnastic exercises, and concluded the festivities of the day by a torch procession to the Wartenberg, opposite the Wartburg.

So far everything passed off with perfect order and decorum. But late in the night an imprudent act was committed on the Wartenberg, which, though not provided for in the programme, proved nearly fatal to the Burschenschaft. It was the burning of 28 illiberal books and pamphlets, together with a bodice, a cue, and a corporal's staff, the symbols of the old fashioned pedantry and tyranny of Germany. This political auto da fé, a mock repetition of the solemn act by which the great reformer committed the papal bull of condemnation to the flames before the Elster-gate of Wittenberg in 1520, might have passed unpunished, and left to its own consequences, in the republics of Switzerland, and the

United States, or in a free monarchy like England. But among the many big and little governments of Germany, whose greatest fault and trouble is an excess of government, it aroused alarm concerning the objects and tendencies of the Burschenschaft, and thus greatly strengthened the political reaction which had set in since the Congress of Vienna, especially in Austria, and even in Prussia. A denunciatory and disrespectful letter of the Prussian Oberregierungsrath von Kamptz, whose collection of police laws was among the number of burned books, to the grand duke of Saxe-Weimar, revealed the indignation which was felt in high places against the students. Upon a calm and impartial representation of the whole affair by the government of Saxe-Weimar, which disconnected the improvisized auto da fé from the Wartburg festival, the storm passed over, but only for a short season.

In the meantime the movement amongst the students enlarged and deepened. On the first anniversary of the Wartburg celebration, the 18th of October, 1818, the representatives of 14 universities assembled in Jena, and founded the *General German Burschenschaft*, on the basis of unity, freedom, and equality of rights and duties. Its object was stated to be "the Christian German (*christlich deutsche*) development of every spiritual and physical power for the service of the fatherland." The constitution of this society, which may be found in full in Haupt's *Landsmannschaft und Burschenschaft*, and also in the fourth volume of Carl von Raumer's *Geschichte der Pädagogik*, is drawn up with considerable care and circumspection, and differs favorably in moral tone from the undignified and ridiculous comments of the *Landsmannschaften*, as they existed before the year 1817. They evidently show the ennobling effect which the German war of liberation exerted upon the rising youth. But such an association, based upon liberal political principles, and extending its net over most of the German universities, appeared dangerous to the reactionists, and created a growing opposition which resulted at last in the dissolution of the Burschenschaft.

The crisis was brought about in March, 1819, by the assassination of Hofrath von Kotzebue, an unprincipled man and writer, then residing at Mannheim, who was justly hated and despised by all the liberals, as a Russian spy and traitor of Germany. Karl Ludwig Sand, an honest and serious, but melancholy, dreamy, and confused student of theology, at Jena, a great admirer of Charles Follen, and member of the Burschenschaft, who had taken part in the festival of the Wartburg, performed the foul deed by a dagger, in mistaken zeal for German liberty, on the wicked maxim that the end justifies the means. While the worthless victim was expiring in his own dwelling, Sand rushed to the street, assembled a crowd, and exclaimed, "Hurrah for my German fatherland, and all those Germans who desire to promote the welfare of pure humanity!" Then kneeling down, he prayed, "I thank thee, O God! for this victory," and made an unsuccessful attempt at suicide, hoping by means of a double crime to open a bloody path for German liberty, and thus to immortalize himself as a second Arnold of Winkelried. During the trial he showed perfect composure, and gloried in his deed, which he declared he had premeditated for six months without the knowledge of others. On the 20th of May, 1819, he was executed by the sword, near Mannheim, before a great concourse of people. His last audible words were, "God gives me much cheerfulness in death—it is done —I die in the grace of God."

It is plain enough that Sand was no common assassin, but a misguided, half insane fanatic. Hence his fate excited as much sympathy as the assassination created abhorrence. Dr. De Wette, at that time professor of Christian ethics, at Berlin, taking the false ground that even an erring conscience is binding and must be obeyed, attempted, not indeed to justify, but to excuse the double crime of Sand, in a private letter to his mother, which, being made known to the King of Prussia, was the cause of his deposition from the professorial chair.

The murder of Kotzebue was regarded by the enemies of the Burschenschaft, although without any legal evidence to justify the charge, as the result of a general revolutionary conspiracy among the academic youth, or at least as the natural fruit of its liberal political tendencies.

The Burschenschaft was prohibited by a resolution of the German Diet, Sept. 20, 1819, and its leaders were made severely to suffer in prison, or exile, for their youthful enthusiasm. Nevertheless, the society continued to exist secretly in several universities, and divided into two branches, the *Arminia*, which favored the principle of constitutional monarchy, and the *Germania*, which was republican in its political creed. The events which followed the French revolution of 1830 seemed to justify a more open and determined action of the students. But these disturbances only led to new investigations, stricter prohibitions, imprisonments and expatriations, especially in 1834 and 1839.

These severe measures increased the distrust of the students against the governments, and that dissatisfaction which broke out so fearfully in the revolutions of 1848, and which can only be radically removed by a wise, benevolent, and liberal policy.

Many of the German students who were compelled to leave their native land on account of liberal sentiments on politics, found a hospitable asylum in the United States, and some of them distinguished themselves as professors, or by valuable contributions to American literature. Among these, three deserve special mention; first, Charles Follen, the teacher of the unfortunate Sand, and suspected, though unjustly, no doubt, for being implicated in the murder of Kotzebue, since 1830 professor of German literature in Harvard University, afterwards Unitarian minister, till he met with a melancholy death in the flames of the steamer Lexington, in 1840; secondly, Dr. Francis Lieber, now of South Carolina, a most accomplished scholar, who is pretty generally regarded in America as the best living writer on political ethics, and the philosophy of constitutional government; and finally, Dr. Frederick Augustus Rauch, the youngest of the three, the first president of Marshall College, at Mercersburg, and author of a well-known psychology, which would have been followed, no doubt, by a number of still more important philosophical and theological works, if Providence had not called him hence in the prime of life (1841.)

CHAPTER X.

HEIDELBERG AND TUBINGEN.

The City and University of Heidelberg—Their Various Fortunes and Present Condition—The Theological Faculty—Tubingen—The General Literary, Social, and Religious Character of Wurtemberg—The Pietists—Mode of Study in Tubingen—Preponderance of Speculation—The Tubingen School—Eritis Sicut Deus—Important Change, and Favorable Prospect—Baur, Beck, Landerer, Palmer, Oehler.

HEIDELBERG, the seat of the Protestant university of the grand duchy of Baden, formerly the capital of the electoral Palatinate, rivals Bonn in beauty of situation, being surrounded by wooded hills, vineyards, and promenades, on the charming banks of the Neckar, and commanded by the famous old castle of the electors, which is regarded as the most picturesque and romantic, as the Coliseum of Rome is the most colossal and imposing, ruin of Europe.

Its university, the celebrated *Ruperto-Carolina*, dating from the fourteenth century, is, next to that of Prague, the oldest in Germany, and the cradle from which the first scientific culture of the Southern regions of that country proceeded. It shared all the strange vicissitudes of fortune to which the city and the castle were subjected. At first the seat of dry and stiff scholasticism, then promoting the revival of classical literature through John Wessel, Agricola, and Reuchlin, it became an early battle-field of the Reformation, and the alma mater of Melancthon, Oecolampadius, Bucer, Brenz, and Schnepf. The last three of these students were converted to the Protestant cause by the public debate of Luther on the freedom of the will, on faith and good works, in 1518. At the middle of the sixteenth century, Heidelberg became the classical soil of Melancthonian theology and the German Reformed Church, under the protection of Frederick the Pius, who called Zacharias Ursinus and Caspar Olevianus to the theological chair, and entrusted them with the composition of the Heidelberg Catechism, the most genial and catholic symbol of the Reformed Confession. But since the outbreak of the thirty years' war it suffered most severely, and was several times suspended during the terrible devastations of the beautiful Palatinate; first in 1622, when the ferocious Tilly, after bombarding Heidelberg for a month, took it by storm, and abandoned it to three days' pillage; then in 1688, when Melac, by order of Louis XIV., burned the town, and outrivaled even Tilly in brutality; again in 1693, when another French force repeated, and exceeded, if possible, all former cruelties; and finally during the wars of Napoleon, who paid as little regard to this ancient seat of learning, and plundered its exceedingly valuable library and manuscripts, since restored in part. But the university outlived all these misfortunes, is now again in a flourishing condition, and occupies a prominent and commanding position in the literary world, especially in the department of jurisprudence. Private gentlemen, too, of eminent distinction, as Chevalier Bunsen, and Heinrich von Gagern, have selected Heidelberg for their literary retirement.

The theological faculty was, in the early part of this century, degraded to the lowest order of rationalism, when it stood under the controlling influence of the notorious Paulus, who resembled much more the persecuting Saul, than the converted Paul, and tried to explain away all the miracles of Christ by the unnatural process of a so called natural interpretation. It is not easy to estimate the amount of harm which this man inflicted during his long life upon the churches of Baden, Hesse-Darmstadt, and the Bavarian Palatinate. Still his influence was counteracted, to a great extent, by the profound and vigorous philosophical divine, Daub, and subsequently by the mild and learned Ullmann. Paulus lived to see himself buried alive with his deistic infidelity, and that not only by the better spirit of the age, but also by another infidel, Dr. Strauss, who built his "Leben Jesu" on the ruins of the work of Paulus on the same subject. The professors who compose, at present, the theological faculty at Heidelberg, Rothe, Hundeshagen, Schenkel, Umbreit, are, without exception, men of eminent talent and scholarship, and zealously engaged in building up, in the spirit of Christ, what a former generation had nearly destroyed.

Tübingen, a town of small size, and hilly streets, but beautifully located on the banks of the Neckar, 18 miles distant from Stuttgart, has been for nearly four hundred years the alma mater of the scholars and professional men of Würtemberg. Of this remarkable country we must first make some general remarks.

The kingdom of Würtemberg contains one third less inhabitants than the city of London alone with its two millions and a half. And yet it would be difficult to find a country which, in proportion to its size and the number of inhabitants, gave birth to a greater number of distinguished scholars and literary men. The poets Schiller, Wieland, Schubart, Uhland, Schwab, Kerner, Pfizer, Mörike, Knapp, Bahrdt, Eyth; the philosophers Schelling and Hegel; the Protestant theologians Brentius, Oecolampadius, Andreä, Osiander, Pfaff, Bengel, Oetinger, Planck, Storr, Schmid, Baur, Beck, Dorner, Hoffmann; the Roman Catholic divines Möhler, Drey, Hirscher, Staudenmeier, Hefele, Welte, are all natives of Würtemberg, and most of them—Schiller excepted—graduates of Tübingen, although the most celebrated of them (Wieland, Schiller, Schelling, Hegel, etc.,) spent their public life in other parts of Germany. For the country is so small and poor, that not a few of its ablest sons are obliged to seek their fortune elsewhere. Besides, the Swabians have a strong love for emigration, and may be found in all parts of the world as professors, school-masters, music-teachers, ministers, missionaries, naturalists, mechanics, and farmers. They contributed probably fully one third to the membership of the Lutheran church in the United States.

This literary fertility of Würtemberg may be attributed, in a large measure, to an excellent system of instruction and rigid examination, from the university down to the primary schools which are established in every hamlet, and *must* be attended by all children from 6 to 14 years of age, until they are confirmed.

But it must be owing also, of course, to natural talent and disposition. The Swabians have strong intellects, fertile imaginations, genial humor, and deep feeling, although an old proverb says that they do not come to their wits until they are forty. They are rather slow, it is true, somewhat heavy and harsh, like their dialect, but solid, industrious, persevering, honest, and reliable. What they lack in form, they make up in contents, and, if their outside be unprepossessing, their inside is the more substantial. I nowhere met more earnest interest in science and literature, more sincere kindness of heart and overflowing affection, than in the good old *Schwabenland.* That untranslatable Germanism, *Gemüthlichkeit,* may be found there in all its peculiar charm and attraction.

Würtemberg is also one of the most interesting countries, in a religious point of view, and deserves to be more frequently visited by travellers, on that account, than it is. It has, in proportion to its size, a larger number of pious ministers and laymen, than any part of Europe, except the Wupperthal, in Rhenish Prussia, England and Scotland. It contributes annually more men and means for the promotion of the kingdom of God, than many a Christian country of double the size, and ten times its wealth. It is a singular fact, indeed, that it produced some of the most learned opponents of Christianity, as Paulus, the champion of deistic rationalism; Baur, the head of the pantheistic rationalism; Strauss, the author of the "Life of Jesus," which should rather be called an attempt at the critical destruction of the life of Jesus. When I studied at Tübingen, from 1837 to '39, more than one half of the theological students were tinctured more or less with Hegelian pantheism, and destructive criticism. But the general character of the people is strongly and deeply religious. They cherish with grateful reverence the unbroken succession of the pious divines and ministers, from Bengel to Hofacker, who faithfully taught and preached the way of life during the infidel apostacy of the last and present centuries. They crowd the churches of those who proclaim the whole counsel of God. Besides, a great change has taken place among the ministers and students, and the young generation is growing up under much more favorable influences now than twenty or even ten years ago.

The Protestants of Würtemberg, who comprise two thirds of the whole population, are originally Lutherans in doctrine and discipline, with the exception of a few colonies of Huguenots, which have long since become Germanized. But in mode of worship they always were essentially Reformed, though by no means puritanic, and more recently a Presbyterian element has been introduced into the form of government. The reformation of the country (1535,) was brought about by the coöperation of Lutheran and Zwinglian elements, the former being represented by Brenz and Schnepf, the latter by Blaurer, a native of Constance, and friend of a more simple service after the Helvetic type. At a subsequent period the pietistic movement of Spener, which, it is well known, lays the main stress on regeneration, conversion, and vital piety, in opposition to exclusive confessionalism and dead orthodoxy, exerted great influence in

Würtemberg, but in a modified form. The Würtemberg pietism is combined with solid learning, and a certain mysticism which includes both a theosophic and a practical element. It also has a special taste for speculations on apocalyptic and millěnarian topics, and strongly leans, at least in many of its representatives, to the dangerous doctrine of a final salvation of all creatures, although on a basis essentially different from that of American Universalism.

The revered leaders of this school are Bengel, the great commentator, Oetinger, Steinhofer, Hartmann, Rieger, Roos, Hiller, Storr, Flatt, Steudel, Schmid, and among the more recent preachers the two Hofackers, Kapff, Knapp and Bahrdt. Their writings, especially the commentaries of Bengel and Rieger, the hymns of Hiller, and the sermons of Steinhofer and Louis Hofacker, are to this day rich sources of instruction and edification to the people.

Next to the main body of pietists there are some smaller branches, the followers of Michael Hahn, a second Jacob Böhm, though less profound and speculative, who insisted upon a thorough sanctification, and the followers of Pregizer, who made justification by faith the most prominent article of Christianity.

These pietists of Würtemberg occupied, for a long time, a position in the Lutheran church similar to that of the early Methodists in the Anglican communion, and the government wisely tolerated them. They held, and still hold, separate prayer meetings, mostly conducted by laymen (the so-called *Stundenhalter*, a sort of class leaders, of whom the late Hoffmann and Kullen, of Kornthal, were the most able and popular); but they attended at the same time faithfully the public services, received the sacraments at the hands of the regularly ordained ministers, and, with the exception of the congregations of Kornthal and Wilhelmsdorf, never seceded from the established church, preferring rather to remain in its bosom as a wholesome leaven. Thus they proved a blessing to it, and kept the lamp of faith burning in a period of spiritual darkness. By and by, the church itself awoke from the cold and dreary winter of indifferentism and rationalism, introduced a better hymn-book and liturgy, and began to take part in the benevolent operations of Christianity, heretofore carried on almost exclusively by the pietists, such as the domestic and foreign missionary cause, the support of poor houses, orphan asylums, etc.

Since this revival of the church, the pietists have themselves become more churchly, and given up or modified their former peculiarities, but without falling in with the symbolical Lutheranism, as it prevails now in the neighboring kingdom of Bavaria, and in some parts of northern Germany. Rigid confessionalism finds no congenial soil in Würtemberg. The church of that country calls itself now officially no more Lutheran, but Evangelical. Its best ministers and laymen take an active part in the movements of the Church Diet, the Gustavus Adolphus Society, and the Evangelical Alliance. They support, in fraternal communion with the Reformed Christians of Switzerland, the missionary establishment of Basel, most of whose teachers and pupils are natives of Würtemberg, and may be said to be attached, in principle and practice, to the cause of the evangelical union. The theology which prevails there, has the same character, and is based upon the consensus of the two churches. Some of the most eminent divines of Würtemberg found no difficulty to follow a call to a Reformed university, as Schneckenburger, or to chairs and pulpits in the United Prussian Church, as Kling, Staib, Dorner, Hoffmann.

But it is time to return from this digression to Tübingen. This university is distinguished for its thorough and systematic way of teaching and studying. This is especially the case with the theological students, who live together in one building, the Protestants in the so called *Stift*, the Roman Catholics in the *Convict*, and are supported by the state to the conclusion of their course. It is impossible to find anywhere closer application and more fervent devotion to study. The *Würtemberger Gründlichkeit* has become proverbial, and often degenerates, it must be admitted, into wearisome minuteness and pedantry. The late excellent Dr. Schmid never finished any course of lectures, although he kept the class from five to ten minutes beyond the time, and continued to lecture to the very last day of the session. He would, for instance, spend six hours a week for six months, in explaining grammatically, critically, historically, dogmatically, ethically, practically, etc., the first eight chapters of the Epistle to the Romans, promising to finish the rest the next session.

The prescribed theological course in Tübingen, from which no exception is made, extends over four years, or eight long sessions, there being but five or six weeks' vacation in spring and autumn. But the first two sessions are mostly devoted to the higher branches of philology and philosophy. The students read, in historical order, the great systems of ancient Greek and modern German philosophy, from Plato down to Hegel, with as much earnestness and zeal as if the salvation of the world depended upon the abstruse categories of metaphysics. This preponderance of speculation is no doubt accompanied by serious evils. Many a youth within the last twenty or thirty years has been unfitted for theology and the ministry by his philosophical studies, which ended in the embrace of Hegelian pantheism, and Straussian infidelity. Hence various reforms have been agitated for some time in the method of study, and Dr. Hoffman, now at Berlin, tried to introduce some radical changes into the organization of the *Stift*, although without success.

But the first and principal want seems to be a reform of philosophy itself. Man will never cease to philosophize as long as he retains the inborn noble desire to penetrate from the outside of things to the inside, from the surface to the depth, to rise from the particular to the general, from accidental phenomena to the eternal laws and principles, and to comprehend the scattered fragments of knowledge in the unity and harmony of a system. But the false philosophy which ruled at Tübingen for so long a time, and wrought incalculable mischief among the students, the logical pantheism and heartless, arrogant intellectualism of the Strauss-Helgelian school, should and must give way to a positive Christian philosophy, that bows in humble reverence before the revealed truths of the Gospel, and tends to reconcile reason with a living faith. Philosophy can only be cured by philosophy. It is a law of the devils and demons, says Göthe, that they must get out at the same place where they sneaked in. At the same time exegetical and practical studies should receive more attention than heretofore, and not be treated simply in the spirit of criticism, but with constant regard to the solemn duties of the ministry, and the awful realities of eternity.

The dark side of the university life of Tübingen for the last twenty years, and the sad consequences of the young Hegelian pantheism were graphically pictured, in 1853, by an anonymous, but highly-gifted and pious lady, in a novel under the characteristic title, *Eritis sicut Deus*, the motto of the old serpent. It created, for a time, almost as great a sensation in the literary circles of Germany, as Mrs. Stowe's Uncle Tom among all classes of readers in America. It is a deeply interesting book, on one of the most remarkable phases of German speculation and infidelity. But by introducing living characters, such as Vischer, Baur, Strauss, Schwegler, and even ladies of Tübingen, who can easily be recognized by the experienced reader through the veil of fictitious names, it unfortunately violates the rules of good taste, assumes somewhat the hideous appearance of a libel, and is calculated to enrage the very men whom it should seek most to benefit and to lead back from the labyrinth of error to the sunny path of truth.

The period of this false philosophy and theology may be said to have passed for Tübingen and Würtemberg.

Dr. Vischer, a classmate and friend of Strauss, and an unusually smart and witty, but thoroughly irreverent and frivolous professor of æsthetics, received a serious rebuke some years ago from the government, and was suspended, although only for a season. He has now accepted a call to Zurich. Strauss has long given up, it seems, all interest in theology, and is an unhappy man, divorced from his wife, the former actress Agnese Schebest, and moving from place to place. His pseudo-theology or mythology ended in a theatrical comedy, and the comedy in a tragedy. Zeller and Schwegler have exchanged the theological for philosophical and philological pursuits, for which they are far better adapted, and the former left Tübingen, first for Bern, and then for Marburg. Dr. Baur, the patriarch of the hypercritical "Tübingen school," and the most earnest and learned of them all, is declining in influence as he advances in age. The most popular professor of theology now is his complete antipode, Dr. Beck, who treats all modern novelties with the silence of utter contempt, and professes to know nothing but the Bible as the book of life. The other members of the theological faculty, Drs. Landerer, Palmer, and Oehler, although differing from each other on minor points, are without exception decidedly Christian and evangelical scholars, and promise a better future for the church of Würtemberg.

SECOND PART.

GERMAN THEOLOGY AND RELIGION.

CHAPTER XI.

CHURCH AND STATE IN GERMANY.

The Free-Church System of America—Freedom of Dissent in England—The State-Church System on the Continent—The Roman Catholic Supremacy over the State—Dependence of Protestantism upon the State—The Theory of the Ecclesiastical State-Supremacy Exposed—The evils of State-Churchism—Frightful Amount of Infidelity—Growing Dissatisfaction with the System—The Attempted Dissolution of the Union of Church and State, by the Frankfort Parliament—The New Prussian Constitution, and its Guarantees to the Independence of the Church.

THE glory of America is a free Christianity, independent of the secular government, and supported by the voluntary contributions of a free people. This is one of the greatest facts in modern history. Its significance can only be fully estimated by a careful comparison with the state-churches of Europe, both Protestant and Catholic, beyond which it marks a gigantic progress. Whatever be the defects and inconveniences of the separation of church and state, they are less numerous and serious than the troubles and difficulties which continually grow out of their union, to the injury of both parties. Our self-sustaining and self-governing Christianity calls to mind the heroic age of the church; with this important difference, however, that in the first three centuries she had to maintain her existence, not only without any help from the Roman empire, but against its deadly hatred and bloody persecution, whilst in our republic she enjoys the friendship and legal protection of the civil government, to which she, in turn, imparts moral strength and stability, so that the two powers are here really a benefit and indirect support to each other, without unsettling their distinct boundaries, and getting into continual collision by mutual interference.

We do not assert, by any means, that the American system is perfect, and final; but it is preferable to a hierarchical rule over the state on the one hand, and to a servile subjection of the church to the secular power on the other. Body and soul undoubtedly belong together, and constitute the idea of man. But the body is not the soul, nor is the soul the body. Each has its peculiar members, faculties and functions, and it is very important that both should enjoy freedom for the fulfilment of their mission. The spiritual and immortal part must rule, of course; but not by putting the body in chains, but by affording it healthy and vigorous exercise, and thus making it a willing organ for higher ends. In the perfect kingdom of God there will be no jealousy and collision of powers, but Christ will rule king of nations, as he now ruleth king of saints in his church. In the present order of the world we must render unto Cæsar the things that are Cæsar's, and unto God the things that are God's, without confounding Cæsar with God, or God with Cæsar.

Great Britain, the immediate parent of the United States, maintains two ecclesiastical establishments, Episcopacy in England and Ireland, and Presbyterianism in Scotland, and thus still holds to the theory of state-churchism. But in practice she carries religious toleration and liberty almost as far as her full-grown daughter, especially in the colonies, and the heroic sacrifices of the Free Church of Scotland furnish even a more striking illustration of the vitality and power of the voluntary system than any of our American denominations.

But on the continent of Europe such a thing as a free, self-supporting and self-governing church is hardly known, and exists only in small dissenting sects, which bear no comparison, in numerical strength and importance, with the dissenting bodies of England. In Germany, Austria, Russia, Sweden, Denmark, Italy, Spain, and even in France, and Switzerland, the public religion is interwoven with the state by ten thousand time-honored ties, which it seems impossible to dissolve without endangering the very existence of the church.

The Roman Catholic Church, it is true, has always asserted, in principle, her independence of, and even her supremacy over the state, which she aims to control and make subservient to her interests wherever she has the power. Her centralized organization, compact unity, imposing hierarchy, and magic influence over the mass of her membership, give her a great advantage over divided Protestantism in cases of a collision with the civil government. But in the first place, she claims liberty only for herself, and denies it, wherever she can, to every other form of Christianity, because she identifies her organization with the church universal, and regards every dissent from her creed and discipline as pernicious and damnable heresy and schism. In the second place, by her domineering and hierarchical spirit she rouses the jealousy and opposition of the temporal power and the spirit of nationality so closely connected with it. Some of the greatest popes of the middle ages spoke of the state with the utmost contempt, as if it was of purely human, or even diabolical origin, the result of ambition, conquest, rapine, and murder, and not a divine institution. Hence the long-continued conflict between the pope and the German emperor, even in the days of the highest power of the former. In our days I believe that Romanism is, in point of fact, nowhere so free from government interference as in England (the Ecclesiastical Titles-bill to the contrary notwithstanding,) and the United States, because these countries the general principle of religious freedom is most fully developed. In France, Gallicanism, which substitutes servility to the temporal prince for servility to the pope, still exists legally, although Ultramontanism is now in the ascendant, and in such countries as Spain, Italy, Mexico, and South America, the Catholic governments frequently rob the sacred property of the church to fill their empty treasury. In Austria, the Romish Church was only quite recently released from the despotic restrictions of the Josephine regime, and time must reveal whether the Concordat of 1855 will improve the morals and prosperity of that large empire or not.

As to Protestantism in Germany, and on the continent generally, it is ruled and almost entirely supported by the state, and this not only as a matter of fact, but on the Erastian principle of the supremacy of the temporal power, or even the territorialistic maxim, *cujus regio ejus religio*, a principle always disowned, and properly so, by the Roman church. This state of things dates from the Reformation. The Protestant princes and magistrates secularized the old church property, assumed the support of public worship, and, at the same time, the supreme authority over it. On this fact the theory was constructed which is still in force in all Lutheran, and in some Reformed churches, that the head of the state is also the head, or *summus episcopus*, of the church within his territory.

Strange bishops, indeed, who never studied theology, who were never ordained, who could never preach or administer the sacraments, and yet claim and exercise supreme authority over the religion of their subjects, fill the highest ecclesiastical offices, and issue or sanction the standards of public doctrine and worship! (Frederick William III. actually composed the new Prussian liturgy himself.) Still more strange, if this supreme governor of the church, as he is called in England, or summus episcopus, as he is entitled in Lutheran establishments, is a mere boy, like Edward VI., or a lady, like queen Elizabeth, and Victoria, of England, or a Romanist, like the kings of Saxony and Bavaria, and the emperor of Austria, or a notorious adulterer like the present king of Würtemberg, or a professed infidel, like Frederick II. of Prussia!

It is true there were not a few wicked popes in Rome, fox-hunting bishops in England, and infidel professors and parsons in Germany. But one inconsistency does not justify another. And then we have to do here with a false principle, and not simply with anomalous exceptions. It is equally true, on the other hand, that many Protestant princes, from the elector Frederick the Wise to king Frederick William IV., were nursing fathers to the church, and exercised their ecclesiastical supremacy in the fear of God and to the best interests of religion. But this only shows the adaptability of Christianity, which will make its independent, indestructible life felt under all outward organizations and in spite of them, and proves nothing for a form of government which places the highest spiritual authority in secular hands, and gives bad princes as much power to destroy the church as it enables good monarchs to build it up. Popes, bishops, and priests have at times made excellent generals, statesmen, and diplomatists, especially in the middle ages; but no sensible man would infer from such exceptions that the clergy should be entrusted with the management of the army, the finances, the foreign affairs, and the police.

Nobody can deny that a truly Christian government is a source of infinite blessing to a people, and if the state were what it ought to be, there could be no serious objection to its union with the church. But how few governments, alas! deserve that praise. They are naturally selfish, and they instinctively subordinate all higher considerations to their temporal and material interests. The world has just seen the strange spectacle—whether right or wrong—of Protestant England and Roman Catholic France and Sardinia, fighting arm and arm with the infidel Turk, against another nominally Christian power. His Catholic Apostolic Majesty of Austria, by a shrewd, shifting, and treacherous diplomacy, managed to keep out of the war, and sacrificed all religious interests to the most selfish state-policy, in spite of the recent concordat of Pius IX. The continental governments not only support theatres and all sorts of shows and amusements, even on Sunday, but many of them actually license gambling hells and houses of prostitution, thus putting the seal of their approbation upon the worst vices. The same government of England which professes and encourages Christianity at home, appropriates from ten to twelve thousand dollars annually to the support of the idolatry of Juggernaut in India, patronizes an institution for the training of Mohamedan priests in Calcutta, and permits the East-India Company, for filthy lucre's sake, to poison the empire of China, i. e., almost one third of the human race, by the infamous opium-trade. "If they do these things in the green tree, what shall be done in the dry?" Of such governments, or misgovernments, rather, as Naples, Spain, and Mexico, we will only say, with Dante, "Look, and pass on."

Now the worst is, that, owing to its union with the secular power, the church becomes in some sense responsible for nefarious acts which she cannot prevent, and has to bear a part of the blame. But this is not the only evil resulting from this mis-alliance. We will mention a few more.

The state-church system tends to secularize the church, to convert it into a sort of higher police, and institution of the government for the intellectual and moral training of its subjects, and to fill the ranks of the clergy with unconverted men, who seek the holy ministry simply from secular motives, like any other state office. In spite of all the orthodox instruction, the masses look upon the holy sacrament of baptism, and the solemn right of confirmation, merely or predominantly in the light of civil acts, which entitle them to the prerogatives of an earthly citizenship; and the time is yet within men's memory when, in several countries of Germany, the majority of theological students and clergymen were either absolutely indifferent, or bitterly hostile to active piety and religion. What a monstrous contradiction!

In the next place, the union of the two powers accustoms the people, moreover, to depend upon the government for the supply of all their spiritual wants, and thus prevents the free and full development of the duty and virtue of Christian liberality and benevolence. The indirect support of the church by the payment of compulsory taxes rather weakens than strengthens the attachment of the masses to the church, while the voluntary system is calculated to make men feel and appreciate more highly the blessings of the Gospel.

In the third place, the system hampers and cripples the energies of the church, and keeps her in a state of continual pupilage, contrary to the truly Protestant idea of the general priesthood and kingship of all believers. In many sections of Germany, especially the northern regions, where Lutheranism prevails, the congregations are almost as passive, dependent, and incapable of self-government, as in the Roman Catholic Church, and Luther's complaint of the want of material for elders and deacons, must be repeated in this nineteenth century, after Protestantism has been in operation for more than three hundred years. The people are only expected to be ruled, and hence they have no chance to learn individual and congregational self-government, which must be gradually acquired like every other art. Nobody ever learned to swim by keeping on the dry land. More recently the church authorities of Prussia, and Würtemberg have made some progress in the right direction, by introducing responsible lay officers, after the model of the Reformed churches, which were always distinguished by greater freedom and independence on the basis of congregational self-government.

Finally, the system fills the church with the most heterogeneous membership, from the highest piety to unblushing atheism and gross immorality; leads to a frequent profanation of the sacraments by their indiscriminate administration, makes discipline almost impossible, tends to beget hypocrisy and infidelity, and brings down a large amount of popular hatred and discontent upon the church, which would otherwise be directed only against the secular government.

It is unfortunately only too true that the majority of the nominal membership in most of the state-churches of Europe, whether Protestant, Roman Catholic, or Greek Catholic, disgrace their baptismal and confirmation vows, and care less for religion than pious heathen, and yet all their children *must* be baptized again on the hypocritical profession of the parents or sponsors. It is only too true that an amount of concealed and open hostility exists there to the church and to Christianity itself, which is almost unknown in the United States, or even in England. The Italian, French, and German infidels, revolutionists, anarchists, if they had the power, would not only dissolve the union of church and state, but destroy the church altogether, which they hate with diabolical hatred, as the supposed backbone of all political despotism. It is to be feared that another general outbreak, like that of 1848, would reënact the mad deeds of the first French revolution, which abolished the Christian religion, and expelled or guillotined its ministers.

The question now arises, Will this union of church and state continue much longer? The signs of the times seem to favor an answer in the negative. The overthrow of the system may lie yet in the distant future, or may be prevented by essential modifications of the system itself. But in its present form it is certainly strongly undermined in public opinion. Even in England, where there is much less cause of complaint, in view of the almost unlimited freedom of dissent, the ecclesiastical establishments have been weakened step by step, so as to embrace now hardly more than one half of the religious population. And yet religion itself seems not to have suffered thereby. On the contrary, even the Anglican and the Presbyterian churches are now in a more flourishing spiritual condition than they were before, having been roused to an honorable rivalry by the activity of the dissenters around them. English institutions and events exert a powerful influence upon the continent, especially the Protestant countries. To this must be added the still more powerful fact of American Christianity, which has now existed for nearly a century in absolute independence of the state, and yet shows more signs of life than any ecclesiastical establishment in Europe.

The liberal party in Germany is pretty well prepared, if not for an entire dissolution of the relation, at least for the broadest development of the principle of dissent after the English model. An entire separation, it is true, would be altogether undesirable under the present circumstances, and could only be the result of great political events, or a radical revolution, such as no peace-loving citizen can desire or help to bring about.

The great majority of pious people in Germany are strongly conservative, also in this respect. They cherish the idea of a Christian state as a sacred inheritance of the past. They value the union especially also for this reason, that it brings the whole population, every child that is born, under the influence and training of the church. They get over the objections and evils above mentioned, by looking to the Jewish theocracy, which was far from being perfect in its membership, and yet of divine institution. They shrink from the prospect of a dissolution of the time-honored bond, as opening the way for the reign of American sectarianism, and the unrestrained power of European infidelity, which is still worse than the former. The ministers fear also for the temporal support of their families, which would be endangered by their being thrown upon the mercy of a people so entirely unaccustomed to the voluntary principle, and in a great measure indifferent or even hostile to the church. They can not, or will not, look beyond the immediate results of a sudden overthrow of the ecclesiastical establishment which, in all human probability, would be disastrous in the extreme.

But, on the other side, many of the best ministers are becoming so utterly disgusted with the evils of the union of church and state that they have no hope but from a free Christianity, which would outlive the storm of a revolution, and in the end regenerate the nation. I heard a prominent evangelical divine of Würtemberg say, "We clergymen are looked upon now by the people as servants of the king and black-robed police officers (schwarze Polizeidiener); but when we shall be free from state support, and state control, they will begin to esteem and love us again as servants of Christ and true friends of the people."

In 1848 the state-church system was on the very brink of destruction. The German Parliament of Frankfort proclaimed full liberty of religion and irreligion, and complete emancipation of the state and school from the church and Christianity. This was evidently a radical measure, and, if we are to judge from the infidel speeches of some of its chief supporters, as Professor Vogt, the atheist and materialist, it looked far more to the freedom of irreligion than to the freedom of the church. It was well enough, therefore, that it remained on paper, with the other acts of that assembly. It helped only to strengthen the reäction, and with it the ecclesiastical establishments, which appear to be more firm now than before the revolution. And yet the state of things has undergone an important change since, after all, and the wild movements of 1848 have not been in vain.

For the new constitution of Prussia, adopted January

31, 1850, and still in force, declares likewise, only in a far more cautious and moderate way than the Frankfort Assembly, and in a manner altogether respectful to religion, the entire freedom of the churches from the state, and the independence of civil and political rights upon the religious profession. As this is a most important fact in modern ecclesiastico-political legislation, we may be permitted to quote, in full, the famous articles of the *Verfassungsurkunde*, which have been called the Magna Charta of religious liberty in Prussia.

ART. XII.—Die Freiheit des religiösen Bekenntnisses, der Vereinigung zu Religionsgesellschaften, und der gemeinsamen häuslichen und öffentlichen Religionsübung wird gewährleistet. Der Genuss der bürgerlichen und staatsbürgerlichen Rechte ist unabhängig von dem religiösen Bekenntnisse. Den bürgerlichen und staatsbürgerlichen Rechten darf durch die Ausübung der Religionsfreiheit kein Abbruch geschehen.

ART. XIII.—Die Religionsgesellschaften, sowie die geistlichen Gesellschaften, welche keine Corporationsrechte haben, können diese Rechte nur durch besondere Gesetze erlangen.

ART. XIV.—Die christliche Religion wird bei denjenigen Einrichtungen des Staats, welche mit der Religionsübung im Zusammenhange stehen, unbeschadet der in Art. XII gewährleisteten Religionsfreiheit, zum Grunde gelegt.

ART. XV.—Die Evangelische und die Römisch—Katholische Kirche, sowie jede andere Religions—Gesellschaft ordnet und verwaltet ihre Angelegenheiten selbständig und bleibt im Besitz und Genuss der für ihre Cultus, Unterrichts und Wohlthätigkeits-zwecke bestimmten Anstalten, Stiftungen und Fonds.

These provisions then guarantee both the freedom of the church and the freedom of the state, and separate the two spheres without infringing upon the sacred rights of ecclesiastical property. But in point of fact the Evangelical Church is still dependent upon state control and state support, and the dissenting sects are placed under various restrictions. The reäctionary party in the Prussian chambers, headed by Ludwig von Gerlach and Stahl, both men of commanding genius and unblemished moral and religious character, made an attempt recently to erase from the constitution the sentence in the twelfth article, which declares the enjoyment of civil and political rights, independent of religious profession, with the view especially to exclude the Jews from civil and political equality with the Christians. But a motion to that effect, proposed by Legationsrath Wagner (the editor of the reäctionary *Kreuzzeitung*, although, strange to say, himself a dissenter from the state religion, viz: an Irvingite,) was not supported by the government, and defeated in the second chamber, February, 1856.

The question, then, for Prussia, now comes to this, whether the articles of the constitution which guarantee full religious liberty, both public and private, and give every recognized ecclesiastical corporation the right of self-government, shall remain a dead letter, or whether it shall be gradually and wisely carried out.

CHAPTER XII.

THE CONFLICT FOR RELIGIOUS FREEDOM.

The Bunsen-Stahl Controversy—Stahl's Views on Christian Toleration—Bunsen's "Signs of the Times"—Opposition to Bunsen—Response to his Plea for Religious Freedom—Position of the King of Prussia, and the approaching Meeting of the Evangelical Alliance in Berlin.

BEFORE we dismiss the consideration of the relation of church and state in Germany, we must take notice of the famous Bunsen-Stahl controversy on religious toleration and freedom, which made so much sensation recently, and affords us a clear insight into the present state of parties concerning this important subject.

The controversy originated with a very able address of Professor Stahl, the distinguished lawyer, and member both of the Prussian *Staatsrath*, and *Oberkirchenrath*, on Christian toleration, delivered at Berlin, March 29, 1855, for the Evangelical Association, in the presence of a part of the court, and a highly intelligent audience, which may be called the Christian aristocracy of Berlin.

The address starts with the assertion that the God of the Old and New Testament is the only true God, and jealous of his honor. So also the revealed religion of the Bible is essentially exclusive and intolerant against all false gods and forms of idolatry. Christianity claims to be the only true and universal religion, out of which there is no salvation, and can, therefore, not be indifferent towards any form of error, which deprives God of his honor, and endangers the salvation of man. Under this view it is diametrically opposed to the modern theory of toleration as proclaimed by Voltaire in France, Frederick II. in Prussia, and Jefferson in America, which places all religions, Christian, Jewish, Mohamedan, and heathen, on a perfect equality, from sheer indifference to religion itself, or from downright infidelity. The heathen Pilate, and Lessing's Nathan the Wise may skeptically ask, "What is truth?" But Christ says, "I am the truth." Hence the cardinal virtue of the Christian is not this toleration of the century of revolution and infidelity, which at times has shown itself most intolerant to Christianity itself, but unswerving devotion to the truth as revealed in Christ, zeal for the glory of the only true and living God, and the propagation of his kingdom for the salvation of the whole world.

Nevertheless, Stahl continues, Christianity includes a toleration far deeper than ever entered the mind or heart of man before, and for this he pleads. True Christian toleration rests on, and consists in, that love and charity which beareth all things, and hopeth all things; that humility which, conscious of its own sin and error, abstains from judging others; that high appreciation of the image of God in man, which the Gospel only can enjoin; and finally, in the conviction that God has reserved the full separation of the tares from the wheat to himself, for the judgment day. All this is perfectly compatible with the strictest and most faithful adherence to divine truth.

But now the difficult practical question arises as to

the duty of a Christian state, in view of the different churches and sects which all claim to be sound forms of Christianity, and to have an equal right to protection.

Here Professor Stahl draws a sharp line of distinction between the Anglo-American, and what he regards as the true German theory of toleration. The former, which he admits is making considerable progress in Germany, amounts to a virtual surrender of the idea of the church as an organic unity, in favor of the principle of independency, and places all evangelical confessions and sects on a perfect civil and religious equality, so that the difference between church and sect disappears altogether. The latter adheres to the idea of the church and the Christian character of the state, and refuses to recognize all sorts of confessions and sects in their corporate capacity, such as Baptists and Methodists, while it is ready to acknowledge the children of God amongst them as brethren in Christ, not because of, but in spite of, their sectarian connection. The mission of German Protestantism is the unity of the church, and not a confederation of sects. Whether this church shall be Lutheran, or Reformed, or United, that is a difficult question to be solved in its own bosom without foreign help; but the result in any case will be one church, and not an indefinite number of coördinate sects. The sound tendency is toward unity and harmony, not to division and distraction. The established church may concede to dissenters the free exercise of their religion, but not the liberty of propagandism to the injury of her own interests. The concession, moreover, in every particular case, must be decided by the state-church authorities, and they have no reason to be very liberal toward domestic disturbers and foreign propagandists.

Nor can the Protestantism of Germany, according to Stahl, permit itself to be drawn by English dissenters into a radical and passionate war against Romanism. The "Evangelical Alliance," while it professes the greatest liberality toward all Protestant sects, still inconsistently adheres to the uncompromising hostility of old Puritanism against Popery, as if it was no part of Christ's kingdom at all, but identical with anti-Christ. But German Protestantism, with all its essential difference, has a bond of union with the Catholic Church, before and after the Reformation, and must aim at a final reconciliation of the schism.

This, according to Stahl, is the highest and most comprehensive form of toleration and catholicity, not in the Romish sense of compulsory uniformity, but in the sense of free fullness and totality. It looks to the ultimate comprehension of the three great confessions into which Christendom is now unhappily, but providentially, divided, viz: the Roman Catholic, Lutheran, and Reformed (he leaves out of sight the Greek communion,) so as to constitute at last one undivided economy of the kingdom of God, to which their separate missions prepare the way. The Roman Church has the peculiar mission to represent and preserve the visible unity and historical continuity of Christianity up to the apostolic age. Calvinism is distinguished for its profound fear of God, its energetic faith, its missionary zeal, and tries to build up a world of Christian institutions on the basis of the holy congregation of believers. Lutheranism unfolds the deepest mysteries of faith, and labors to show the harmony and interpenetration of the divine and human, the spiritual and natural in the person of Christ and his holy sacrament. These peculiar charismata must all be preserved and taken up into the final constitution of the church universal.

The expectation of such a church, concludes Stahl, which is elevated above all earthly confessions, and yet combines all their excellences, makes us truly tolerant, not in the indifference, but in the most conscientious fidelity to the divine truth, and to the particular branch of Christ's kingdom, in which we were born, and to which we are sworn.

There is much in these views to which we can heartily subscribe. There can be no doubt among sound divines that Christianity is the only true and absolute religion, and that its development must lead at last, not to a mere friendship and brotherhood of sects, much less to division and distraction, but to one flock under one shepherd, to an organic union of all believers, to one holy catholic kingdom, that shall include in its divine harmony everything that is true, and good, and noble, and beautiful in the different branches and periods of the militant church.

But the surest and quickest way to this very end is just the freest development of Christianity, with all its energies and powers, and not a mechanical square-and-compass system, which only retards its real progress. Stahl is mistaken as to the means. He confounds the free spirit of the Gospel with the legalism of the Jewish dispensation. The New Testament furnishes not one single passage in favor of the state-church system, and still less in favor of any compulsion in matters of conscience and religion. Christianity was born free from the state, and though living in this world, it is not of this world, and must be propagated by spiritual means, in a free, uncrippled way. And then, his view of the extent of the church is too contracted. He does great injustice to several branches of Protestantism which have as good a mission to fulfil as he concedes to three denominations only, taking the Reformed in a very restricted sense. We are no advocates for any particular sect; but history teaches that Methodism has done, and still does, as good a work for England and America, as Spener's Pietism for Germany, and that the Baptists, whom Stahl despises as mere disturbers, are more active in the distribution of the Bible, and the spread of the Gospel to the heathen, than any Lutheran state-church. It is very possible, also, that greater religious movements may yet arise from the inexhaustible fountain of Christianity, than even the Reformation of the sixteenth century, without permission from any minister of worship, or Oberkirchenrath. Protestantism, if it is to maintain itself at all, must take a far more spiritual and comprehensive view of the church, than Romanism. It becomes necessarily inconsistent, or stops half way, when it takes a stand, open or concealed, direct or indirect, against religious or civil liberty.

Stahl's views in connection with some cases of actual persecution for conscience sake, called forth the "Signs of the Times," (2 vols., 1855,) by Chevalier Dr. Bunsen, formerly Prussian ambassador at London, now residing near Heidelberg, in literary retirement. He regards Stahl's tract on religious toleration as a concealed plea for intolerance, which would justify, in principle, the most bloody persecutions of the Romish Church. He takes up the pen for religious liberty in opposition to all intolerance, whether it proceed from Romanism or Protestantism. His views may be summed up in the following points.

1. The absolutism of the state strengthens the absolutism of the hierarchy.

2. Protestantism never developed itself vigorously and nationally, except where it produced civil liberty as the legitimate fruit of ecclesiastical reform.

3. Civil liberty can only succeed on the basis of self-government, and this is impossible without liberty of conscience, and the religious rights of the congregation.

4. The hierarchy or priestcraft, claims freedom of conscience only for itself, and instinctively opposes it in others.

5. Religious freedom never led yet to political revolution; but its oppression has done so in France and elsewhere.

6. Intolerance and persecution are a curse to any government and people, but especially so to a Protestant government, because they involve an inward contradiction.

With all these positions Bunsen still holds to the state-church theory, and especially to the Prussian Union. He simply pleads for the fullest toleration of all dissenters, provided, only, that they do not violate the laws of the state, or of public morality. His position, therefore, is substantially English, and not American, although he speaks with the highest respect of the United States, and especially of the influence of Puritanism and Congregationalism on civil and religious liberty. But we regret to say that our esteemed friend has mixed up with his noble and spirited defence of religious and political freedom, a good deal of theological neology and latitudinarianism, which would be rejected as unsound and dangerous, both in England and in this country. He makes too little account of confessions and creeds, and spreads the mantle of union so far, that Luther, Lessing, Hegel, and Göthe, may dwell under it in peace, and commune at the same table of the Lord.

Hence the orthodox party denounced Bunsen, forgetful of his former services to evangelical religion, in most unsparing terms. Hengstenberg, in his *Vorwort* for 1856, treats the "Signs of the Times" as a perfectly worthless book, filled only with idle wind, (why, then, make such a fuss about it ?) He calls the author an apostate from Christianity to radicalism and pantheism, applies to him the passage of the unclean spirit, who returns with seven others worse than himself, compares his Christian phrases with the kiss of the traitor, and yet calls on him, in conclusion, to repent! This is strong enough, in all conscience. Leo, of Halle, handled him with equal severity. Stahl wrote a lengthy reply, (*Wider Bunsen*, 3d ed., 1856,) which his admirers and sympathizers hailed as a complete extinguisher; and it must be admitted that, as a logical reasoner and skillful dialectician, he is superior to his more brilliant opponent, exposes many weak points very successfully, and fortifies his own position in regard to toleration and the

Prussian Union, apparently with more consistency on the conceded basis of state-churchism. He charges upon Bunsen the attempt to deprive Germany of its best possession, the church, and forcing upon it the worst feature of America,—the curse of sectarianism,—without giving it the American faith and practical Christianity.

But the general principle of religious liberty met with a hearty response throughout Germany, and its advocacy made the celebrated ex-diplomatist suddenly one of the most popular men in those very circles where he was formerly disliked on account of his religious views. His Signs of the Times passed through three editions in a few weeks. Public opinion pointed him out already as the future minister of public worship in Prussia. The "*Protestantische Kirchenzeitung*," of Berlin, boldly declared, in a review of his book (N. 7, 1856,) "The liberty of conscience is a power of the present age, an idea which takes hold, with divine irresistibility, of all hearts and of all nations, from which no man and no state can escape for any length of time." That the liberal political organs of the press should fall in with this view, and even go beyond it, was to be expected as a matter of course. But what is more significant, is the fact that some decidedly evangelical divines, as Dr. Schenkel, of Heidelberg, and Dr. Dorner, of Göttingen, have openly come out for Bunsen, and against Stahl and Hengstenberg.

A third party which has mixed in the controversy, takes middle ground between the two extremes. So Dr. Krummacher. He agrees with Stahl in his attachment to an established church on decidedly orthodox, though less exclusive grounds, but asks, at the same time, full toleration for dissenting sects of an evangelical character, has greater sympathy with the Reformed Christianity in and out of Germany, and favors the Evangelical Alliance, whose professed object is the promotion of religious liberty throughout the world.

This seems to be also the position of the King of Prussia, who was formerly an intimate friend of Bunsen. He painfully feels the weight of the ecclesiastical supremacy of the crown, and declared once publicly that he wished the time would soon arrive when he could place it back into the proper hands, and let the church manage her own affairs independent of, though in friendly union with, the state. Although he heard Stahl's famous address before the Evangelical Association, and allows him and his small, but powerful party a very large share in the present management of the church and the state, he expressed himself, on several occasions, decidedly averse to all religious intolerance and persecution, and recently extended, even against the advice of his minister of worship, and the views of the reäctionary party, a cordial invitation to the Evangelical Alliance to meet at Berlin in 1857. This, too, is a sign of the times.

CHAPTER XIII.

THE ESTABLISHED CHURCHES.

Numerical Proportion of Roman Catholics to Protestants—Mixed Religious Character of most German States—The three Protestant Churches—Lutheranism—The Reformed Confession—The Evangelical Union.

EVER since the peace of Westphalia, (1648,) which brought the thirty years' war to a close, and secured to the two contending parties full liberty of worship and equality of civil rights, Germany was almost equally divided between Roman Catholicism and Evangelical Protestantism. The former is numerically stronger, (21,092,000,) but the latter, (16,415,000,) makes up the deficiency by a decided intellectual superiority. The Greek Church is confined to the Sclavonic population of Austria, and a small part of Prussia. The Jews are scattered everywhere in considerable numbers, especially in the large cities. Upon the whole, the south of Germany is predominantly Roman Catholic, the north predominantly Protestant. In Austria about five-sevenths, in Bavaria about two-thirds, of the population profess the papal creed. Prussia numbers ten millions of Protestants, and six millions of Catholics, while the kingdom of Saxony, the Saxon Principalities, and Mecklenburg, are almost entirely Lutheran. In Hanover, Würtemburg, Baden, Hesse Cassel, and Hesse Darmstadt, Nassau, Oldenburg, and the four Free Cities, the Protestant Confession has likewise the preponderance. But there is hardly a single state in Germany where the two churches are not mixed, the Catholics being subject to a Protestant, or the Protestants to a Catholic monarch. In Saxony, we have the singular anomaly, that a Roman Catholic Prince rules over an almost entirely Lutheran population. In Austria, according to the census of 1850, the whole population of the empire amounted to 36,398,620, and, as to its religious character, stood as follows: 25,509,626 Roman Catholics, 3,505,686 United Greeks, 2,751,846 Schismatic Greeks, 1,869,546 Reformed (mostly Magyars,) 1,213,897 Lutherans, 46,278 Unitarians or Socinians, 455 Separatists, 853,304 Jews.

The Roman Catholic Church in Germany, as everywhere else, is one in its visible organization, although its intercourse with the Roman head was, and is, in part, still subjected to various restrictions by the territorial governments, especially in Austria before the Concordat of 1855. Its actual membership, however, is fully as heterogeneous as that of Protestantism. It includes, perhaps, less skepticism and infidelity, but far more ignorance and superstition.

The Protestant Church in Germany, owing to its close connection with, and subordination to, the state, is cut up into as many sections as there are separate kingdoms, grand duchies, duchies, principalities, and free cities. Each little government has its own ecclesiastical organization, with its separate polity, worship, and administration, perfectly independent of the others. The

Church Diet, it is true, is a very large and imposing representation of the evangelical ministry and laity of Germany; but it has no official and legislative character, and the confederation of all the German Protestant establishments, which it contemplated originally, was never realized. Territorially, then, there are actually no less than thirty-eight Protestant churches within the limits of the German Confederation. So in Switzerland, each canton has its independent Reformed Church, without any official connection whatever with that of the neighboring canton.

But this is, after all, merely a geographical and political boundary line, such as keeps, for instance, the Episcopal communion of Scotland apart from that of the Church of England, or the various denominations in Canada from the corresponding denominations in the United States.

Theologically, there are only three branches of German Protestantism as connected with the state, the Lutheran, the Reformed, and the Evangelical United Church. Although territorially divided, they have respectively the same confessions of faith, a similar form of government, a common inheritance of hymns and liturgies, and keep up a free exchange of theological ideas, teachers, and students, much more so than in any other country. A theological professor, for instance, may be called from Würtemberg, or Switzerland, to Prussia, or the reverse, without the least difficulty, while a similar exchange between the seminaries of different denominations in our own country, although they may stand in ecclesiastical correspondence, hardly ever takes place.

The Protestantism of Germany, with the exception of a few cities on the confines of Switzerland, and Holland, was originally all of the Lutheran type; and if the high Lutheran party had not attempted to annihilate the milder and more liberal Melanthonian school, Calvinism would probably never have taken deep root in German soil. But the violent Lutheran controversies in the second part of the sixteenth, and the beginning of the seventeenth century, resulted in the transition of a large portion of the Melanthonians to the Reformed Confession.

This was the case in the Palatinate, Zweibrücken, Nassau, Hesse, Witgenstein, Solmes, Wied, Hanau, on the lower Rhine, Jülich-Cleve-Berg, Westphalia, Lippe, East-Friesland, Anhalt, Dessau, and Brandenburg. The electors of the Palatinate, and of Brandenburg, (subsequently the royal house of Prussia,) became the principal protectors of the Reformed Church in Germany, which, after the revocation of the Edict of Nantes, received considerable accession from the Huguenot refugees of France.

In 1817, at the third centenary celebration of the Reformation, the king of Prussia, Frederick William III., united the Lutheran and the Reformed churches in his kingdom under one government and worship, and gave them the name of the *Evangelical* Church. This example was followed by most of the countries where the two denominations were represented, viz: Nassau, (1818,) Bavaria on the Rhine, (1819,) Baden, (1821,) Hesse-Cassel and Hesse-Darmstadt, (1822,) Saxony-Weimar and Hildburghausen, (1826,) and Würtemberg, (1827).

But Bavaria proper, Austria, and the kingdoms of Saxony, and Hanover never introduced the union.

This amalgamation of the two sister churches of the Reformation has been, and is still, a source of infinite trouble and controversy, of which we shall speak more fully in a separate chapter. The real object of the movement has not yet been attained. For instead of making one out of two, it has resulted, so far, in the addition of a third church.

Of these three branches of German Protestantism, the Evangelical or United Church, is the strongest; but symbolical and exclusive Lutheranism is at present making considerable progress, especially in Bavaria, the eastern provinces of Prussia, Mecklenburg, and Hanover, and this will rouse the Reformed communion to renewed zeal and united effort.

CHAPTER XIV.

THE DISSENTING SECTS.

Religious Liberty—General Condition of the Dissenters—Three Classes of Sects—The Moravians—The Old Lutherans—The Mennonites—The Baptists—The Methodists—The Swedenborgians—The Irvingites—The Hoffmannites—The Socinians—The Friends of Light—The German Catholics—The Mormons.

Religious liberty, in the full sense of the term, includes three elements, liberty of conscience, liberty of association and public worship, and liberty of proselytism. The first exists in Germany to the fullest, the second to a limited extent, the third is prohibited by law, although it cannot, of course, be prevented altogether. But while dissent is restricted in its practical operation, the liberty of religious conviction and theological teaching is carried to an excess within the bosom of the established churches, so that they embrace, in fact, as already remarked, the most heterogeneous material, from the stiffest orthodoxy to the lowest rationalism, that would not even be tolerated in any of our more respectable Unitarian congregations. This is just the reverse of the normal and natural order of things. Instead of true liberty in connection with discipline and order, as we have it in America, these state churches of Europe present us compulsion with confusion and contradiction. If the existing religious and theological differences were freely permitted to assume a separate organized form, they would relieve the establishment of so many contradictory and discontented elements. Then each body could exercise discipline, and be in fact what it professes to be in name. It is perfectly vain and preposterous to think of ruling a moral and spiritual constitution like the church as you would a police or an army, especially in a nation, which in every kind of intellectual life and culture, occupies such a high, free and independent position as the German.

The dissenting bodies are not near as large and influential in Germany, as in England. This is owing partly to the want of full liberty outside of the establishments, and the excess of liberty within them, to which we have just alluded; partly to the fact that the reflective and contemplative mind of the German has less disposition to embody religious and theological differences in an outward form and organization, than the more practical Englishman. Still the number of Dissenters is increasing of late, and receives encouragement from the growing influence of English and American institutions and sects. They receive, of course, no support from the state, and have to sustain their operations by the voluntary principle and assistance from abroad. New sects are subjected to a great many vexations and annoyances, amounting at times to real persecution, especially in those states where Romanism prevails, and also in some Lutheran countries, as Mecklenburg, until they are invested with corporate rights.

The German sects may be divided into three classes,

the evangelical, the mystic, and the rationalistic. To the first belong the Moravians, the Old Lutherans, the Mennonites, the modern Baptists, and the Methodists; to the second the Swedenborgians, and the Irvingites; to the third the Socinians, the Lightfriends, and the German Catholics. The Rationalists generally are not a sect, but a theological school and party in the Established Churches, which was once stronger than the orthodox party, but is now rapidly diminishing.

1. The *Moravians*, or *Herrnhuters*, whose founder, Count Zinzendorf, must be ranked among the greatest names in church history, are of native German growth, and a small, but most lovely and thoroughly evangelical denomination. They agree with the doctrines of the Augsburg Confession, and although they form a separate organization, they are remarkably free from sectarian pride, bigotry and exclusiveness. Faith in the atoning death of Christ, and love to him and all his followers of whatever name, are the fundamental articles of their Christianity. Their worship is of the liturgical order, and their government a peculiar combination of Episcopacy, and Synodical Presbyterianism. They live in separate peaceful communities, (Herrnhut, Barnby, Niesky, Gnadau, Konigsfelden, Neuwied, &c.,) which have exerted, and still exert a happy influence upon the surrounding country, and were the salt of the national churches in the period of the great apostacy. Although their former zeal has considerably abated, they still keep up their extensive missionary operations in heathen lands, their boarding-schools and other useful institutions, which secure to them such an honorable place in the history of evangelical Protestantism.

The great divine, Schleiermacher, received his early training among the Moravians, and learned there the love of the Saviour, which accompanied him through the labyrinth of skepticism, and gave him comfort and peace in the hour of death.

2. The *Old Lutherans* are seceders from the Evangelical church of Prussia, and took their rise in opposition to the Union as introduced in 1817, which they regard as a sacrifice of the truth and a union between Christ and Belial. They adhere to all the tenets of the Lutheran symbols with scrupulous tenacity, and look upon the Reformed church as essentially heretical and rationalistic. But their hatred against the Union is still more intense. Their leaders in the opposition to the state church were Dr. Scheibel, formerly professor of theology in Breslau, who died at Nuremberg in 1843; Dr. Huschke, professor of law in the same university, and Dr. Guericke, of Halle. Their strength lies mainly in the provinces of Silesia, Saxony and Pomerania. They were at first fined, imprisoned and annoyed in various ways under Frederick William III. Their persecution is the darkest and most disgraceful page in the history of the Prussian Union. But it would be unjust to make this prince responsible for all the brutalities of his soldiers and police-officers. It must be admitted also, that the seceders often provoked severe measures by the fanatical violence of their attacks upon the established church.

Several of their leading ministers, as Ehrenström and Grabau, emigrated with their people to the United States. The former ran into the wildest excesses, and perished at last in the gold mines of California. The latter still presides like a pope over an extremely bigoted, though zealous and well-drilled, Lutheran congregation in Buffalo. Still others identified themselves with the more moderate Old Lutheran Synod of Missouri and Adjacent States.

With the accession of the present King of Prussia, all persecution against these seceders from the Union ceased, and by a decree of July 23, 1845, they were formally recognized as a dissenting sect, with full liberty of worship. Their membership amounts to from 20 to 30,000 souls. Their largest congregations are in Breslau and in Berlin.

But the Old Lutheran secession has been quite overshadowed and almost forgotten, since confessional Lutheranism raised its head within the bosom of the evangelical church of Prussia itself. The followers of this movement are called New Lutherans, in distinction from their more ultraistic, but more consistent predecessors. They differ very little in doctrine from the Old Lutherans, but they still adhere to the union with the state, they wish to enjoy all the benefits of the establishment, and aim to Lutheranize it as much as they possibly can. (In the United States, on the contrary, the term New Lutheranism is identical with what is also called American Lutheranism, in distinction from genuine, strict, symbolical Lutheranism.)

3. The *Mennonites*, so called from Menno Simonis, a Romish priest of Friesland, who joined the Anabaptists in 1536, and led them from their fanatical extravagances into the state of an orderly religious community, num-

ber about 14,000 in Prussia, and live principally in the regions of the lower Rhine, without exerting any influence upon the general course of religion. In Holland, where they are more numerous, they have become Arminian.

4. The *Baptists*, who excite considerable attention in Germany at the present time, are not the descendants of those wild fanatics of the sixteenth century, who preached and practised anarchical doctrines, and were so vigorously opposed by Luther and all the Reformers, but of quite recent date, and we may say of English and American origin. The first congregation was formed in Hamburg in 1834, by Mr. Oncken, an American Baptist. Assisted by men and means from the United States, they have since made some progress in Berlin, Elberfeld, and in Würtemberg, but almost exclusively amongst the lower classes of society. They attack not only the institution of infant baptism, but also the mixture of the church with the world, and insist upon the necessity of discipline, which attracts many serious persons to them. They complain a great deal of persecution, especially in Mecklenburg, and sent a delegation recently to the king of Prussia, who expressed his surprise at their representations, and declared himself decidedly in favor of full religious toleration.

5. A few years ago (1850) the *Methodist Episcopal Church* of the United States, encouraged by the rapid success of their missionary operations among the German population in this country, sent Dr. Jacoby and a few other German missionaries to the fatherland, in order to convert it to American Methodist Christi-

anity. They have already built a church in Bremen, where they have a good opportunity to direct a part of the German emigration into the channel of their church, before they reach their new home. From this centre of operations they expect to extend the net of their labors gradually, wherever they can find a safe foothold. They also publish a religious newspaper, and Dr. Jacoby wrote a Handbook of Methodism for the benefit of the Germans. The Albright Brethren, a German Methodist sect of this country, have imitated the example of their stronger brethren, and sent a missionary to Würtemberg, who reports favorably of his success.

Public opinion in Germany is very much divided as regards the degree of toleration which should be allowed to such foreign emissaries. I am confident, however, that, in Prussia, the Methodists will not meet with any serious obstacle, if they carefully abstain, as they ought to do, from all improper interference with the rights and duties of the established churches. The religious destitution is so great in the larger cities as Berlin, Hamburg, Bremen and Frankfort, that they will find plenty of room for missionary work, for which the Methodist system is peculiarly adapted.

We proceed now to the mystic sects.

6. *Swedenborgianism* exists in Germany more as an opinion than as a sect. Dr. Tafel, a respectable scholar and librarian at Tübingen in Würtemberg, translated and published the numerous writings of Emmanuel Swedenborg, but without much success. For some time a talented and self-denying clergyman of the Evangelical Church in that kingdom, Gustavus Werner, a former

classmate of the infidel Dr. Strauss, labored as a travelling evangelist for the propagation of the peculiar opinions of this remarkable system, opposing, although with great caution, the Protestant doctrines on the trinity, the atonement, original sin, and justification by faith, urging to works of charity, as the root of faith, and pointing to a Johannean Church of the future, where Jesus-Jehovah would restore the new Jerusalem and the reign of love. His disinterested zeal, his ingenious allegorical interpretation of the Scriptures and his practical benevolence at first attracted to him crowds of admirers; but the excitement has passed away, and he is not likely to accomplish much in the end. His ecclesiastical superiors, after tolerating him for many years, have now forbidden him the use of the public churches, since he declined to sign the Augsburg Confession. The whole number of Swedenborgians in Germany hardly reaches two hundred.

7. The *Irvingites*, between 1840 and 1850, sent some of their ablest men from England to Germany, and succeeded in making a few important conversions. The principal one is that of Dr. Henry Thiersch, formerly professor of theology at Marburg, and decidedly one of the most learned and most pious divines of the younger generation, (he was born in 1819,) who might now exert a powerful influence for good in one of the first academical chairs, had he remained in the church of his fathers. Still his works on Catholicism and Protestantism, on the history of the Apostolic Church, and on Christian family life, have an independent value, derived from his Christianity and solid research, and not from the peculiarities

of his new connection. As a writer he stands between Irvingism and the Evangelical Church, as Tertullian stood between the Montanist sect and the Catholic Church of the second century. With all his abilities and zeal, Thiersch has not been able to make many converts.

The Irvingites have only a few congregations on German soil. The most important is that in Berlin, which includes some influential members; e. g. Mr. Wagner, the editor of the famous "*Kreuz-zeitung*," the chief organ of the high-state and high-church party in Prussia. The excitement about the new apostles, prophets, and evangelists reached its height during the commotions of 1848, but has since greatly diminished.

8. In the year 1854 a new sect, of a mystic and apocalyptic character, arose among the Pietists in Würtemberg, which has as yet no distinctive name. Their leader is Dr. Hoffmann, of Ludwigsburg, son of the founder of the pietistic colony of Kornthal, and brother to the distinguished court-preacher of Berlin. He is a gentleman of much talent, learning and piety, and was elected, in 1848, a member of the Parliament of Frankfort in opposition to his rival, the notorious Dr. Strauss. But he always was eccentric in his opinions, and more recently he fell out entirely with the state of things in Europe. He regards the church in its present mixture with the world, as the modern Babylon which is hopelessly hastening to destruction, dimly foreshadowed by the revolutions of 1848, and directs his eyes to the holy land, where the true children of God must collect to prepare the way for Christ's

second coming. This he calls the *Sammlung des Volkes Gottes.* His friends made preparation for an emigration to Palestine. They actually applied to the Sultan to make them a present of that country, but he has not yet seen fit to part with it. The Eastern war excited great expectations in them, which have not, however, been realized thus far.

All these sects base themselves more or less on the Word of God, and are animated by Christian piety. Very different, and of all least worthy of protection, are the rationalistic, which we must notice in conclusion.

9. The *Socinians*, or original *Unitarians* of the sixteenth century, still maintain a number of congregations with a semi-rationalistic creed, in the Austrian province of Siebenbürgen, or Transylvania. Their days as a sect are long since past, but their opinions on the divine unity, the person of Christ, the atonement, etc., found their way extensively into the Lutheran establishments, the Reformed Churches of Geneva, France, Holland, the Presbyterians of England, and the Congregationalists of America. German Rationalism is a consistent development of Socinianism, and divests it of those supernatural elements (the necessity of a divine revelation, the deification of Christ after the resurrection,) which Laelius Socinus and his nephew, Faustus, taught in strange connection with naturalistic principles.

10. The *Lightfriends* (*Lichtfreunde*) are a few independent rationalistic congregations in the Saxon province of Prussia. They owe their origin to the excitement between 1841 and 1848, caused by Ulich of Magdeburg, a preacher of considerable popular elo-

quence and managing talent, but of the lowest views on Christianity. They became for a while the depositories of all religious and political discontent and opposition to the Prussian government, until they were swept away by the current of the Revolution of 1848. One of their leaders, Wislicenus, of Halle, emigrated to America. It is deeply humiliating, that a superficial rationalism, which was supposed to be dead and buried, could create such a commotion in a state like Prussia, and on the classical soil of the Lutheran Reformation. But the emptiest wagons often make the greatest noise.

11. The same may be said of the so-called *German Catholics*, (*Deutsch-Katholiken*) who date their existence from the famous protest of the suspended Romish priest, John Ronge, against the superstitious veneration of the seamless coat of Christ at Treves, in 1844. Never was a man more overrated, than this Ronge, at his first appearance. He was glorified as a second Luther, and his letter from Laurahütte was hailed as the trumpet of a new reformation, which would give the finishing stroke to Popery. But the movement which spread for a while with great rapidity among the Catholics, especially in Silesia, only revealed the large amount of rationalism and infidelity which exists in the Roman Catholic Church, under the mask of orthodoxy and pious ceremonies.

It is true, some priests and laymen were carried away by a pure desire after reform, and wished to retain the fundamental articles of the old Catholic creed. They gathered around Czerski, who, however, was himself rather weak and inconsistent; or they fell in subsequently with one of the Evangelical churches. For a short time, two scholars, also of established reputation, Theiner and Regenbrecht, gave in their adhesion. But the main current of this German Catholicism, or New Catholicism, was purely negative, and ran more and more into shallow humanitarianism and revolutionary politics. The revolution of 1848 brought complete freedom to the new sect, even in Bavaria and Austria. Ronge was even elected to the parliament of Frankfort, and joined the extreme radical party, but was unable to command any influence; ran off to England with another man's wife, and sank into his native obscurity. His congregations, after the triumph of order over revolution, broke up in rapid succession, or were suppressed by the governments, which was a very unnecessary and impolitic measure in view of their low state of consumption. In Vienna they quietly returned to the Roman Church; in other cities they joined in part the Protestant Churches. The short history of this inglorious sect, shows the utter inability of rationalism to build up a religious community.

12. The *Mormons* have not been able yet to make any converts in Germany, while in England, Denmark, Sweden and Norway, they met with considerable success. But the singular fortunes and persecutions, the high claims, and the rapid progress of this American edition of Mohamedanism, and the perplexities which it will probably cause yet to our national government, excite a great deal of interest and curiosity amongst German scholars, indeed much more than it actually deserves.

CHAPTER XV.

THE SKEPTICAL ERA OF GERMANY.

The great Apostacy to Rationalism and Infidelity—Its various Causes—The German Classics in their relation to Christianity—Gothe and Schiller—Witnesses of Truth during the Skeptical Era—Reinhard, Storr, Knapp—Klopstock, Herder, Hamann—The Romantic School—Von Muller, Schelling, Hegel—Claudius, Stilling, Lavater—The Moravians and the Pietists.

THERE was a time when the religious condition of Germany seemed to warrant the opinion so widely prevalent, till recently, among Christians in Great Britain and the United States, that it was a semi-heathen country, abounding in pedantic book learning, wild speculations, unpractical theories, dreary rationalism and godless infidelity. The same land which produced the faith of the Reformation, and rendered all glory to Christ, exalting his grace far over all human works, and his word above all human traditions, gave rise also to the most subtle and dangerous forms of unbelief and Anti-Christianity. Other nations have likewise fallen into the iron embrace of skepticism, especially the French, who, like the Pantheon of Paris, are moving backward and forward from the worship of Popery to the worship of Voltaire, and seem to be unable to find a sound medium position between despotism and licentiousness. But in no country has infidelity clothed itself in such an array of learning, assumed such a serious aspect, spread more generally among the professional and higher classes, and led to more disastrous results among the people, than on the native soil of Protestantism. But the greater the conflict, the greater also the victory. God overrules the wrath of man for his praise. "Truth, like a torch, the more it's shook, it shines."

Truth crushed to earth will rise again,
The eternal years of God are her's;
But error, wounded, writhes in pain,
And dies amid her worshippers.

The great apostacy of Germany from the gospel, commenced about a hundred years ago. English deism; French materialism, Voltaireism and Rousseauism; the reign and influence of the highly gifted, but thoroughly infidel Frederick II., of Prussia; the shallow popular philosophy of Wolf; the historical skepticism of Semler; and the French Revolution, were the principal causes that combined to undermine and overthrow the old orthodoxy, which was too stiff, pedantic and weak to resist the strong current of the age.

The Pietists and Moravians, it is true, adhered to the ancient faith and preserved it for better times, but they were small in number, and confined themselves almost entirely to a practical, subjective Christianity, without taking an active part in the intellectual war and revolution of ideas which was then going on.

The second part of the last and the beginning of the present century was, indeed, in many respects, a great advance on the literary semi-barbarism of the preceding age, and forms the classical period of German literature and art. Only think of the immortal creations of Kant, Fichte, Schelling, Hegel, in philosophy; of Klopstock, Winckelmann, Lessing, Herder, Wieland, Jean Paul, Göthe, Schiller, in poetry and prose; of Haydn, Mozart, Beethoven, in music! But in theology and religion, that period, although a necessary transition from a lifeless, contracted orthodoxy to a deeper, broader, and more scientific conception of Christianity, was the most dreary and chilly in the history of Protestantism. Many of the ablest writers, who exerted an incalculable influence upon the rising generation, and will forever figure among the first German classics, were unfortunately either altogether indifferent, or decidedly hostile to Christianity.

Göthe, for instance, undoubtedly the greatest poet since Shakspeare, and the most universal and the most cultivated of all poets, was a refined heathen, without even a desire after salvation, which characterized the noblest minds of Greece and Rome, but perfectly contented with himself and the world of nature. His theoretical knowledge of Christianity, as displayed in the wonderful tragedy of Faust, and in the confessions of a beautiful soul, inserted in Wilhelm Meister, as well as his former intimacy with the pious Stilling and Lavater, makes his case only the worse. He studiously avoided that indirect and suggestive teaching of virtue and goodness, which is the highest prerogative of art; and the religious tolerance in which he entrenched himself at last, was in fact nothing but cold indifference.

His great friend and rival, Schiller, was a pure-minded and noble-hearted genius, abounding in elevated moral sentiment, and always longing after something higher and better than earth can give; but his religious views did not rise above the Pelagian rationalism of Kant, and so great was his ignorance of the real nature and infinite value of Christianity, that he deplored, in a mistaken interest for poetry, the downfall of the gods of Greece, and entertained the absurd idea, that the theatre might take the place of the church. To his excuse it must be said that the sermons in hundreds of churches in his days had no more religion, and far less spirit and interest, than theatrical performances. No wonder that they were forsaken more and more, and that such men as Stolberg, Frederick Schlegel, Werner and Novalis, sought and found at least some sort of religion in the bosom of Romanism.

Thus a deistic and Pelagian rationalism, which emptied Christianity of all its supernatural contents, and retained from it only the truths of natural religion, took in a short time possession of the theological faculties, the pulpits, the consistories, the educational institutions, and the thrones of princes. It altered or removed the orthodox text books from colleges and schools, and even the venerable hymns and liturgies which breathed the piety of the pentecostal days of Protestantism, were exchanged for the watery and prosy productions of sentimentalism. From the higher regions of society and learning, the unbelieving spirit gradually worked its way down to the people. All the revolutionary forces, which at that time were employed in France for the destruction of the political order of things, were in Germany directed against religion and the church. Had the governments of that country not confined its talents so much to a literary existence, and given them more room for free expansion in the political and social sphere, it would never have produced so many rationalistic and infidel theologians and ministers. Many of them would have chosen much more congenial fields for the exercise of their zeal for destruction and innovation.

Yet it must not be supposed that Germany, even in its darkest period, was a complete desolation, without green spots and fresh fountains of living water. There were some venerable divines, like Reinhard, Storr, Knapp, who, although affected to some extent by the spirit of the age, defended the necessity of a supernatural revelation and the divine authority of the Bible with great learning and ability. Klopstock, the German Milton, although inferior to the sublime genius that inspired the "Paradise Lost," sung the glory of the Messiah. In Herder's enchanting paradise of all the flowers of humanity, Christianity bloomed after all with the brightest colors and sweetest fragrance. His eccentric friend, Hamann, "the Magus of the North," uttered hieroglyphic oracles, which sounded like prophecies of a new creation. Jacobi maintained, in the name of philosophy, the insufficiency of reason and the necessity of faith. The romantic school of Schlegel, Tieck, Novalis, revived a taste for the poetry of religion, and chastised with withering irony the conceited folly of a Nicolai. John von Müller, the German Tacitus, found at last in Jesus Christ the centre of the history of the world, and the only key to the solution of its mysteries. Schelling and Hegel dug out a deeper channel of speculation, which was far remote, indeed, from the simplicity of the gospel, but promised at least to show the beautiful harmony of the highest truths of philosophy with the leading doctrines of Christianity, and to dethrone the rationalistic common sense from its usurped dominion. Claudius, Stilling, and Lavater, preserved a childlike piety in an age of prevailing skepticism, and proved, in their persons and writings, a blessing to thousands. The Pietists and Moravians kept the lamp of faith burning in dark places. And finally the common people, in spite of all the efforts of the blind leaders to deprive them of their dearest treasure, retained a certain traditional piety, nourished by the German Bible, the catechisms, hymns, and devotional works of the sixteenth and seventeenth centuries.

Thus, there was a sufficient amount of salt left to keep the body from spiritual decay and corruption. The fact is, that in the very time of the deepest national humiliation of Germany under the yoke of the Corsican conqueror, the intellectual and moral powers for a successful emancipation and regeneration of Germany were fast ripening, especially in Prussia, which had sunk lowest, to rise highest among the German states.

CHAPTER XVI.

THE REVIVAL OF EVANGELICAL THEOLOGY AND PIETY.

The War of National Independence—The Centennial Jubilee of the Reformation—The Theses of Harms—The Evangelical Union of Prussia—Influence of Schleiermacher and his Theology—The School of Schleiermacher and Neander, and other Evangelical Divines—The Reformation of the Pulpit—The Restoration of ancient Hymns and Liturgies—The return of Philosophy and other Sciences to the Spirit of Christianity.

DR. KAPFF, of Stuttgart, one of the best men living, opens his Report on the religious condition of Germany, which he prepared for the meeting of the Evangelical Alliance, held at Paris in 1855, with the following remark: "If Germany some thirty or forty years ago resembled the early dawn of morning, where the sun shone only on the highest tops of isolated mountains, it is now approaching the middle of the day, but a day obscured by many a dark cloud; infected by poisonous vapors from the deep, and threatened by heavy thunder storms. Yet towards evening there shall be light; fresh waters shall flow from Jerusalem; the Lord will rule King over all the lands, and all the nations shall serve him with one heart."

The great revival of evangelical Christianity in Germany is generally dated from the national struggles for independence against the usurpation of Napoleon. They were, however, themselves the result of an internal movement already at hand, and in turn gave it a new, powerful impulse. The memorable events of 1813 kindled an extraordinary patriotic enthusiasm, and a noble, though vague, desire for an entire political, moral and religious regeneration of the Fatherland. It was after the battle of Leipzic that the Protestant king of Prussia, the Roman Catholic emperor of Austria, and the Greek Catholic czar of Russia formed the Holy Alliance, by which they took God to witness that they would henceforth only reign for the happiness of their subjects and the triumph of the Christian religion. Whatever may be thought of the manner in which they kept this solemn vow, whatever be their subsequent guilt in making this alliance subservient to the interests of despotism, there is not the slightest reason to doubt their sincerity and pious emotion at the time they formed it.

A few years afterwards, (1817,) followed the enthusiastic celebration of the third centennial jubilee of the Reformation, and although it displayed more admiration for Luther as a national hero and German patriot, than a proper appreciation of him as a man of faith and religious reformer, yet it directed the interest and research of the age to the great movement of the sixteenth century, and elicited a series of works which made its story as familiar as household words.

In connection with it must be mentioned the ninety-five theses of Harms, who assailed with the faith of Luther the wide spread rationalism, as an abuse and caricature of true Protestantism.

Still more important was the introduction of the

Evangelical Union in Prussia, in 1817, which was followed by a similar movement in other states.

In the meantime a deeper and more spiritual philosophy and theology had already arisen, and gathered new strength every day in its struggle against rationalism.

Here the immortal name of Schleiermacher shines pre-eminent, and marks a new epoch in the history of German Protestantism. It is impossible here to enter into a detailed account of this extraordinary genius, whose biography will be at the same time a history of the corresponding period of Germany. For he passed through all the movements of his age, and took an active part in the national rising of Germany, the jubilee of the Reformation, the union of the Lutheran and Reformed confessions, and in every great philosophical and religious question which agitated his country till his pious death in 1834. The sublime speculation of Plato, the calm pantheism of Spinoza, the keen criticism of Kant, the subjective idealism of Fichte, the romantic poetry of Tieck and Schlegel, the bold neology of Semler, the sentimental piety of Zinzendorf, the stern supralapsarianism of Calvin, were all mastered by him and worked up into a most original system, which is certainly far from being orthodox, either in the Lutheran or Reformed sense, but a wonderful creation of philosophical and theological science, a complete annihilation of the shallow rationalism which preceded it, and a near approach to a truly evangelical theology, in which the living person of Jesus Christ, the God-man and Saviour, is the soul and centre, and the Pauline doctrines of sin and grace the two opposite poles.

It seems to be incredible that a man who removed from the New Testament the pedestal of the Old, who numbered the miraculous conception, the resurrection and ascension of Christ and his return to judgment, among the things comparatively indifferent to saving faith, who denied the existence of the devil, and taught the final salvation of all creatures, should have been a blessing to the church and lead the rising generation to the fountains of life. And yet such is undoubtedly the fact and his lasting merit, which will hardly be denied by the most orthodox divines in Germany. But Schleiermacher can only be understood and properly appreciated in close connection with the two ages between which he stood, as the last in the generation of skeptics, and the first in the succession of believers.

Schleiermacher's best disciples, animated by his free spirit, and for this very reason not dependent on his letter, made a still nearer approach to the Christianity of the Church and the Bible, and a series of learned and pious divines arose, whose influence goes far beyond the limits of Germany.

Neander reproduced the history of Christ's kingdom, as a living witness of the divine and leaven-like power of the gospel, as a source of instruction and edification for all ages. Tholuck and Olshausen laid open with reverent minds the treasures of the New Testament, as the word of God, after it had so long been misinterpreted by profane hands, as the word of fallible men. Hengstenberg, who, however, never belonged to the school of Schleiermacher, defended the divine inspiration and authority of the Old Testament, which had been so rudely assailed by the Rationalists, and founded the *Evangelical Church Gazette*, as a powerful weapon against all forms of infidelity. Twesten and Nitzsch improved the dogmatic system of Schleiermacher by bringing it more in harmony with the Evangelical and Scriptural system of truth. Ullmann, Lücke, Bleek, Sack, Müller, Schmid, Rothe, Dorner, Lange, and a number of other distinguished theological writers labored for the same cause of building up on a stronger foundation what neology had destroyed.

The result was, that in the course of thirty or forty years the chairs of nearly all the German universities were filled with men imbued more or less with a believing spirit, and laboring successfully in rearing up a pious and zealous generation of ministers, who will scatter the seed among the people, and thus, with the help of God, build up once more the walls of Jerusalem in the land of the Reformation.

The glad tidings of salvation began to resound again from pulpits, where for years before Pelagian moralists had fed the congregations with husks. Powerful preachers arose like Louis and William Hofacker, and the Krummachers, father, uncle, and son, who unfolded the plan of salvation and led the thirsty souls to fountains of living water. A new taste and zeal was awakened for the sacred hymns and prayers of a better age, which began to be restored to their proper position in the sanctuary in place of the insipid productions of a prosy and chilly rationalism, while Spitta, Knapp and Bahrdt, tuned their harp for new songs of Zion.

Nor was this reform confined to theology and religion

proper. The human sciences, too, which, superficially tasted, had led away from God, began to return, in some of their profoundest representatives, to the source of all truth and wisdom. The aged Schelling slowly matured, in mysterious silence, his new system of a positive philosophy that should unfold the sense of, and defend the truth of revealed religion. Baader worked out, in aphoristic flashes of genius, a peculiar theosophy, and Emil von Schaden followed both in the path which promised to show the sacred harmony of natural and revealed truth. Fischer, and Fichte the younger, labored successfully in the service of Christian theism in opposition to Hegelian pantheism. History was now treated by Leo, Ranke and others in a much better spirit, and from a far higher stand-point, as a theatre for the unfolding of the plans of divine wisdom and mercy. The prevailing tendency of the general literature of Germany for the last thirty or forty years, differs essentially from the negative and destructive literature of the preceding age, and looks, in various forms and degrees, towards a reconciliation of science with faith, of reason with revelation, of modern culture with old and ever young Christianity, the unfailing source of truth and life.

It must not be supposed, however, that this was an easy triumph. On the contrary, it was and is still a most powerful conflict between Christ and Anti-Christ, faith and infidelity, theism and pantheism. This very conflict, which is not yet ended, makes the last period of German theology one of the most instructive and interesting chapters in the internal history of the Church.

CHAPTER XVII.

THE CONFLICT OF CHRISTIANITY WITH THE LATEST FORMS OF INFIDELITY.

Reaction of Infidelity—Pantheism and Transcendentalism—The Tubingen School of Baur, Strauss, etc.—The Hallesche Jahrbucher, Feuerbach and Vogt—The Apologetic Literature in Defence of the Gospel History and Primitive Christianity—Young Germany, Heine, Borne, etc.—The Friends of Light—The German Catholics—The Revolution of 1848—Reaction, and increased Efforts for Religious and Social Reform—The Evangelical Church-Diet—The Gustavus-Adolphus Society—The cause of Foreign Missions—Future Prospects.

"In Germany," says the late Archdeacon Hare, "the mighty intellectual war of Christendom has been waged for the last half century, and is now going on." Neology had entered so deeply into the various ramifications of society, and especially the higher literary circles, the seats of controlling power and influence in Germany, that it required years of the most persevering labor to turn the current. In the same proportion in which orthodoxy and true religion revived, the enemy, disturbed in his possession, rose in self-defence, and invented new modes of attack.

The old deistic rationalism of common sense, represented by such men as Paulus, of Heidelberg, Röhr, of Weimar, Wegscheider, of Halle, and Bretschneider, of

Gotha, gave way to a more refined, and dangerous pantheism and transcendentalism, arrayed in the armory of the Hegelian philosophy. Strauss, the representative of the left wing of this system, as applied to theology, resolved, in his notorious "Life of Jesus," (1835,) the entire gospel history into mythological fables, and recommended the worship of human genius, as the only real divinity! His more cautious friends, Baur, Zeller, Schwegler, (the so-called Tübingen school,) applied this destructive work of criticism to the whole apostolic and post-apostolic literature, and arrived at the conclusion, that all the books of the New Testament, with the exception of five, were the fabrications of the second century, and that the Christianity of the Church, far from being the product of Christ himself, resulted as a compromise from the protracted conflict of the early heresies, in which Gnosticism plays the most prominent part. The "Hallesche Jahrbücher" taught this pantheistic philosophy and infidel theology without any reserve, denying the existence of a personal God, of the personal immortality of the soul, and deifying poor sinful man. Feuerbach employed all his ingenuity to prove that theology was only a reflection of anthropology, and all religion a dream of the human fancy. The latest form of this pseudo-philosophy and pseudo-theology is the crude materialism taught by Karl Vogt in the abused name of natural science.

It seems to be impossible to carry the opposition to Christianity further than this infidel wing of the Hegelian school has done, without running into direct blasphemy, or madness.

Yet after all, the productions of these writers, especially the Tübingen critics, to whom must be accorded the credit of a rare amount of learning, power of combination, and a certain degree of earnestness, have done perhaps more good than harm, by bringing matters to a crisis, by drawing a sharper line of distinction between the opposite parties, and by eliciting an extensive apologetic literature relating to the history of primitive Christianity, and the fundamental articles of faith. The work of Strauss, on the Life of Jesus, alone called forth a host of replies, direct and indirect, from Neander, Tholuck, Ebrard, Lange, Hoffmann, Lücke, etc., some of which are of permanent value, and mark a great progress in the scientific understanding of the gospel history.

While this contest was going on in the theological and philosophical world, a new school of light literature arose after the Revolution of 1830, under the name of the *Young Germany*, headed by Heine, Börne, Gutzkow, Mundt, and Wienbarg. It united German pantheism, or rather atheism, with French wit and frivolity, and proclaimed, in poems, novels and literary criticisms, the downfall, not only of the Christian religion, but also of the Christian morality, and the triumph of the infamous doctrine of "the emancipation of the flesh." It exchanged the Bible doctrine that man was created in the image of God, for the blasphemous notion that God is no more than the image of man, and from the dizzy height of self-deification it sank down into the abyss of brutish licentiousness. It is characteristic that the principal preachers of this infernal gospel were

Jews, who crucified the Messiah afresh, the very opposite of those pious Israelites of our age, like Neander and Stahl, who embraced him as the only Saviour of fallen man.

Fortunately, these champions of the flesh, with all their brilliant talents, found an insurmountable barrier in the moral seriousness of the German people. They were thrown out of decent society, and found a more congenial home in the atmosphere of Paris. Some of them have since turned their attention to more worthy pursuits. Even Henry Heine, the most gifted of them, after long keeping swine, like the prodigal son, began to see his folly, on his hopeless sick-bed in Paris, and thought of a return to his forsaken God. His memoirs, published in 1854, a year before his death, contain some very remarkable confessions on the bankruptcy of his former views, and the beauty and grandeur of the Bible.

Although the ordinary rationalism was long considered dead and buried, even by the Hegelian pantheists, it suddenly rose again in the movement of the so-called Friends of Light, headed by Uhlich, of Magdeburg, and in "German Catholicism," under the leadership of Ronge. The former originated in the bosom of Protestantism, the latter seceded from Romanism. Both were purely negative, and ran more and more into a shallow humanitarianism and revolutionary politics.— Yet they made an immense commotion amongst the middle classes in Northern Germany, between the years 1844 and 1848, and filled all the newspapers with their hollow noise.

In the midst of these intellectual conflicts, the sudden

downfall of Louis Philippe's government in February, 1848, gave the signal for the outbreak of the revolutionary forces in Germany, which had been gathering ever since the reactionary measures of the Congress of Vienna, and were nourished by the rationalistic and infidel literature of the age. This revolution, which brought even Austria and Prussia to the brink of dismemberment, gave a fair chance to all the radical spirits, discontented with Church and State, to show whether they were able to construct a new and better order of things. But rationalism and pantheism exposed their utter incompetency for any positive work of social reform, and covered themselves with disgrace. Even the National Assembly of Frankfort, which embraced a large amount of the professorial wisdom of Germany, and raised for a while the most sanguine expectations of a great national regeneration, refused to open its sessions with prayer, and decreed a separation of the State and School from the Church, not in the American sense of a peaceful co-existence of the spiritual and temporal powers, but in the infidel sense of an emancipation of the German people from Christianity. No wonder that it broke up at last in confusion and shame.

The follies, abuses and distractions of the radical and infidel parties, caused the failure of these revolutions, and called forth a successful reaction. Princes, statesmen, lawyers, and the higher classes generally, who had been very indifferent, or even hostile to the Church, before 1848, learned wisdom from sad experience, and, either from honest conviction or from political motives, favored religion as the only safeguard of public order, and cure for the diseases of society, which had come fearfully to light in the recent commotions. The conservative party in nearly all the German States, especially in Prussia, raised the standard of Christianity, of which many had been ashamed a few years before.

The places of high influence and trust were filled with pious men. Rationalism disappeared from nearly all the theological chairs in the universities, and is fast disappearing from the teachers' seminaries and the management of common schools. The students and candidates for the Gospel ministry know that much more is required from them now than theoretical learning, if they are at all to succeed in their high calling.

The interest in philosophy and speculation which had occupied the German mind for so many years, almost to the exclusion of practical pursuits, declined so rapidly, as to give room even for complaint of the opposite extreme. The rising generation of scholars are mostly believers in Christianity. Practical questions now engross the attention. Societies for the better observance of Sunday, introduction of family worship, the promotion of temperance, the improvement of prison discipline, the care of dismissed convicts, Young Men's Christian Associations, useful libraries for the people, benevolent institutions for the laboring classes, colliers, sailors, emigrants, the poor and the orphans, establishments for deaconesses, and all those efforts and means for the religious and moral reform of society, which are comprehended under the name of Inner Missions, are multiplying in every direction. All these operations have a common centre in the German Church Diet, which was formed in the revolutionary year of 1848 over the graves of Luther and Melanthon, and has since travelled as a powerful evangelist over the leading cities of Germany, gathering to its meetings the most distinguished divines, ministers and laymen, and kindling everywhere the sacred fire of evangelical faith and charity. In 1853, this Diet, consisting of two thousand ministers and laymen from all parts of Germany, solemnly professed anew the Augsburg Confession, in the city of Berlin, and the royal heir of the infidel Frederick the Great, the protector of Voltaire, attended its session. This fact alone shows a gigantic progress of evangelical truth, and gives effectually the lie to the assertion of the eloquent champion of French Romanism, the Count Montalembert, who only a year before had declared: "Go now, and count the number of Protestants in the country of Luther who would be willing to sign the Confession of Augsburg: they could all be contained in one small borough."

Another encouraging sign of the times is the enlarging activity and usefulness of the Gustavus-Adolphus Society, which, though not so decidedly orthodox and evangelical in its profession and composition as the Church Diet, does the good work of the merciful Samaritan, gives material aid to hundreds and thousands of feeble evangelical denominations in Roman Catholic countries, especially in Austria, and promotes the general interest of Protestantism. Its annual contributions are now exceeding the sum of 80,000 Prussian dollars, and the last anniversary, held at Bremen, (1856,) was unusually spirited.

The interest in foreign missions is likewise increasing every year; and many of the most devoted evangelists in East India, China, and Africa, have proceeded from Basel, Barmen, and other missionary institutions, which are now regarded with growing favor by the people.

These are some of the facts which show a change in the religious aspect of Germany, brought about within the last ten or twenty years. In some cases there is danger even of injuring the cause of sound religion by extreme high church tendencies, which may ultimately work into the hands of Romanism, and by identifying it too much with political ultra-conservatism and reactionism, which might in the end provoke a new convulsion of society more dangerous than the one of 1848.

On the other hand, it cannot be denied that there is yet an immense amount of infidelity and smothered hostility to all authority in Church and State amongst the middle and the laboring classes, only waiting for a new chance of outbreak. Some regions have been so terribly devastated by the architects of ecclesiastical ruin, that it will require many years of the most self-denying labor to re-build the walls of Zion.

There are not wanting excellent and highly intelligent men, who entertain but little hope for the ultimate fate of their fatherland, who are disposed to fear, that the recent improvements may be swept away sooner or later by a new flood of Anti-Christianity more terrible than any which has gone before, until the coming of Christ will bring about, in a supernatural way, a true and lasting reformation of the Church and of society.

Such pious pessimists, however, may be found in any

country, even in the United States, which seem to be emphatically a land of hope and promise. We are no prophet, nor the son of a prophet, and would ever be mindful of the truth, that man proposes, but God disposes, and that his ways are past finding out. But a comparison of Germany of the present day, with the Germany of the past generation, is certainly calculated to fill an unprejudiced lover of the kingdom of Christ with deep gratitude to God and joyous hopes for the future.

CHAPTER XVIII.

LUTHERANISM AND REFORM.

General Character of the Difference between Lutheranism and Reform—Its National Basis—Relation of both to Romanism—Doctrinal and Theological Difference between the two Churches—Difference in Constitution and Discipline—Difference in Worship and Ceremonies—Difference in Practical Piety.

LUTHERANISM and Reform are the two great branches of evangelical Protestantism, which date from the Reformation itself, and to which all other denominational divisions and controversies of Protestantism are subordinate. They may be compared to the two sections of Catholicism, the Greek, and the Roman, although the difference in our case is much more freely and fully developed.

The two churches of the Reformation do not absolutely contradict each other, but admit of an ultimate reconciliation. They agree in all the essential articles of faith, and even some of their most prominent differences are more of a theological and scholastic, than of a religious and practical nature. Hence the union—movements which, under various forms, such as the Prussian Union, the German Church Diet, the Evangelical Alliance, occupy so large a space in the modern history of Protestantism, especially in Germany. But they represent, on the other hand, two distinct ecclesiastical individualities, or types of Christianity. The difference is by no means confined, as some suppose, to the doctrine on the Lord's Supper, and the divine decrees. On the contrary, it runs through the whole system, and affects more or less the entire theology, organization, worship, and practical piety. It rests, we may say, on a different psychological constitution, and national basis, as much so as the distinctive peculiarities of the Greek, and the Latin Churches may be traced back to the difference between the ancient Greek, and Roman nationalities.

Lutheranism is essentially of German growth and intimately identified with the German language and nationality. Hence it loses more or less its original features and assimilates itself imperceptibly to the Reformed Confession, whenever it is transplanted by emigration to French, English, or American soil, as a mere glance at the Anglicized portion of the Lutheran denomination in the United States, compared with the foreign German synods of Missouri and Buffalo, sufficiently shows. The name itself is significant. The Lutheran church is not only called after its human founder, but is animated and controlled by his genius and influence. The Germans may be said—*sit venia verbo!*—to worship three idols, Luther, Frederick the Great, (the *alte Fritz,*) and Göthe, the first for his religious, the second for his military, the third for his poetical genius. Luther is the most truly German, as well as the most honest, pure-minded and noble-hearted of the three, and worthy of all honor and praise which it is lawful to bestow upon a mere man who after all, combined with extraordinary virtues and excellences, violent passions and strange inconsistencies. He is revered by German Protestants as the master spirit of the Reformation, as a Christian Elijah, as the divinely commissioned prophet and apostle of Germany. The almost magic influence of his name may be strikingly seen in the fact, that even those numerous American Lutherans who disown every distinctive doctrinal feature of Lutheranism, and are pure Zwinglians or even downright rationalists in their views on baptism and the eucharist, still cleave tenaciously to this traditional veneration of the name, and are as sectarian in practise as the strictest old Lutherans who revere the *Formula Concordiæ*, as the perfection of theology. But the Lutheran church has always included also a Melanthonian school which is more liberal, moderate, and favorably disposed towards a union or friendly intercourse with the Reformed church. In the seventeenth century, it was almost suppressed, but it still lived in Calixtus, acquired new strength and importance in the pietistic movement of Spener and Francke, and has now the ascendency we may say in all the United Churches.

The Reformed Church, on the other hand, is far more independent of a particular personality and nationality. The number of its founders is larger, and none exerted such a commanding and absorbing influence upon its genius, as Luther upon the Lutheran communion. Zwingli, Œcolampadius, Bullinger, Farel, Calvin, Beza, Ursinus, Olevianus, Cranmer, Knox contributed their share to its establishment and constitution, but none, not even

Calvin, could or would impress his name upon it. It took its rise, it is true, in German Switzerland, and found a home afterwards in the Palatinate, on the Lower Rhine, in Friesland, Hesse, Brandenburg and Prussia. But it developed itself with more marked peculiarity and on a larger scale in the French, Dutch and English nationalities. To get a proper idea of the power and extent of the Reformed communion, we must especially keep in view the national Church, and the dissenting bodies of England, the various branches of Presbyterian Scotland, and the leading evangelical denominations of America, which are all different modifications of the Reformed principle, as distinct from Romanism, and Lutheranism. In Germany, it has always been modified more or less by Lutheran, or rather Melanthonian influences, both to its injury, and to its advantage, so that it presents there neither that strict discipline, congregational self-government and practical energy and power, nor the rigorous extremes of the Calvinistic bodies. With all her defects, the German Reformed church is more elastic and pliable than her sisters of other nations, and occupies, so to speak, a central position between Lutheranism and Calvinism, affected by the good elements of both, and capable also to exert a modifying influence in turn upon both.

If we now proceed to the consideration of the distinctive theological and ecclesiastical features of the two Confessions, we may derive them in great part from the different relation they sustain to mediæval Catholicism from which they seceded, and consequently also to the Romanism of the present day.

The Lutheran church generally speaking, is more conservative toward the past, than the Reformed, which, agreeably to its name, carries the principle of reform much further, in some of its sections, Puritanism especially, to the extreme of Ultra-Protestantism. The former retained from the ancient system what was not expressly prohibited by the Bible; the latter drew a sharper line of demarcation between the Word of God, and the traditions of men, followed more strictly and exclusively the directions of the Scriptures, and aimed at a complete renovation of the life of the church, with the view to conform it as much as possible to the doctrine and practice of the apostolic age, regardless of the intervening history from the sixteenth up to the second century.

In this respect, however, the Church of England occupies a peculiar position. She adheres still more closely to the Catholic organization than Lutheranism, although she belongs upon the whole to the Reformed family, and shows unmistakable traces of the impression which Calvinism not only, but even the Puritan Revolution of the seventeenth century made upon it. Anglicanism is a compromise between Catholicism and Protestantism held together by the royal supremacy.

Then again, the opposition of the two Confessions to Romanism is directed against different aspects of it. The one attacked mainly the Judaism, the other the Paganism in the Papacy. "Away with legalism and self-righteousness!" was the war-cry of Luther. "Away with idolatry and moral corruption!" was the motto of Zwingli, Calvin and Knox.

Let us now specify the difference in the various branches of ecclesiastical and religious life.

In the department of doctrine and theology, the closer affinity of Lutheranism to Catholicism shows itself especially in the articles on the church and the sacraments, and the rule of faith by the greater weight which it allows to tradition. Most of the Lutheran symbols are silent about the supreme and exclusive authority of the Scriptures, which, in the Reformed creeds, is made a fundamental principle. The central dogma, moreover, of the former, is the doctrine of justification by faith alone, called by Luther, the "articulus stantis et cadentis ecclesiæ," while the latter are based upon the more comprehensive doctrine of the absolute sovereignty and free grace of God, and upon the solemn sense of our perfect dependence on him, and our sacred obligation to serve him alone in a holy life and conversation. The Lutheran theology has throughout a more idealistic and speculative tendency, aims to harmonize divine and human truth, revelation and reason, knowledge and faith, and when deviating from the sound path, runs naturally into mysticism, transcendentalism and pantheism. The Reformed theology is more realistic and practical, keeping God and the world, Scripture and tradition, church and state strictly apart, and is more exposed to the opposite danger of deism and a sort of dualism. Hence the Lutheran dogma of the real presence in, with and under the material elements, of the ubiquity of Christ's body, and the oral manducation of it by the unworthy, as well as the worthy communicants; while the Reformed symbols separate carefully, at times almost abstractly and mechanically, the sacramental sign from the sacramental grace, and teach only a spiritual, though nevertheless real fruition of the exalted Saviour through the indispensable medium of faith. Hence also the leaning of the Lutheran christology to the Eutychian confusion, and of the Reformed to the Nestorian separation of the two natures in Christ's person.

Secondly, as to government and discipline, the Reformed, especially the Calvinistic or Presbyterian communions, are far more consistently Protestant than the Lutheran churches. Luther and Melanthon troubled themselves very little about this question. They confined themselves to a reformation of faith and theology, and left the corresponding changes in the organization to the course of events. They permitted the temporal princes to assume and exercise the episcopal supervision. Thus the Lutheran establishments became most intimately interwoven with the state, and in fact entirely dependent of it, and are generally destitute of discipline within, while they carefully exclude dissent from without, especially in Sweden, where no other religion is tolerated to this day. The congregations remained almost as passive as in the Roman church. They have, in Europe, not even the right of electing their pastor. They are exclusively ruled by their ministers, as these are ruled by their provincial consistories, always presided over by a layman, the provincial consistories by a central consistory, or Oberkirchenrath, or whatever may be its name, and this again by the minister of worship and public instruction, who is the immediate executive organ of the ecclesiastical supremacy of the crown.

The Reformed, on the contrary, wherever they were not crippled in their legitimate development, made earnest with the doctrine of the universal priesthood of believers, reorganized the constitution of the church on a scriptural and popular basis, introduced the office of lay-elders and deacons, together with a strict discipline, thus creating what is a most important feature, a congregational and synodical self-government, and strove after greater independence, and at last entire separation of the church from the state. While Lutheranism is monarchical, and extremely conservative in politics, the Reformed church became the fruitful soil of civil and religious liberty, on a constitutional, monarchical, or republican basis, as may be seen by a mere glance at Switzerland, Holland, England and the United States, which are the freest and most prosperous governments in the world. Romanism may be called the church of priests; Lutheranism the church of ministers and theologians; Calvinism the church of congregations and a free people.

Thirdly, as to worship and religious customs and ceremonies, Lutheranism, like the Episcopal church, adhered more closely to the stated liturgical and sacramental system of Catholicism; removing, however, the sacrifice of the mass, the idolatry of saints, and popularizing the services by transferring them into the vernacular language, and giving to the sermon the central place. It draws the fine arts into the service of religion, and has produced a body of hymns and chorals which, in richness, power and unction, surpasses the hymnology of all other churches in the world.

The Reformed communion is much poorer in this respect; it confined itself for a long time to the use of the Psalms, and aimed at the greatest sobriety and simplicity of worship, which, in Presbyterianism and Puritanism, is certainly carried to excess. Mrs. Beecher Stowe, though herself a Puritan, in describing the wondrous beauties of nature in Switzerland, makes the significant remark: "One thing is certain; He who made the world is no utilitarian, no despiser of the fine arts, and no condemner of ornament, and those religionists, who seek to restrain everything within the limits of cold, bare utility, do not imitate our Father in heaven. The instinct to adorn and beautify is from him; it likens us to him, and if rightly understood, instead of being a siren to beguile our hearts away, it will be the closest of affiliating bands." It should not be forgotten, however, that even the Puritan simplicity has its peculiar solemnity and charm for a certain class of minds, and proceeds from a high degree of intellectuality, spirituality, and independence from outward helps to devotion. To the Reformed churches, especially of Great Britain and America, belong the great merit also of having promoted the sanctification of the Lord's day, and cultivated the sermon and the gift of free prayer to an extent which was never known before, or even now in any country on the continent of Europe.

Finally, if we look to practical piety, it seems to us as clear as daylight, that the Reformed churches, owing to their more fully developed Protestantism and individualism, include a much greater proportion of converted people, or personal subjective piety, than the Lutheran, and are unsurpassed in liberality, missionary zeal, practical energy and activity, power of self-government and vigor of discipline, love of religious and civil freedom, and earnest, faithful devotion to the service of Christ. We need only point, in support of this assertion, to the host of Reformed martyrs in France, Holland and England, to the flourishing spiritual life in the Wupperthal, to the astounding sacrifices of the Free Church of Scotland, and to the great fact of the self-sustaining and self-governing Christianity of America with its restless activity, to the British and American Bible, Tract, and Missionary societies, and to the progressive march of Reformed Christendom in the extreme West and extreme East, in every new colony and every heathen land.

But on the other hand it should not be forgotten that the Lutheran piety has also its peculiar charm, the charm of Mary, who "sat at Jesus' feet and heard his word." If it is deficient in outward activity and practical zeal, and may learn much in this respect from the Reformed communion, it makes up for it by a rich inward life. It excels in honesty, kindness, affection, cheerfulness, and that *Gemüthlichkeit*, for which other nations have not even a name. The Lutheran church meditated over the deepest mysteries of divine grace, and brought to light many treasures of knowledge from the mines of revelation. She can point to an unbroken succession of learned divines, who devoted their whole life to the investigation of saving truth. She numbers her mystics who bathed in the ocean of infinite love. She has sung the most fervent hymns to the Saviour, and holds sweet, child-like intercourse with the heavenly Father.

We see, then, that each confession has its peculiar mission, virtues and merits, and however deeply we may regret the split which divided the forces of the Reformation, and exposed it to the attacks and ridicule of the enemy, yet in view of a history of three hundred years, we must say that the evil has been providentially overruled for good, and that both branches of evangelical Protestantism, with their subdivisions, have accomplished a great work for the promotion of Christ's kingdom on earth.

CHAPTER XIX.

THE EVANGELICAL UNION.

Unity, an essential Attribute and Duty of the Christian Church—Early Attempts to unite the Lutheran and Reformed Confessions in Germany—The Marburg Conference—The Wittenberg Concordia—Bucer and Melanthon—The Lutheran Confessionalism—Zwingli and Calvin—The Electors of Brandenburg and the Prussian Symbols—Indifferentism of the Eighteenth Century—The Revival of Faith in the Nineteenth Century—Catholic Spirit—King Frederick William III. and the Prussian Union of 1817—Introduction of the Union in other German States.

BUT now the question arises, shall Lutheranism and Reform forever continue separate, or be united into one family, and in what form? Are the true tendencies of Protestantism to increased division, distraction, and ultimate dissolution, or to consolidation, peace and harmony? If the latter be the case, then it seems to be the duty of the land of the Reformation which gave rise to the great split, to take the lead also in the attempt to reunite, theologically and ecclesiastically, the scattered forces of evangelical Protestantism, and thus to complete the work of the sixteenth century.

This leads us to speak of an important movement which originated in Prussia in 1817, in connection with the third centennial celebration of the Reformation. It certainly marks an epoch in the history of German Protestantism, and will result in some good, even if it should fail under its present form. In order to understand it properly, we must trace shortly the preparatory steps which looked to the same object.

Unity is an essential attribute of the Church of Christ, as much so as holiness and catholicity; and to promote it and realize it more and more, is one of the first duties of Christians. The Romish church confounds unity with uniformity, and maintains it at the sacrifice of the free development of nationality and individuality. Protestantism, on the other hand, promotes freedom and variety at the expense of unity and harmony. The Reformers themselves originated the principal divisions which have since been embodied in so many confessions and denominations. But they felt at the time that it was wrong for brethren to quarrel, and were anxious to heal the distractions in their own camp, as far as supreme regard to truth and conscience would permit.

The attempts to unite the Lutheran and the Reformed branches of Protestantism on German ground, did not originate with the royal house of Prussia, but are almost as old as the division. The Union has as many *testes veritatis* in the divided churches of the Reformation, as the Reformation itself in the Catholic middle ages. It was the object of the famous Conference held at Marburg in 1529, where the leaders of the German and Swiss Reformations agreed upon fourteen fundamental articles of faith, but parted on the sole question of Christ's real presence in the Eucharist.

Martin Bucer labored incessantly for the union of the two parties, and succeeded, in 1536, to induce Luther and Melanthon to sign a compromise with the Swiss, called the Wittenberg Concordia, which, however, concealed rather than reconciled the difference, and was therefore but of short duration.

In Poland the Bohemians, Lutherans and Reformed actually effected at least a temporary *Consensus* at Sendomir in 1570.

Melanthon, in the latter part of his life, became more and more favorable to a union with the Reformed, and altered even the Augsburg Confession in 1540, with the express purpose to suit it to them, and thus to make it a union symbol for all the Evangelical churches of Germany and Switzerland.

But the exclusive Lutheran party gained the ascendancy towards the end of the sixteenth and during the seventeenth centuries. Of them Hase remarks in his Church History, (p. 527, seventh ed.): "The Reformed divines were always favorable to a fraternal recognition; whilst the Lutheran divines would rather hold communion with the Papists, and declared the hope that Calvinists could be saved, to be a diabolical invention."

Still the Melanthonian school was never entirely extinguished in the Lutheran body, and adhered to the conciliatory spirit of the master. Calixtus, Leibnitz, Spener, Zinzendorf, were all favorable to the principle of a union of the Christian confessions, and exposed themselves for this reason to the bitter reproaches of the champions of the scholastic orthodoxy and sectarian bigotry of their age.

As regards the Reformed, they were always willing to recognize the Lutherans as brethren, notwithstanding the difference of opinion on some articles of faith. This appears already from the conduct of Zwingli at Marburg. Calvin, while at Strasburg, signed even the Augsburg Confession, acted on several conferences in concert with Melanthon, kept up an intimate correspondence with him till his death, and was anxious to promote union and harmony among Protestants as far as it could be done without sacrifice of truth. The German branch of the Reformed church seemed to offer less difficulty than any other to a union with the Lutheran, since, from its origin, it stood in the closest connection with the Melanthonian school, and was regarded by Frederick the Pious, of the Palatinate, and many others, as its legitimate continuation, although modified to a considerable extent by Calvinistic influences.

The Electors of Brandenburg especially, since the transition of John Sigismund from the Lutheran to the Reformed confession, (1614,) cherished from political and religious motives the idea of a union of the contending parties. His grandson, Frederick William, surnamed the Great Elector, was married to a Dutch princess, Louise Henrietta, of eminent talents and piety, and regarded it as the mission of Prussia, in connection with Reformed Holland and Reformed England, to strengthen and protect the general cause of Protestantism. The Brandenburg-Prussian symbols, the *Confessio Marchica*, or *Sigismundi*, (of the year 1614,) the *Colloquium Lipsiacum* (1631,) and the *Declaratio Thoruniensis* (1645) look all in the same direction.

But owing to the prevailing polemical spirit and dogmatical exclusiveness of the seventeenth century, all attempts to realize the unity of evangelical Protestantism

16

failed. It was the will of Providence that the several confessions should first fully develop their distinctive peculiarities and fulfil their separate mission in the departments of doctrine, discipline and worship.

The latter part of the eighteenth century buried the controversy between Lutheranism and Reform, and even the doctrinal differences between Romanism and Protestantism, in the flood of indifferentism and infidelity which overrun the Continent of Europe. The confessional war was absorbed by the question, whether Christianity itself was not a fable, and the church an obsolete institution of the dark ages.

The reviving faith of the nineteenth century moved first in the broad channel of general Christianity, which precedes the particular ecclesiastical confessions. Even pious Catholics (think of Bishop Sailer, the princess Gallitzin and others) moved hand in hand with pious Protestants (Hamann, Claudius, Lavater, Stilling, etc.,) against the common foe of infidelity.

In this general Christian faith, and in harmony with the spirit and traditional policy of several of his royal and electoral ancestors, the Reformed king of Prussia, Frederick William III., after the emancipation of Germany from the French yoke, and shortly before the celebration of the third centennial jubilee of the Reformation, issued on the 27th of September, 1817, the memorable declaration, that he wished to unite the separate Lutheran and Reformed confessions in his dominions into one renewed Evangelical Christian Church, and would set an example in his own congregation at Potsdam, by joining in a united celebration of the Lord's

Supper on the approaching festival of the Reformation, hoping that the example may be generally imitated by his subjects in the same spirit, and that the time may soon come when all true Christians would be united in one faith, love and hope, as one flock under the common Shepherd of souls. The execution of the plan was commended to the provincial consistories, synods, and the pious zeal of the clergy.

Bunsen, who calls this event the most important work of Frederick William's reign, not only, but of the whole century, tells us, (Signs of the Times, vol. ii. p. 178,) that the king matured the idea on his visit to England in 1814, impressed with the imposing, national, conservative, pious and independent character of Anglican Protestantism, and that he made the first arrangement for a union and a new liturgy in the palace of St. James.

The good motives of the king are universally conceded. He was a monarch of only moderate talents, and somewhat contracted in his political creed, but of sound practical sense, honest character, righteous disposition and sincere piety, which had been much benefited by great disasters and great victories. He united in his reign the period of the deepest humiliation of Prussia with the period of her national, political, and religious regeneration, and died (1840) universally esteemed and beloved by his subjects, with the motto of his life, "My time in trouble, my hope in God," (*Meine Zeit in Unruhe, meine Hoffnung in Gott.*)

Nor was this Union by any means an arbitrary measure of Frederick William III. "It fell"—to use the words of a distinguished historian—"into his hands as the ripe fruit of his age." The Synod of Berlin, led by the greatest modern theological genius, Schleiermacher, who was far too independent to follow a movement because it proceeded from a court, and who was even suspected for his liberal views on politics, and nearly the whole clergy and laity of Prussia, readily fell in with the royal decree as a timely work, from which the greatest benefit might be expected to the cause of evangelical Protestantism. It was then generally believed and hoped that the time of the unhappy religious dissensions had forever passed, that the two sister Churches of the Reformation were agreed in every essential article of Christianity, in opposition to Romanism, and infidelity, and that their differences were too insignificant to prevent a hearty communion and co-operation in the work of the common Master.

Not only in Prussia, but in most of the German States where the two Confessions were sufficiently represented to justify a similar movement, the example of the king was followed. Thus the Union was introduced either by resolution of Synods, or by a general vote, in Nassau, 1817, the Bavarian Palatinate, 1818, Baden, 1821, and even in Würtemberg in 1827, where the Reformed had hardly an existence. But Saxony, Hanover, Bavaria proper, Mecklenburg, were too exclusively Lutheran, Switzerland too exclusively Reformed, to fall in with a movement, which otherwise, even there, met with decided sympathy, and they adhered to the former state of things.

The Protestants in Austria, who live under an absolute Roman Catholic government, and are only in very remote connection with the general life of Protestantism, were not affected by the new epoch, and continue to exist as two separate branches, the Church of the Helvetic Confession, and the Church of the Augsburg Confession.

Thus, if the Union contemplated the absorption of all the Protestants of Germany into one Church organization, it has by no means succeeded yet. For the Confessional Churches still exist in Switzerland and a considerable part of Germany, so that we have now three leading Protestant denominations instead of two. But a beginning had to be made somewhere, with the expectation, of course, that the movement would gradually affect the entire Protestant, and as the concluding hope of the royal Prussian declaration of 1817 implies, even the entire Christian world.

We have now to consider the leading features and obstructions in the subsequent development of this scheme of ecclesiastical Union.

CHAPTER XX.

THE CONFLICT OF UNIONISM AND CONFESSIONALISM.

Controversies growing out of the Union—Their Causes—The Proclamation of 1817—The New Prussian Liturgy, and the Old Lutheran Secession—The explanatory Decree of 1834—The Rise of New Lutheranisn in the Prussian Establishment—The Confessional Separation in the Oberkirchnrath, 1852—The Union—Decree of 1853—The proposed General Synod of Prussia—The preparatory Conference of 1856—Present State of Parties, the anti-confessional Unionists, the Confessional Unionists, and the High-Church Confederalists—Prospects.

THIS well-meant work of union and peace gave rise to a great deal of agitation and controversy, and is just now the burning question of German Protestantism, especially in Prussia, the principal battle-field, on which the religious and political problems of Germany must be solved. The theological war now raging about the union or disunion of Lutheranism and Reform, reminds me sometimes of our violent pro-slavery and anti-slavery agitation which seems to deepen every year, throwing the brand of discord into our States, Territories, and Churches, and seriously endangering the permanence of our National Union. It is to be hoped that the cause of union and peace may triumph, in some form or other, over sectional and sectarian division and strife. But its present condition is certainly critical in both cases, while it must be admitted, on the other hand, that the very opposition has revealed the intrinsic strength and tenacity of the Union, which may possibly outride all the storms, and be benefited by them in the end, so as to be delivered from its present objectionable features, and to assume a more free, natural and homogeneous character.

The troubles connected with the Evangelical Union are owing partly to the intrinsic difficulty and far-reaching importance of the work itself; partly to the serious defects in its origin and execution. Instead of growing out naturally of the inner life of the Church, it originated with temporal princes, and was introduced (like the Reformation itself in many countries) by virtue of the ecclesiastical supremacy of the crown, which may be conceded to it by human right, but never by divine right, the Church being born free as a supernatural constitution, with the inherent right and duty of self-government. It is true, the great mass of the ministry and people fell heartily in with the measure, but to a very large extent from sheer indifferentism, or at least simply from a vague and latitudinarian catholicity of feeling. For, at that time German Protestantism had hardly arisen from a death-like slumber, and had almost lost the consciousness of the distinctive doctrines and practices which originally separated the two Confessions of the Reformation, and which were now to be merged forever in the Union. Hence it was to be expected that the further progress of Protestantism in the positive and churchly direction would revive the old confessional controversies, and in the same measure shake the fabric of a Union, which was not the result of an inward theological solution of the questions at issue, but a measure of state policy and the product of pious desires.

Another objection to the Union is, that it wished to comprehend the entire Protestant population, and hence is composed, like every state-church, Lutheran or Reformed, of the most heterogeneous materials, which will necessarily get into conflict and collision as soon as the slumber of indifferentism is broken. But it is hard to see how this objection is to be removed, except by a separation of the time-honored connection of church and state, and a perfectly free development of religion, which would inevitably result in the breaking up of the Union, or any other ecclesiastical establishment, into an indefinite number of denominations and sects.

As the Union had proceeded from a German Reformed king, the opposition to it came from revived Lutheranism, which, owing to its closer affinity with the Catholic system, is constitutionally more exclusive and intolerant of dissent, than the Reformed communion. Harms had predicted it in 1817 in one of his 95 Theses, where he says—I quote from memory—"They wish now to enrich the Lutheran Church as a poor servant by a wealthy match. But pray do not perform the marriage ceremony over the bones of Luther; for they will be roused to life by the very act, and then woe to you."

It would lead us too far, of course, to present a detailed history of the Union. We will point out simply the leading facts in order to enable the reader to understand the present confused condition of things. We may distingnish four epochs in the movements, and connect them with four short but important official documents, (*Cabinetsorders*,) two of which were issued by Frederick William III., and two by his present successor, Frederick William IV.

1. We commence with the original proclamation of the Union, dated September 27, 1817. This must be regarded as the Magna Charta of the Prussian Establishment under its present form, and Prof. Stahl is wrong in claiming this honor for the decree of 1834, which is simply an explanation of the true meaning and import of the decree of 1817. It opened the way simply for the Union as regards government and worship. It left the doctrinal question undecided, and did not even mention the symbolical books which then had almost entirely gone out of use. But it contemplated neither a doctrinal absorption nor a mere confederation, but a real union of two bodies so as to constitute a higher third. It declared expressly that the plan proposed was neither a transition of the Reformed Church to the Lutheran, nor of the Lutheran to the Reformed, but the exhibition of one Evangelical Church, renewed in the spirit of the Master, and grounded in the Holy Scriptures. It was thought that minor theological differences might continue to exist without interfering with the general fellowship and harmony.

In order to carry out the Union, the late king contemplated two things, the gradual introduction of Presbyterian and synodical government, which is characteristic of the Reformed Church, and of a new liturgy, which was substantially taken from Lutheran sources. The former was established already before in the western provinces of Westphalia and the Rhine, where the Reformed element has the preponderance; but in the eastern provinces, where Lutheranism prevails, it has existed so far only as a partial experiment. The latter was accomplished, but called forth the first opposition to the Union itself.

In 1821, the King issued the new liturgy, which he made himself, in connection with his court preachers and a pious layman; for the clerical commission entrusted with this work since 1814, led to no satisfactory result. It was, however, subsequently submitted to consistories for revision in 1829, and is now undergoing another revision. Although breathing a pious spirit and marking a considerable improvement upon most of the liturgies then in use, it is still very defective, and hardly satisfies the wants of the present time.

The introduction of this guide of public worship was to realize and cement the Union among the people. But it met with great opposition, partly from friends of the Union, as Schleiermacher, who justly doubted the right of a king thus to interfere with the internal affairs of the Church, and disapproved of the arbitrary measures of the government in its introduction; partly from the Reformed congregations in the Wupperthal who wished to retain more freedom in the religious services; but especially from a few Lutheran ministers and laymen in Silesia, Scheibel, Huschke and Steffens, who objected to the virtual suppression of several characteristic Lutheran tenets in the eucharistic and other forms of the king's liturgy. For the work, although selected mostly from ancient Lutheran sources, was so constructed as to suit equally the Reformed, and substituted for the old Lutheran formula of distribution, "This is the *true* body of Christ," the declarative words, "*Christ says*, this is my body."

The harsh treatment of these dissenting Lutherans, whatever may have been their faults, is the dark spot in the history of the Prussian Union. Their leaders were fined, imprisoned and vexed in various ways, till the accession of the present King in 1840, who strongly disapproves of all compulsion in the sphere of religion, and permitted the Old Lutherans, as they are called, to organize themselves into a separate ecclesiastical body, without giving them, however, a share in the national church-property. A number of them, in the times of their severest trials, emigrated to the United States, where they belong to the Synods of Buffalo and Missouri.

2. The opposition to the liturgy, and the Old Lutheran troubles, called forth the second royal decree, on this subject, dated February 28, 1834. It goes a step beyond the first as regards the doctrinal aspect of the Union, and was intended to prevent further separation, by declaring the continued validity and authority of the symbolical books of the two confessions. The Union is here pretty much reduced to a "spirit of moderation and mildness," (*Geist der Mässigung und Milde,*) which should hold fast to the fundamental agreement of the two churches, and the principle of church communion, notwithstanding the doctrinal differences still existing. This order of 1834 then, must be regarded as a concession to confessionalism, and more particularly to Lutheranism.

The confessional tendency grew more and more in opposition to a false anti-symbolic and semi-rationalistic liberalism, and especially in opposition to the wild revolutionary spirit which was let loose in 1848, and threatened for a while to sweep away the Church itself.

Since that time there arose in the bosom of the Evangelical Church itself, and in close connection with the political reaction, a powerful Lutheran party, headed by Hengstenberg, Stahl, Göschel, von Gerlach, and others. These New Lutherans, as they are called in distinction from the Old Lutheran seceders, profess a high regard for the Reformed Church, where it exists in its original vigor and purity, and concede to it peculiar excellences, such as, to use the words of Stahl, "the sanctification of the congregation, the building up of a well defined system of Christian institutions and Christian life on the basis of a vigorous congregational faith, and an energetic, aggressive, life-reforming Christianity." Hengstenberg and Gerlach are themselves of Reformed origin, and Stahl is married to a Reformed lady. But they hate and abhor rationalism and latitudinarianism in every form, and object to every scheme of Union, which does not full justice to the ancient confessions. They also regard the Lutheran system as more orthodox, churchly, conservative and catholic, and better adapted to the genius of the German nation, than the Reformed, and hence their personal sympathies are all on the side of Lutheranism. But instead of seceding from the established Church of Prussia, as the Old Lutherans did, this party labors to make the Union itself more and more subservient to the interests of high church Lutheranism, or at least to reduce it to a mere mechanical confederation on strictly confessional ground.

3. The present king of Prussia so far yielded to the pressure of this influential party, as to allow, by an order of March 6, 1852, a confessional division in the *Oberkirchenrath*, the highest ecclesiastical tribunal of the Evangelical Church in Prussia, which he founded in 1850, with the view to give it more independence. Accordingly, in the session of this body on the 14th of July, 1852, Uechtritz, Neander, (the bishop, not the historian,) Strauss, Muehler, Twesten and Richter, declared themselves Lutherans, friendly to the Union, in the sense of the royal order of February 28, 1834, which maintains the Union without weakening the authority of the old confessions. Bollert and Snethlage professed the Reformed faith, with the same assent to the Union, as existing in Prussia *de jure* and *de facto*. Stahl, with whom the scheme seems to have originated, declared himself a pure Lutheran, without any qualifying clause. The same course was pursued by Cappell, (although he was originally Reformed,) when he entered the Oberkirchenrath a few weeks later. Nitzsch was the only member who represented the principle of the Union in the confessional sense, by declaring that he belonged to both churches, viz.: the *consensus* of both. He received subsequently a strong support in the person of Hoffmann, formerly president of the Evangelical Missionary establishment at Basel, and now Court-preacher and general superintendent at Berlin, and member of the Oberkirchenrath.

4. This arrangement of 1852 seems to resolve the

Union of the two confessions into a mere confederation of three parties, the Lutherans, the Reformed, and the Unionists or Evangelicals proper. But it called forth vigorous protests from the Prussian Universities, which show how deeply rooted the Union sentiments are. The King himself issued a new order in July 12, 1853, the last official royal document on this subject, which may be regarded as a reaction against confessionalism as far as this tends to undermine the Union. He declares there, that the decree of 1852 was intended simply to secure to the confessions all proper guarantee and protection within the established Church, but by no means to abolish or even to disturb the Union of the two evangelical denominations, founded by his father, and to create a schism in the national Church. He directs the Oberkirchenrath in Berlin and all the provincial consistories to resist such inferences, and to maintain the Union.

This declaration leaves no doubt as to the determination of the King to carry on the work commenced by his father. His reply to an address of the Lutheran Conference held at Wittenberg in October, 1853, is still more decided, and reveals a great deal of dissatisfaction, on his part, with the restless and exclusive spirit of the stiff Lutheran party. He has even recently expressed his full sympathy with the objects of the Evangelical Alliance of all evangelical Protestants, and invited the leaders of this movement in England and Scotland, to hold their next general conference at Berlin, to the great dissatisfaction of the New Lutherans, who are strongly opposed to the principles of religious liberty, and to all connection with English Dissenters, such as the Baptists and Independents.

Another still more important step of the king, is the resolution to call a General Synod during the year 1857, for the purpose of taking up and carrying on the work of the General Synod of 1846, which was interrupted by the revolution of 1848. The Confessionalists have no confidence whatever in deliberative bodies, either in politics or religion, and expect from it nothing but idle talk and agitation. Hengstenberg, Stahl and Herr von Raumer are absolutists in church and state; they think that all help must come from above, from the government, and that the congregations in their present homogeneous and indifferent characters cannot be safely entrusted with any participation in legislative measures. But the King, although by no means a strong and determined character, but yielding and conciliatory to a fault, is bent upon this Synod.

He summoned, therefore, a preparatory Evangelical Conference of fifty-seven delegates, which met in one of the palaces of Berlin, in November, 1856, to take into consideration the same questions which will claim, in a final manner, the attention of the proposed synod, viz.: the introduction of a Presbyterian form of government into the congregations of the Eastern provinces, the revival of the institutions of deacons and deaconesses, the revision of the present liturgy, the reform of the laws of marriage. Most of these topics affect directly or indirectly the very constitution of the Union. Although the Conference has no legislative, but merely advisory power, it will pretty much determine the course of the

Synod, unless this should be composed of different material.

It was expected that the positive Unionists, or the party of Nitzsch, Müller, Hoffman, Tholuck, Krummacher, von Bethmann Hollweg, etc., would have the preponderance. But I learn from private letters of members of the Conference and others, that the party of the high church Confessionalists to their own agreeable disappointment, have in the first sessions carried the day, especially in the question of congregational self-government. It is possible, that the Unionists yielded that point, in order to secure the more influence in other questions. But it is very unlikely that the high church Lutheran tendency in Prussia, backed as it is by a similar movement in Saxony, Bavaria, Hanover, and Mecklenberg, can be stopped. It is the nature of a movement that it moves and moves until its inward life and energy is exhausted. Principles must work themselves out, and it is worse than useless to stop their legitimate development.

5. The state of church parties in Prussia then, at the moment we write (December, 1856,) is this:

Rationalism proper is dead, and has not a single representative in the Evangelical Conference now assembled in Berlin.

The anti-confessional or latitudinarian Unionists, who base themselves on the Bible simply, without the church symbols, and embrace, besides the left wing of Schleiermacher's school, a number of liberal divines of different shades of opinions, held together by the mutual opposition to the reactionary tendencies in religion and politics, are deprived of power and influence in the highest councils; but they still live, are numerically strong in the ministry and laity, and hope for a radical change in their favor in case of an accession of the Prince of Prussia to the throne, who is known to be opposed to high-church tendencies, and rather loose and indifferent in matters of religion. But, as he is only two years younger than the king, his brother, such an event is neither probable nor desirable.

The evangelical Unionists, or the *consensus* party, which takes for its doctrinal basis the Bible, and the common dogmas of the Lutheran and Reformed Confessions, is strongest in the universities, but in the minority in the Oberkirchenrath.

The strict Confessionalists, who regard the Union as a mere confederation of the two Confessions under a common state-church government, and who are for the most part strict symbolical Lutherans and monarchical absolutists, although comparatively small in number, have at present the ascendancy in the seats of power and influence. It can hardly be disputed that the ultimate tendency of their zealous efforts is the dissolution of the Union altogether. A few of them have a strong leaning to Romanism, and would at any time prefer a union with Popery to a union with the Reformed confession. Their Lutheran brethren of other states have quite recently, in a conference at Dresden, resolved upon the reintroduction of auricular confession. "Straws show which way the wind blows."

In the case of a dissolution of the Prussian Union, which though not very probable, is by no means impossible, both the Lutheran and the Reformed churches

17*

would be reorganized on their separate confessional basis. But the majority of the people would not be prepared to go back to the old state of things which they regard as for ever surmounted by the Union of 1817. The radical Unionists would perhaps run into the principle of independency. The orthodox Unionists would strive to build up a United Evangelical Church, on the consensus of the two confessions, with a small membership, perhaps, at the beginning, but—as an intelligent correspondent of the New York "Independent" said some time ago—"with more theological learning at her command than any other church on the globe."

None of the three parties is willing to separate itself from the connection with the state, each striving to obtain the lion's share in the control of the establishment. But all the apparent indications to the contrary notwithstanding, the principle of freedom of religion and public worship, as already remarked, is making slow but sure and steady progress all over Europe, and the time may not be far distant, when the present relation of church and state will undergo a radical change.

The present state of the Prussian Union is very excited, confused, unsatisfactory and critical. But it must not be forgotten, that its very troubles and agitations are indications of life and energy, as the somewhat similar movements of the low-church, high-church, and broad-church parties in the Anglican Communion, and must result at last in good. For nothing can be considered a failure which essentially belongs to the ever progressing historical development of Christ's kingdom on earth. The great merits especially of the German evangelical Union-divines for the solution of the doctrinal differences between the two great divisions of Protestantism, and for the promotion of all branches of sacred science and literature, are immortal, and have already made an impression upon the more recent French, Dutch, English, Scotch and American theology, which can never be effaced.

Whatever may be the ultimate fate of the Prussian and other ecclesiastical establishments, the work of Union itself, lies deeply in the wants of the church and the present age, and will go on therefore, in some form or other, until the Lord, in his own good time, will crown the feeble efforts of his people and realize, in a far better form than we can conceive, the precious and unfailing promise of the one flock under one shepherd.

A proof of the existence of the deep rooted tendency of the better spirit of the age towards a union and consolidation of Christendom, we have in the important facts of the Evangelical Church Diet of Germany, and the Evangelical Alliance of England, both of which are altogether independent of state-church control, and look towards a free voluntary harmony and coöperation of the various sections of evangelical Protestantism.

P. S.—Since the above was written, we received full reports of the "Evangelical Conference" of Berlin, from which we learn that it closed its sessions December 5, 1856; that it turned out much more favorable to the cause of the Union, than was at first expected; and that it led upon the whole to important and encouraging results.

CHAPTER XXI.

THE EVANGELICAL CHURCH DIET.

General Character and Object of the Kirchentag—Its Origin in the revolutionary year 1848—The Sandhoff Conference—Dr. von Bethmann Hollweg—First Meeting at Wittenberg on Luther's and Melanthon's grave—Peculiar Solemnity and Importance of the First Meeting—Its Results—Relation of the Church Diet to the Evangelical Alliance, and to the Evangelical Union.

THE German Evangelical Church Diet has now been in existence since 1848, and become one of the most important and encouraging facts in the history of modern Protestantism. A condensed account of its origin, history, influence and prospects, based upon the official reports of its proceedings, as they were published from year to year, upon personal observations made at its seventh meeting at Frankfort on the Maine, and upon intercourse and correspondence with its founders and leading members, must be both interesting and instructive to those who wish to become fully acquainted with the present state of theology and religion in the land of the Reformation.

The Kirchentag, or Church Diet, is a free association of pious professors, ministers and laymen of Protestant Germany, for the discussion of the religious and ecclesiastical questions of the day, and for the promotion of the interests of practical Christianity, embraced under the term *Inner Mission*. It meets annually in one of the leading cities of Germany, and is at present by far the largest and most respectable representation of Evangelical Christianity in that country. Its doctrinal basis is the Bible, as explained by the ecumenical symbols and the evangelical confessions of the sixteenth century. It comprehends thus far only four Protestant denominations, the Lutheran, German Reformed, United Evangelical, and the Moravian brotherhood, but it holds intercourse at the same time with foreign Evangelical Societies and Churches of Switzerland, France, Holland, England, Scotland, and the United States, as far as they may choose to have themselves represented at its meetings, by official delegates on the above general Christian and positive Protestant basis. The Church Diet is no formal or official union of these denominations, but a free confederation simply of many hundreds and thousands of their ministerial and lay members, although it looks undoubtedly to a stronger consolidation and coöperation of the original Churches of the Reformation against their common enemies from without and from within. All parts of Germany, especially Prussia and Würtemberg, the two leading Evangelical States, send delegates to this body, and amongst them their very best men. But the rationalists and semi-rationalists, as well as those rigid Lutherans who refuse to hold any ecclesiastical communion with the Reformed and the Unionists, oppose it,—the former, because it is too orthodox and churchly for them; the latter, because it is not confessional and churchly enough, in their sectarian and exclusive sense of the term.

This assembly may be regarded as the practical fruit of that vigorous evangelical theology which, for the last twenty or thirty years, has risen in successful opposition to the most learned and dangerous forms of infidelity. The leaders of that theology, as Tholuck, Nitzsch, Müller, Hengstenberg, Dorner, Ullmann, Hoffmann, Ebrard, Lange, etc., are also amongst the principal founders and supporters of the Kirchentag. But the war, victoriously waged in the field of science and literature, must now be carried into the congregations and the practical life of the people. This work must be continued and completed by the rising generation of ministers trained by orthodox and pious professors, by the various Church-governments, and by free associations, of which the one under consideration is by far the largest and most influential.

The German Church Diet took its rise in the eventful year 1848, when all the thrones of Europe—save those of England, Belgium, and Russia—trembled, and the very foundations of civil and religious society seemed to give way, to make room, as was to be feared, to a reign of rationalism, atheism and Satanism. It appeared after the storms and earthquakes of revolution, as a rainbow of peace and promise, on the horizon of Germany, and has outlived the commotions and mushroom creations, the bright hopes and dark fears of the memorable year of its birth.

It is true it was prepared long before by the pastoral conferences, which, since the days of a revival of religious life, assembled annually pious ministers and laymen in various parts of Germany; and also by the desire of many of the most distinguished divines, for a closer union and independent action of the national churches, held under the bondage of as many secular governments. But the imminent danger of an approaching dissolution of all order in that revolutionary year on the one side, and the labors of the Parliament of Frankfort for a political regeneration of Germany on the basis of unity and constitutional liberty, on the other, matured this desire and suggested the plan of a great meeting of all the true friends of Christianity, for mutual consultation on the present crisis of the country, and for forming a confederation of the Protestant Churches without destroying their distinctive features or interfering with their internal affairs; in fine, a sort of evangelical defensive and offensive alliance against the growing flood of infidelity and destruction.

These ideas sprang up simultaneously, as with the instinct of historical necessity, in different minds, amongst which Dr. von Bethmann Hollweg, of Berlin, Dr. Dorner, then at Bonn, Dr. Ullman and Hundeshagen, of Heidelberg, Dr. Wackernagel, then at Wiesbaden, Bonnet, Heller and Haupt, in or near Frankfort, were the most active; and in several local pastoral conferences, especially one held at Bonn, on the 11th of May, 1848, one at Berlin, on the 21st of June, and two at the Sandhof, near Frankfort-on-the-Maine, on the 3d of May and 21st of June, of the same year.

At the last mentioned meeting many perplexities arose, and doubts were started as to the success of such a serious undertaking, when a true Christian nobleman, von Bethmann Hollweg, who was subsequently elected president of the Kirchentag at every one of its meetings, quieted their fears and re-animated their courage by pointing to the never-failing source of all true strength. "It is the Lord, my friends," he said, "who builds the Church. Never forget this! Whether the assembly spoken of will accomplish what we desire and hope, no one can tell. Our resolution must be an act of faith. Like Peter, we shall have to walk on the sea; but we know also that the Lord does not suffer any one to perish who trusts in him. If we look merely upon ourselves and upon the scattered, distracted and weak members of the Church, we would have indeed to despair. But if we raise our eyes in faith to Him, who is the Lord, we may venture it."

Finally, the Sandhof Conference, after a session of nine hours, resolved to call a general free assembly of distinguished ministers and laymen of the Lutheran, German Reformed, and United Confessions, to be held at Wittenberg, over the grave of Luther, for the purpose of consulting on the true interests of the Evangelical Church of Germany at the present crisis, on the basis of the evangelical faith. An invitation to this effect was issued, signed by nearly fifty names from all parts of Germany, well known for their distinguished merits, high standing and excellent Christian character.

Accordingly, the first Kirchentag, consisting of five hundred members, eminent divines and ministers, (Nitzsch, Müller, Heubner, Hengstenberg, Lehnerdt, Sack, Sartorius, Krummacher, Ball, Wichern, etc.,) statesmen and lawyers, (von Bethmann Hollweg, Stahl, von Gerlach, Götze, etc.,) and plain Christians of all classes of society and parts of Germany, especially from Prussia, met as one brotherhood on the 21st of September, 1848, in that venerable town so well known as the cradle of the Reformation, in that very church to whose doors its signal, the ninety-five theses, were once affixed, and on the tombstones of Luther and his friend, Melanthon, whose last desire and prayer was for the unity of distracted Christendom. The old lecturer's chair of the former university was used as the rostrum, adorned with the portrait of Luther, and with the significant motto of the Reformation, "*Verbo solo—fide sola*," (On the word alone—through faith alone.) A fervent prayer of the late venerable Dr. Heubner, then president of the theological seminary at Wittenberg, and the singing of the celebrated war-and-victory hymn of the evangelical faith, written by Luther a year before the Diet of Augsburg, opened the proceedings. It faithfully expressed the feelings which pervaded this first meeting from beginning to end, much better than we could do it, and may, therefore, claim a place here in the admirable translation of Thomas Carlyle.

A safe stronghold our God is still
A trusty shield and weapon;
He'll help us clear from all the ill
That hath us now o'ertaken.
The ancient Prince of hell
Hath risen with purpose fell,
Strong mail of craft and power
He weareth in this hour,
On earth is not his fellow.

With force of arms we nothing can,
Full soon were we down-ridden;
But for us fights the proper man,
Whom God himself hath bidden.
Ask ye, Who is this same?
CHRIST JESUS is his name,
The Lord Zebaoth's Son,
He, and no other one,
Shall conquer in the battle.

And were the world all Devils o'er
And watching to devour us,
We lay it not to heart so sore,
Not they can overpow'r us.
And let the Prince of ill
Look grim as e'er he will,
He harms us not a whit,
For why? His doom is writ—
A word shall quickly slay him.

God's word, for all their craft and force,
One moment will not linger,
But spite of hell, shall have its course,
'Tis written by His finger.
And though they take our life,
Goods, honor, children, wife,
Yet is their profit small;
These things shall vanish all,
The Church of God remaineth.

The significance of the first Kirchentag will be better understood, if we recollect all the revolutionary storms, wars and rumors of war, by which it was surrounded. The frightful murder of Lichnowsky and Auerswald had just been committed in the streets of Frankfort, and broken the remaining moral strength of the national assembly; the excesses of the revolutionists and destructionists had reached their height, and the future looked dark and gloomy as it never did before. With such prospects before them, the assembly at Wittenberg felt the whole weight of its awful responsibility; past differences were forgotten, and the disciples of one common Master pressed together into a close adhesion and holy brotherhood as they awaited the issue of their own yet dimly apprehended mission. Surrounded, as they were, by the sacred associations of the most remarkable period in modern church history, they looked less to Luther's name, so long abused by dead churches, than to Luther's God, and were animated by the very spirit of repentance and faith, of humble self-distrust and strong confidence in Christ which had animated the reformer, without suffering themselves to be distracted by the minor domestic controversies which disfigured the great work of the sixteenth century.

"It was," says a well informed and esteemed English friend, on this meeting, (Mr. Tho. H. Gladstone, in an article on the Kirchentag for the London Eclectic Review, April, 1855,) "it was indeed a new and interesting sight to behold the learned professor seated side by side with the simple-minded Christian, the dignified ecclesiastic taking brotherly counsel with the humble lay-missionary or provincial school teacher. It was no less a strangely novel spectacle to see the strongest upholders of the respective orthodoxies, Lutheran and Reformed, forgetting doctrinal differences in the harmony of Christian purpose and Christian love; still more to see the object of their common jealousy, the

"United" Church, as well as the Moravian and other dissenting communities, completing the picture of Christian union and brotherly love by being admitted to their association without question of their ecclesiastical polity or church rule. All seemed to point to the dawning of a better day. And the tempest of persecution with which the Church was assailed, appeared already converted into a blessing, in the recognition of its essential unity, and the sense of the mutual dependence of its parts as members of that mystic body which is one in its living Head. This feeling of Christian fellowship was heightened to the sublime, and received an expression too deeply affecting ever to be erased from the memory of those who witnessed the scene, when, at a solemn moment on the last day, the earnest Krummacher, in one of his fervent addresses, pledged the members to stand true to one another in the day of persecution, which seemed about to burst upon them, and received in the prolonged affirmation of the whole assembly, the assurance that they would bear each other as members of one family in their hearts and prayers, would receive each other in the day of persecution to house and home till the storm should be overpast, and would account as their own sister and their own children the widows and orphans of the brother who should seal his testimony by the martyr's death."

The results to which this deeply solemn and interesting assembly arrived in three days session (from the 21st to the 23d of Sept.,) were :

1. An invitation addressed to all the Protestant Churches of Germany, to hold on the 5th of November,

1848, the Sunday following the anniversary of the Reformation, a day of general prayer and humiliation, in order to begin the work of the regeneration of Protestantism with the same spirit of true evangelical repentance, with which Luther commenced the Reformation, and which he so clearly expressed in the very first of his ninety-five theses.

2. A resolution to form a confederation of all those German Churches which stand on the ground of the reformatory confessions, not for the purpose of an amalgamation of these churches and an extinction of their peculiarities and relative independence, but (*a*) for the representation and promotion of the essential unity and brotherly harmony of the evangelical churches; (*b*) for united testimony against every thing unevangelical; (*c*) for mutual counsel and aid; (*d*) for the decision of controversies; (*e*) for the furtherance of ecclesiastical and social reforms, especially Inner Mission; (*f*) for the protection and defense of the divine and human rights and liberties of the evangelical church; (*g*) for forming and promoting the bond of union with all evangelical bodies out of Germany.

We see from all this, that the first Kirchentag was animated by a truly Christian spirit, placed itself wisely on the most solid basis, viz.: the Gospel and the Reformation, evangelical repentance and evangelical faith, and proposed the noblest practical aims, which are well worthy of the united efforts of all Protestant Churches, in and out of Germany. It is evident, from its subsequent history, that the Lord has eminently blessed it for the good of his Church, although its original plan of an official confederation was never realized, and silently dropped.

But before we follow its progress, we must say a few words on the relation of the Church Diet to a somewhat similar body, the Evangelical Alliance. This originated two years earlier, in August, 1846. It met first under the name of the "World's Convention," in the city of London, and consisted of nine hundred and twenty-one members; forty-seven of which were from the Continent, eighty-seven from North America, the rest from England and Scotland. It convened again in London during the World's Fair, in 1851, a third time at Paris, in 1855, and is to meet at Berlin in 1857, at the special invitation of the King of Prussia.

Both the Kirchentag and the Alliance are no union of Churches, but a union of Christians, laymen as well as ministers; no legislative assembly, but simply a free association with moral power. Both afford an admirable occasion for Christians from all parts of the world, to hold fellowship and consult with each other about the common interests of the Redeemer's kingdom. Both tend thus to promote the true unity of the spirit, and to strengthen the interests of divided Protestantism. But they differ at the same time in the following points:

(1.) The one is an essentially German, the other an essentially English and Scotch plant.

(2.) The former has at least a *semi*-official character, and looked at first to a confederation of the churches of the Reformation, which the latter never contemplated.

(3.) The Kirchentag is an association simply of four denominations, Lutheran, German Reformed, United, and Moravian, although it receives delegates also from foreign evangelical bodies; while the Alliance at its first meeting, was composed of representatives of about fifty denominations, among which the Scotch Presbyterians and the English Baptists seem to have had thus far the controlling influence.

(4.) The Kirchentag never pretended to make a new creed, but took for its doctrinal basis the Bible and the original Confessions of evangelical Protestantism from the period of the Reformation; while the Alliance issued a new symbol in 1846, consisting of nine short articles, which express the fundamental doctrines of Protestantism, in such a manner as to exclude none of the leading Protestant sects except Universalists, Unitarians, and Quakers.

(5.) The Kirchentag aims at an internal regeneration of Protestantism over against infidelity and vice within its own borders; while the Alliance had from the beginning a special reference to the foreign foe, and intended to erect a bulwark against the progress of Romanism and Puseyism.

(6.) The Kirchentag is more extensive and practical in its operation, as it embraces all the important questions of the time and the whole field of Inner Mission; while the Alliance confined itself so far mainly to the preparation of reports on the condition of the various churches of Christendom, and to the promotion of religious liberty throughout the world, in opposition to the intolerant and persecuting spirit of Rome.

The relation of the Church Diet to the Evangelical Union, will appear, from what has been said already.

While it is no amalgamation of churches and creeds, and has neither the official authority, nor the benefits of an ecclesiastical establishment, it is far more homogeneous and thoroughly evangelical in its composition, free in its character and mode of operation, and has a purely religious origin and history. It was not made, but it grew; it is not the project of a temporal prince, a measure of the state-church authorities, as the Union, but it took its rise in the heart of the church itself, at a time of a general upheaving of the very foundations of society, and was carried on and sustained so far without any assistance of the temporal arm, by the free spontaneous coöperation of the most vital forces of German Christendom.

CHAPTER XXII.

HISTORY AND RESULTS OF THE CHURCH DIET.

The Eight Meetings of the Kirchentag—Mode and Character of the Proceedings—The Church Diet of Berlin, and the solemn Adoption of the Augsburg Confession—Merle d'Aubigne's Remarks in behalf of the Reformed Church—The Kirchentag of Frankfort-on-the-Maine, and its principal Reports—Fraternal Correspondence with the German Churches of America—The Kirchentag of Lubeck—Prospects of the Church Diet—Its general Results and happy Influence—The Work of Inner Mission and Dr. Wichern.

SINCE 1848, the Kirchentag met every year in September, with the exception of 1855, when it would have assembled at Halle, according to appointment, had it not been providentially prevented by the sudden appearance of the cholera in that city. The following is a list of the places of meeting, with the number of regular attendants, exclusive of the large crowd of spectators:

1.	Wittenberg,	a. 1848,	members	about	500
2.	Wittenberg,	1849,	"	"	700
3.	Stuttgart,	1850,	"	"	2000
4.	Elberfeld,	1851,	"	"	1800
5.	Bremen,	1852,	"	"	1400
6.	Berlin,	1853,	"	"	2000
7.	Frankfort-on-the-Maine,	1854,	"	"	1800
8.	Lübeck,	1856,	"	"	400

The next Kirchentag is to take place, on urgent invitation, at Stuttgart in 1857 or 1858, as the central committee may decide. The fluctuation in attendance is owing mostly to the local situation of the respective places. The small number of regular members at Lübeck, for instance, can easily be accounted for, partly by the extreme Northern location of this city, and partly by the raging of the cholera in it a short time before the meeting took place. We are confident, that should Providence not prevent the proposed assembly at Stuttgart, the large Stifts-Kirche will be crowded to overflowing, and the members will be as hospitably and affectionately entertained as they were in 1850.

As to the general nature of these meetings, they have far less of a business character, but are much more instructive and edifying than our synodical assemblies. They are exclusively occupied with spiritual affairs, and have nothing to do with money matters and cases of discipline, which unavoidably take up so much time in our self-governing legislative Church-councils. The Kirchentag lasts four days, two of which are devoted to the congress of Inner Mission, of which we shall say more hereafter. Dr. von Bethmann Hollweg and Prof. Stahl, two learned and pious jurists and statesmen, were annually re-elected Presidents, except at Frankfort, where the Rev. Dr. Hoffman took the place of the absent Stahl. The business of the Kirchentag during the year is managed by the select central committee, the leading members of which, von Bethmann Hollweg, Stahl, Nitzsch, Hengstenberg, Snethlage, Hoffman, von Mühler, Jordan, reside in Berlin. They select the principal topics for discussion, and the speakers or reporters six months before the meeting, so as to give them full time for careful preparation. At the day and hour appointed these speakers read their papers on the subjects assigned them. Then follows a free discussion, and if necessary, a resolution for the adoption of measures proposed for the carrying out of the object in view. Owing to the great number of speakers, they must generally be limited to five or ten minutes. Some leading members, as Wichern, Krummacher, Sander, Stahl, Nitzsch, Kapff, speak often; others, as Hundeshagen, Ullmann, Rothe, Bähr, prefer to sit silent. There is also room given, for short addresses, to the delegates from foreign churches and religious societies. The official minutes contain the reports in full, and an abstract of the debates and proceedings. We need not add, that devotional exercises open and close each session, and that most, if not all, the pulpits of the place of meeting, are filled by distinguished orators every evening and during the intervening Sunday.

Besides the general sessions, a number of separate sessions are held early in the morning and late in the evening for particular objects connected with the Kirchentag, as the promotion of the better observance of Sunday, the reform of prisoners and prison-discipline, the establishment of houses of refuge, the cultivation of religious art, etc.

Finally, the Kirchentag has become the nucleus and occasion for the meetings of the Reformed Conference, of the Missionary, Bible, Tract, and other benevolent Societies, so that it is impossible for the most anxious and persevering visitor to attend more than one-third of these gatherings. The excitement and commotion is so great, that it would be better to extend the Diet over one or two weeks, instead of condensing such a large amount of religious life and social enjoyment into the short space of four days.

It would lead us far beyond our proposed limits to give a detailed account of all the meetings of the Kirchentag from the first held at Wittenberg to that of Lübeck. We must confine ourselves to the principal topics of interest in the last three meetings.

The Church Diet of Berlin, in 1853, was the most important of all in a doctrinal point of view. For it solemnly and almost unanimously adopted the Augsburg Confession of 1530, as the fundamental symbol (*Grund-Symbol*) of the entire Evangelical Church of Germany in all its branches, with the distinct understanding, however, that the tenth article on the Lord's Supper, should not exclude the Reformed doctrine on the subject, and that this whole act should not interfere at all with the peculiar position of those Reformed Churches which never adopted the Augsburg Confession. The measure was supported by Sartorius and Stahl, in the name of the Lutheran, by Krummacher, in the name of the Reformed, and by Nitzsch, in the name of the United Church. After a very interesting discussion, which occupied the whole of the 20th of September, the two thousand members who filled the garrison church of the Prussian capital, signified almost with one heart and one mouth, their assent to the most venerable and most catholic Confession of German Protestantism, and then burst out in the German Te Deum, "*Nun danket alle Gott.*" The joyful news of the decision was carried with the greatest haste to the king, who received it with every expression of delight, and was hailed with enthusiasm by the pious Protestants throughout Germany, while the Roman Catholics were disagreeably surprised by this unexpected testimony of doctrinal unity and strength among their opponents. This act of confession, coming from such a vast assembly, including the most respected and influential men from all parts of Germany, was no doubt a powerful protest against Romanism, and still more against Rationalism, and marks an epoch in the history of German Protestantism.

And yet while we concede the great importance of this fact for Germany and for Lutheranism, we are not in the least surprised that some Reformed members present, as the late Dr. Henry, the author of the Life of Calvin, Professor Heppe, of Marburg, and Dr. Merle d'Aubigné, of the city of Calvin, were not altogether satisfied, and would have greatly preferred the resolution, if, instead of simply guarding the Reformed conscience in reference to the interpretation of the Augustana, it would have included a formal recognition of the Heidelberg Catechism, or the Helvetic Confession, or some other Reformed symbol. Dr. Merle, the author of the popular history of the Reformation, abstained from voting on this subject, and in an interesting speech, after bestowing due praise upon the Augsburg Confession, made some significant remarks from the stand-point of general Protestant Christianity against German and Lutheran sectionalism.

"I have no objection," he said, "to the Augustana, nor to the Lutheran Church, which I honor and love like a child, having learned much from Luther and his associates. But I fear an excess in the Lutheran spirit, and can, therefore, wish it nothing better than an intimate confederation—I do not say union which has a peculiar technical sense—with the believing, living and more free Reformed Church. I fear first the increase of a traditional, ceremonial, hierarchical element in Lutheranism, which may all be found in much greater perfection in the Church of Rome; and secondly, an isolation from, and condemnation of other children of God who live of the same Word of God. Luther had two hands, the one with which he turned off Zwingli at Marburg, that was his left hand; and the other with which he signed the Wittenberg Concordia, that was his right hand. And finally, I fear that Lutheranism may withdraw too much from practical life. Its passivity must be melted with the activity of the Reformed Christians. Three great colossi of mankind are now shaken to the very base, Mohammedanism, India and China; and in every case Reformed Christianity has a hand. The Reformed element has grown mightily since the Reformation. A mustard seed then, it is now a large tree, spreading its branches over the face of the globe. The modern progress of Christianity in Great Britain and North America is especially astounding. The sceptre of the future development of humanity lies in the hands of the Reformed Confession. Now, my dear Lutheran brethren, let us rather unite under the banner of our common Head for the conversion of the world, with the inscription: *Hoc signo vinces!* As far as I am concerned, I would place the Gallicana, or the Helvetica, or the Heidelbergensis, on a par with the Augustana. But whatever you may do, let us who are redeemed by the blood of atonement, members of all confessions to the ends of the earth, be one in the Father, in the Son, and in the Holy Ghost."

The seventh Church Diet, held at Frankfort-on-the-Maine, in 1854, September 22d to 27th, derived special importance from the variety and fullness of its reports, as well as from the place of meeting in the old imperial city, in whose immediate neighborhood (the Sandhof) the Kirchentag itself was born six years before, and in the same church of St. Paul, where, in 1848 and 1849, the famous Parliament discussed, with the assembled learning of German professors and patriots, the political regeneration and reorganization of Germany on the basis of liberty and unity, and where, in August, 1850, the representatives from Europe and America held the third General Peace Congress. This building was thus within a few short years the witness of angry debate and of heavenly worship, of political clamor and the eloquence of peace and good will to the Church and the world. Of the sixteen hundred and sixteen published names of regular members, eleven hundred and twenty were theologians and ministers, and four hundred and ninety-six laymen, of all ranks of society, and from all parts of Germany and foreign countries. A dense crowd of spectators of ladies and gentlemen filled the galleries at every session. The evening sermons which were preached in the different churches of the city by Krummacher, Tholuck, Hoffmann, Kapff, Bahrdt, Mallet, Ebrard, Sander, Grandpierre, and other distinguished pulpit orators, were so largely attended, that hundreds had to return home for want of room. This fact may show what a salutary influence this assembly may exert upon the place of its meeting, as well as upon the hundreds and thousands of visitors from abroad.

The first paper read before the Frankfort Church Diet, after the introductory services and the annual report of the President, von Bethmann Hollweg, was a most able, pointed and stirring essay of about two hours in length, on the right use of the Bible in the church, the school and the family, by the Rev. Dr. W. Hoffmann, now court preacher and general superintendent at Berlin. The speaker declared the whole Bible, from beginning to end, (exclusive of the Apocrypha) to be the Word of God in human form and speech, an organic whole, unfolding the divine plan of redemption, the infallible rule of faith and practice, and pointed out the ways and means by which a universal Bible-custom (*Bibel-sitte*) and a universal Bible-life (*Bibel-leben*) should be introduced into all the churches, schools, and families of Germany. He advised the ministers to study the whole Bible, not only from commentaries, but on the old principle of the self-interpretation of Scripture, and on their knees, so as to be filled with the Holy Ghost and with the majesty and power of the Word of the living God. Then their sermons will be truly scriptural, i. e., not merely quote passages from the Bible, but unfold its great ideas and realities of the divine plan of redemption, bring near the powers of the world to come, and make the Word of God alive in the hearts of the hearers. Concerning the third point he said, every Christian household should become an *ecclesiola in ecclesia*, a temple of the living God. There never yet was a Bible-life, in the full sense of the term, in the families of the Church, except by way of exception. Before the invention of the art of printing, it was impossible; the Reformation made an attempt to introduce it, but could not carry it through. But now, when a copy of the Bible is in almost every family, it can and ought to be fully realized, that it may exert its sanctifying influence over all branches and ranks of society, and make the German nation emphatically the people of God in the new dispensation. Thus the Church would cease to be merely a Church of theologians and preachers, and become truly a Church of the people. The meetings of the Church Diet would become free feasts of thanksgiving and praise to the great Author of the book of books. Let us all wish and pray that He may kindle this Bible-life amongst us and make it shine in all its pentecostal glory.—This address was exceedingly well received, and ordered to be extensively circulated, so as to reach, if possible, every minister, school-master and father of a family.

The second report by Dr. Julius Müller, of Halle, assisted by Advocate Thesmar of Cologne, related to the law of divorce, a subject of great practical importance for Germany, and wound up with the resolutions which were unanimously adopted: (1.) That the civil governments of Protestant Germany be respectfully requested to reform the matrimonial legislation, and to abolish all causes of divorce not sanctioned by the word of God. (2.) That the Protestant clergy decline to marry such persons as had been divorced on unscriptural grounds. This subject was subsequently agitated in the Prussian Chambers, and the result was, that some at least of the fourteen, say fourteen reasons of divorce which the Prussian *Landrecht* recognizes since Frederick II., were abolished. But there is great room for additional improvement in this direction all over Germany.

Then followed an interesting and animating discussion on infant baptism, introduced by an original essay of Dr. Steinmeyer, of Bonn, without leading, however, to any definite results.

Dr. Wichern, of the Rough House, near Hamburg, opened the Congress for Inner Mission on the third day, in his usual fervent and heart-stirring manner, with a lengthy, instructive and encouraging report on the great theme of his life. He discoursed, out of the fullness of his experience and enthusiasm, on the training of laborers for Inner Mission; on the propriety of forming evangelical brotherhoods and sisterhoods, without the Romish addition of vows, celibacy and meritorious works; on new institutions for destitute children; on the recent labors for promoting family worship, the sanctification of Sunday, for providing every married couple with a copy of the Bible; on the spiritual care of the poor, the orphans, sailors, emigrants, mechanics, and destitute classes of society; on prison discipline, the temperance movement; in fact on nearly every topic of moral reform and Christian charity, which now arrests the attention of serious and benevolent men in Germany.

The ecclesiastical care of the poor, next occupied the attention, on the basis of a paper presented by superintendent Lengerich of Pomerania.

Then came, on the fourth day of the session, a most valuable and popularly written report of Prelate Dr. Kapff, of Stuttgart, against gambling houses and lotteries. It is a notorious fact, that two or three little German governments disgrace themselves by tolerating, for filthy lucre's sake, faro-banks in fashionable watering places, especially Baden-Baden, and Homburg, to the temporal and moral ruin of hundreds of families. One of the best acts of the unfortunate German Parliament of Frankfort, was the abolition of these miserable establishments in January 8th, 1849. But with the triumph of political re-action, they were restored, and even increased in number. The Electorate of Hesse sanctioned in 1853, or 1854, four new ones (Neuheim, Hofgeismar, Wilhelmsbad and Neundorf); and yet this government, then under the control of the unpopular Hassenpflug, (called by his enemies *Hessenfluch*, also *Hass und Fluch*,) wanted to be pre-eminently Christian, abusing the holy name of order and of Christianity for the promotion of political tyranny and bigoted churchism! It was, therefore, highly proper, that the assembled piety of Germany should give free utterance to the indignation of all good men against this abomination, and this, too, at Frankfort, which lies in the immediate neighborhood of these gambling-hells. The Church Diet unanimously, and without any discussion, resolved upon a petition to the respective governments for the suppression of all games of hazard, faro-banks and lotteries, within the limits of the German confederation. The petition was favorably acted upon by the *Bundestag* of Frankfort, but the miserable little governments, basing themselves upon their sovereignty, refused, thus far, to abolish those nurseries of vice and misery. Prussia alone promptly responded to the appeal of the Kirchentag, and at once suppressed the gambling establishments at Aix-la-Chapelle.

The last session of the Frankfort meeting was devoted to the consideration of the relation of the evangelical Churches of Germany to the German Churches of America, and the spiritual care of the German emigrants. The writer of this book, then on a visit in Europe, had been requested to prepare the report on this subject; and spoke of the general significance of America for the future development of Christianity and civilization; of the particular mission of the German evangelical Churches in the United States; and finally on the duty of the mother Church in Europe toward her daughter in America, with special reference to the thousands and hundreds of thousands of emigrants who annually flock to our shores, to become either a disgrace, or an honor to their native country, and a curse, or a blessing to their adopted home, according to the moral and religious character they bring with them from Germany. In the discussion which followed, and in which Kapff, Krummacher, Sander, Kaiser, Conze, Grandpierre, of Paris, Cappadose, of the Hague, von Bethmann Hollweg, and others, took part, the kindest Christian interest was expressed in the state and progress of Christianity in the new world, and a new impulse given to the societies and efforts which have for their object to provide for the spiritual destitution of the German emigrants, and to make them good citizens and pious Christians. The meeting unanimously resolved to enter into fraternal correspondence, and as far as possible into an exchange of delegates with the German and Anglo-German Churches of America, and concluded with the solemn singing of Zinzendorf's beautiful hymn on the union of all believers, alluded to at the close of the preceding report, ("Lass uns so vereinigt werden, Wie Du mit dem Vater bist," etc.)

The resolution was subsequently carried out. The officers of the Church Diet sent a truly Christian and fraternal address written by the president, Dr. von Bethmann Hollweg, to all the American Churches of German descent and evangelical profession, comprehended in the plan of the Kirchentag, namely, the Lutheran, German Reformed, Evangelical United, and Moravian. The letter was responded to in the same spirit. The German Reformed Church of the United States, at a Synodical meeting held at Chambersburg in 1855, sent not only a written reply, but also three delegates, two clergymen, (Rev. Dr. B. Schneck and Rev. B. Bausman, of Pennsylvania,) and a lay-elder (Mr. G. S. Griffith, of Maryland,) to the Church Diet at Lübeck.* This fact is now recorded in history as a

* I may be permitted here, without impropriety, to quote a passage from a very friendly private letter of the President of the Church Diet, Dr. von Bethmann Hollweg to me, dated from Rheineck, Nov., 14, 1856, which shows how kindly this delegation from America was appreciated by the German brethren:

delightful testimony of the communion of faith and love which, in spite of the ocean, still binds together the Churches of the German and Swiss Reformation and their children and brethren in the new world, whither the star of Christ's kingdom is taking its way. Besides there are important practical interests which strongly recommend such a correspondence. For the German Churches on both sides of the Atlantic should certainly coöperate in bringing the large and increasing tide of German emigration to America under Gospel-influences, and giving it such a direction and shape, as to make it an honor to their old, and a blessing to their new home. It is to be desired, that the General Synod of the Lutheran Church of the United States, and the German Evangelical Association of the West, should imitate the example of the German Reformed Church, and have themselves represented by a personal delegation at the next Kirchentag of Stuttgart, where it may confidently expect a most warm-hearted Christian welcome.

The eighth Church Diet, having failed to meet at Halle in 1855, on account of the sudden outbreak of a violent epidemic, took place in the free city of Lübeck, in the extreme North of Germany, in September, 1856. For local and other reasons, it was apprehended by

"Wenn der Lübecker Kirchentag überhaupt zu den gesegnetsten gehörte durch die fühlbare Nähe des Herrn, seine gute Hand in allen Verhandlungen, und den Geist der Eintracht, des Friedens, der Liebe und Kraft, der sie durchwehte, so gehörte zu seinem schönsten Schmuck, zu den schönsten Gaben, die der Herr ihm verlieh, die Gegenwart der Abgeordneten aus Ihrer Kirchengemeinschaft und die herzliche Weise, wie ihr Sprecher, Herr Dr. Schneck, der vaterländischen Kirche die Bruderhand reichte."

many, that this meeting would prove a failure, especially since it was known that the cholera had raged there during the summer. But this fear was not realized. The attendance, it is true, was much smaller than at any previous meeting, especially from the central, western and southern regions of Germany. Still it was a respectable and imposing assembly of about four hundred clergymen and pious laymen. Several foreign countries and churches also, as the Free Church of Scotland, the Presbyterian Church of Ireland, the Reformed Churches of Holland and France, besides various benevolent societies were worthily represented. The three delegates of the German Reformed Church of America were all on the spot, and express themselves in their official and private reports highly delighted with all the proceedings, as well as with their personal reception. Concord and harmony reigned from beginning to end. The distracting church question, which agitates at present the Prussian establishment to its very centre, and on which even the presiding officers of the Kirchentag are by no means entirely agreed, was fortunately not permitted to disturb the truly Christian tone and feeling, or to overshadow the essential agreement in all the fundamental articles of the Christian faith. The subjects, although not of such absorbing interest, as on former occasions, were judiciously selected and ably discussed.

The first topic related to the revival of evangelical Church-discipline, and was opened by a veteran divine, Dr. Sack, formerly professor at Bonn, now Consistorial-rath at Magdeburg, a son of the former Reformed court-preacher at Berlin, who was one of the chief promoters of the Union in Prussia in 1817.

Discipline, we are sorry to say, has almost entirely ceased in Germany, and it is difficult to see how it ever can be properly exercised, as long as the Church remains so intimately interwoven with the State, and as long as the sick and dead members so far outnumber the living Christians. The State-Church system drills every body mechanically into the Church, but permits them afterwards to believe and profess and act as they please. The State cares only for the outward appearance and the legal aspect of the case, but cannot produce an inward change, and the church, which is the proper moral and religious agent, is constantly cramped in its free action by the secular government, and not unfrequently paralyzed by the bad example of the head of the State, who is at the same time the *summus episcopus* of the Church. In Würtemberg, for instance, excommunication for adultery sake, would have to commence with the King, who is generally known to be habitually addicted to that grievous sin.

On the second day, Dr. Schmieder, the successor of the venerable Dr. Heubner, as head of the Theological Seminary of Wittenberg, read a lengthy address on the call to the ministry. Our German brethren complain both of the want of efficient, and an excess of indifferent ministers. Many study for the sacred office merely from utilitarian and mercenary motives, to the injury of the church and themselves, while many, who have the proper spirit, refuse to obey the internal call, to the loss of religion. The clergy proceed almost exclusively from the middle and lower classes. Count Zinzendorf still remains almost a solitary example of a missionary nobleman. The cause of this evil was found in the prevalence of materialism among the higher classes, the love of gain, and an aversion to the solemn duties of the ministry. But another cause should have been found in the close union of church and state as it exists in Germany. The excellent pastor Meyer, of Paris, remarked, that there were at present twenty-three vacant parishes in the Reformed Church of France; that they had the son of a wealthy banker who served as a faithful village-pastor; and that they had many excellent ministers, who were the children of street-sweepers. "If they only come," he said, "we care not whether they come from above or below. Yes, let them come from *above, far above,* from the Lord and Head of the Church."

The third topic of discussion was the question, How shall the Church oppose the influence of materialism in modern natural science upon the masses? Dr. Fabri, the author of the "*Briefe gegen den Materialismus,*" 1856, one of the very best refutations of this latest form of infidelity, had been very properly selected for the leading report, and seems to have done full justice to his theme.

It is a singular fact, that, after a temporary stagnation of philosophical speculation in Germany, a crude materialism should suddenly spring up, proclaiming in the name of the natural sciences, the irreconcilable contradiction of geology and astronomy with the Bible, and flatly denying the very existence of an immortal spirit in man. This seems to be the opposite extreme to the transcendental idealism which formerly prevailed, and yet there is a connecting link between the two in such books as Feuerbach's *Wesen des Christenthums.* But to the credit of Germany, it must be said, that quite a number of works, both scientific and popular, have already appeared against this pseudo-philosophy of a Vogt, Moleschot, Burmeister, Büchner and other infidel naturalists of the day.

Fabri takes the ground, that materialism is no philosophy at all; that it must logically end in nihilism; that it must be met, not with governmental coercion, but with the weapons of reason; that theology and natural science do not necessarily contradict each other, but can be harmonized without torturing any of their principles or data. Dr. Stahl, in the discussion, denied that materialism was a product of Protestantism, as it existed under the papacy long before the reformation. Much as he respected and admired the investigations of science in the sphere of nature, he regarded it as transcending its reasonable limits, when it presumed to define and explain the domain of spiritual and eternal truth. It can discover planets, but it cannot tell us whether they are inhabited. It can invent the telegraph, but it cannot explain the essence of electricity, much less the hidden mysteries of God.

The last days, as usual, were devoted to the discussion of the various benevolent operations of the Congress for Inner Mission. Here the most important and interesting part was an address of Dr. Wichern, nearly three hours in length, on the sphere of woman in the evangelical Church, where the distinguished Christian philanthropist gave a graphic picture of the present position, trials, claims and duties of woman.

As already remarked, the next meeting of the Kirchentag is to be held in Stuttgart, either in 1857 or 1858, as the central committee on further deliberation may deem best.

We think it likely, that the meeting will be put off till 1858, for in the autumn of 1857, the Evangelical Alliance will assemble for the first time on German ground, and attract no doubt a great deal of attention. Some of the best friends of the Church Diet believe that it will sooner or later be brought to a close either by the course of events which may supersede it, or by the growing confessional strife and doctrinal exclusiveness which is adverse to union and confederation of different confessions. Some of its leading members and founders, as Stahl and Hengstenberg, become more high-church Lutheran every year, and are alienated in the same proportion from their brethren who occupy United or Reformed ground. In 1855, it was apprehended also, that the burning political difference on the Russian and Turkish question which divided the two presidents, Dr. von Bethmann Hollweg and Professor Stahl in the Prussian Chambers, might seriously overcloud or break up the proposed meeting at Halle, which, however, was providentially prevented. The Eastern war is now concluded, and with it the bitter political controversy to which it gave rise. But the general difference between the monarchical absolutism of the high-church Lutherans, and the constitutional liberalism of the Reformed and the moderate Unionists still exists, and the controversy about ecclesiastical union or disunion rages more fiercely than ever in Northern Germany, especially in Prussia.

But no one can tell what may take place in the short space of one year. Events may happen in Germany, which will show the necessity of a closer union amongst evangelical Christians even more strongly, than the revolutionary storms of 1848, which gave rise to the Church Diet. Besides, this has a host of friends, who will do all they can to keep it up. In Würtemberg especially, which has stood aloof so far from the confessional war, the Church Diet is universally popular among the pious of the laity, as well as of the clergy, and the proposed meeting at Stuttgart, though it should be the last, will be one of the most enthusiastic, a worthy end of a worthy beginning.

But whatever be the final fate of this assembly, it has already a glorious history of nine years, and forms one of the most interesting and edifying chapters in the annals of Protestantism.

This leads us to sum up, in conclusion, the benefits and results of the Church Diet.

As regards the official and authoritative confederation of all the Protestant State-Churches of Germany, which the Diet proposed at its first meeting in Wittenberg, as a safeguard against the fearful dangers and evils of that particular time, we must say, that this object has not been attained, and was almost entirely lost sight of in its subsequent meetings. The sudden change in the political condition of Germany, the defeat of the revolutionists and anarchists, and the restoration of the old order of things, are the immediate causes of this failure. But the idea of one evangelical Church of Germany still lives, and may perhaps be realized better in the end on the ruins, than on the basis of the existing rotten establishments. On the other hand, however, it may be questioned, whether such an official confederation of churches is at all desirable, and whether the mission of Protestantism, for the present at least, lies not rather in the direction of a free, voluntary association of Christians in their individual capacity, preparatory to a comprehensive church-union. At all events, the past and present power of the Church Diet rests on the principle of free association and communion, while by passing over into an official body, it would have become inevitably connected with all the evils of state-churchism.

In some sense, however, the desired confederation may be said to exist in a body distinct from the Kirchentag, but called into existence by its influence. We mean the Conference of Eisenach, which consists of a small number of official delegates from the various church governments of Protestant Germany, and meets, since 1852, annually or bi-annually, as circumstances may require, at Eisenach, for consultation on subjects and measures of common interest to all. But its deliberations are private, and subject to the final sanction or rejection of the respective authorities. The most important work of this Conference, so far, is the preparation and publication of one hundred and fifty standard hymns, with their melodies, for public worship, which should form the nucleus of the hymn-books of the different Churches, and thus promote unity in the place of the endless confusion produced by the arbitrary alterations of hymns and chorals.

In the meantime the Church Diet has accomplished, in a free form and altogether independent of State-control, much more than an official State-Church Confederation, in all probability, could have done under similar circumstances.

Deprived of legislative authority and even pecuniary means, the Kirchentag has all the moral power of faith and truth speaking in love, of remonstrance with the authorities and of appeal to the people at large. It exerted a most salutary influence upon the cities and neighborhoods in which it met. It travelled like a living evangelist to the centres of leading influence in Germany. It gave a powerful impulse to the course of evangelical piety and active Christianity all over the land. It discussed topics and started measures of the greatest theoretical and practical moment. Several of these were already mentioned above. To them must be added, from previous meetings, the discussions on Christian education, the relation of Church and State, the political duties of ministers, the sanctification of Sunday, the reform of worship, the introduction of a common hymn-book for all Germany, the relation of voluntary societies to the ministerial office, the Romish question, the treatment of dissenters, the spiritual care of the poor, the emigrants, the prisoners, the travelling journeymen, etc. It interceded in behalf of the persecuted Madiai at Florence, in connection with English and French Protestants, and protested against several crying abuses in certain countries and churches of Germany. It has become a nucleus for a large number of benevolent and reformatory societies which cluster around it. It has promoted the cause of Christian union, not only at home, but also abroad, by receiving delegates from, and forming connections with the Protestant Churches of France, Holland, Belgium, Scotland, Geneva, the Canton de Vaud, the British Evangelical Alliance, the American Tract Society, and the German Churches of America.

But one work must be mentioned with special praise, which may be called the adopted child of the Kirchentag, and has been most fruitful and blessed in immediate results. We mean the cause of "Inner Mission," to which it devotes two days, or fully one half of the time of its annual meetings. This is undoubtedly one of the most important movements of the age, and is alone sufficient to immortalize that assembly in the history of practical Christianity and Christian philanthropy. The term, Inner Mission, comprehends much more than what we mean by Home Missions, or Domestic Missions. It aims at a relief of all kinds of spiritual and temporal misery by works of faith and charity, at a revival of nominal Christendom, and a general reform of society on the basis of the Gospel and the creed of the Reformation. It is Christian philanthropy and charity applied to the various deep-rooted evils of society, as they were brought to light so fearfully in Germany by the revolutionary outbreaks of 1848. It comprises the care of the poor, the sick, the captive and prisoner, the laboring classes, the travelling journeymen, the emigrants, the temperance movement, the efforts for the promotion of a better observance of the Lord's-day, and similar reforms, so greatly needed in the Churches of Europe.

Dr. Wichern is the chief author and moving spirit of this great work in its modern German form. For as to its essence, of course, it is as old as Christian charity itself. It was with considerable difficulty, and only after a most eloquent speech, that he succeeded in urging it upon the serious attention of the Church Diet at its first meeting in 1848, and in making it one of its regular and principal objects. The movement spread with wonderful rapidity. There is now hardly a city in Protestant Germany or Switzerland, where there is not a "Society for Inner Mission," or an "Evangelical Association" for the promotion of the various works of Christian benevolence. "That which, in 1848"—says an English philanthropist—"was a germ of thought lodged in the mind of one man, is now a principle actuating human minds, instigating Christian endeavors, and giving birth to benevolent enterprise in a hundred forms throughout the fatherland, and wherever, in Europe, in America, or in Australasia, Germany may find a home." Dr. Wichern presents a general survey of the progress of the work at every meeting of the Kirchentag, and urges to renewed efforts with ever fresh vigor and with an earnestness and enthusiasm that is not from this earth.

We cannot better conclude this article, than by quoting the last words of Wichern's report at the Church Diet of Frankfort. "The Inner Mission," says this great and good man, "is the work of John, not the Baptist, but the apostle who leaned on the bosom of the Lord. According to the word of this apostle, we should all love each other as brethren, who confess the only saving name of Christ. But in this brotherly love we should also burn, like John, in the pursuit of the apostate youth, for the recovery of those who are wandering on the abyss of destruction. The love of God shed abroad in our hearts, uniting the disciples into one body, going forth like a burning light into the world, and converting the dreary deserts round about us into a paradise of God—such Johannean love is the hope and the strength of Inner Mission. May God bless this work, in midst of envy and strife, for the establishment of peace."

CHAPTER XXIII.

THEOLOGICAL SCHOOLS AND CHURCH PARTIES.

The Classical Period of German Theology—Its prevailing spirit—Variety of Schools—The Age of Rationalism and Supernaturalism—Dr. De Wette—The Age of Schleiermacher and Hegel—Division in the Hegelian Ranks—The Tubingen School.

GERMANY may boast of two classical periods of theology which exerted a powerful influence upon the other Christian nations, the theology of the Reformation, and the theology of the present age. Between the two lies the orthodox stagnation of the seventeenth, and the rationalistic revolution of the eighteenth centuries. The theology of the Reformation was a conflict of evangelical faith with superstition and ecclesiastical despotism; the theology of the present age a conflict of the same faith with infidelity and intellectual licentiousness. In the first case, genius and learning were concentrated in a few individuals, especially Luther and Melanthon, whose influence for this reason was the more commanding and comprehensive, as a tree which rises on the plains, in solitary grandeur, spreads the longest branches and casts the widest shade; in the second case, the intellectual powers are divided among a larger number and greater variety of minds.

No country and no age has produced, within so short a time, so many eminent commentators, church historians, and speculative divines as Germany did during the first half of the present century. Some of them have died within our recollection, as Schleiermacher, in 1834; Olshausen, in 1839; Marheineke, in 1847; De Wette, in 1849; Neander, in 1850; Höfling, in 1853; Gieseler, in 1854; Lücke, in 1855. But many of the veteran leaders are still on the field of action, and train a new generation of ministers and divines, less brilliant in talent and learning than they, but animated for the greater part by a decidedly Christian spirit, and having the advantage of starting with the results of a successful conflict with infidelity in its most dangerous forms.

Germany sent forth some of the worst infidel works of all times, and we are far from the hope that the triumph over false theology and philosophy is completed. Though beaten in scientific circles, rationalism, pantheism and atheism still extensively obtain in popular and practical forms, among the higher and lower classes of that country, as any American may infer from a large portion of the German immigrants, and their newspaper organs in our large cities. But to represent Baur, Strauss, and Feuerbach, as the true types and exponents of German theology, as was done recently in a series of articles in one of our leading religious journals, on the authority mainly of an infidel partisan book of Schwarz, is simply a caricature, and not less unfair and unjust, as if a German would hold up to his countrymen a Channing, Parker, and Emerson, as the genuine representatives of American theology and religion.

To classify the divines of Germany is no easy task. As political freedom cannot exist without parties, which may be compared to the fly-wheels of the machinery, and the counter-weights of the balance beam, so the free and vigorous development of philosophy and theology necessarily implies a variety of schools and tendencies, which are related to each other either as antagonistic and antipodal, or as supplementary and balancing forces. Frail as we are, parties and schools will always have their severing, embittering and dislocating effects, and the noblest instincts of our nature, as well as the tendencies of divine grace, look, not towards uniformity indeed, but towards harmony and union of tempers and views. But such divine harmony can only be the result of the freest and fullest development of all the elements included in the idea of humanity under its social and religious aspects.

Owing to the subjectivity and speculative turn of the German mind, and its fertility in originating new opinions and stand-points, it presents, in its theology and philosophy, as great a number of schools as practical England and America exhibit denominations and sects. We will endeavor to lead the stranger through this labyrinth to an elevation from which he may survey the largest and most interesting modern battle-field of theological theories and systems of thought.

To avoid confusion, we must distinguish three phases in the German theology of the present century, the age of Rationalism and Supernaturalism, the age of Schleiermacher and Hegel, and the age of the revived denominational controversies, or the conflict of Unionism and

Confessionalism. In the last stage of development, the theological schools coincide with the church parties that agitate the German state churches at the present time.

I. At the end of the last and the beginning of the present century, German theology was divided into the two hostile armies of Rationalists and Supernaturalists. The former maintained the sufficiency of natural reason, (*ratio*, hence the name,) and rejected everything in the Bible which they could not comprehend with their common sense. They would not admit, with Shakspeare and the deeper minds of all ages, that "There are more things in heaven and on earth, than were dreamt of in *their* philosophy." Göthe, in the second part of *Faust*, characterizes them admirably in these lines:

> Daran erkenn 'ich den gelehrten Herrn:
> Was ihr nicht tastet, steht euch meilenfern;
> Was ihr nicht fasst, das fehlt euch ganz und gar;
> Was ihr nicht rechnet, glaubt ihr, sei nicht wahr;
> Was ihr nicht wägt, hat für euch kein Gewicht;
> Was ihr nicht münzt, das, meint ihr, gelte nicht.
>
> (Herein I recognize the high-learned man!
> What *you* have never handled, no man can;
> What *you* can't grasp, is sheer nonentity;
> What *you* cannot account for, cannot *be;*
> What *your* scales have not proved, can have no weight;
> What *you've* not stamped, can never circulate.)

The Supernaturalists, on the other hand, maintained the necessity of a divine revelation, the inspiration and authority of the Bible, and the fundamental doctrines of orthodox Protestantism. Yet in their philosophical views they differed but slightly from their theological antagonists, who gradually gained the ascendancy and occupied for a considerable number of years the chief seats of power and influence.

The leaders of Rationalism, properly so called, were Paulus of Heidelberg, Wegscheider and Gesenius of Halle, Röhr of Weimar, and Bretschneider of Gotha. The ablest defenders of Supernaturalism of the elder school were Reinhardt of Wittenberg, afterwards court preacher in Dresden, Storr, Flatt and Steudel of Tübingen, and Knapp of Halle.

Between the two extremes stood those who styled themselves Rational Supernaturalists, or Supernaturalistic Rationalists, according to the preponderance of the one or the other element. They may be compared to the moderate school of English and American Unitarians.

The most distinguished champion of an undecided medium-position between Rationalism and Supernaturalism, was the late Dr. De Wette, a man of eminent ability, fine taste, extensive learning and honorable character, whose translation of the Bible is a work of abiding merit for scholars. He was constitutionally a skeptic, of the order of Thomas, but he never attained in this life to the full conviction of the apostle, who exclaimed at last at the feet of the risen Saviour, "My Lord and my God!" With the understanding he denied the divinity of Christ and the authority of the Bible, with the heart he was disposed to believe it. He painfully felt this conflict, and gave it a touching expression in the following lines written a short time before his death:

Ich fiel in eine wirre Zeit,
Des Glaubens Einfalt war vernichtet.
Ich mischte mich mit in den Streit;
Doch, ach! ich hab'ihn nicht geschlichtet.

(I lived in times of doubt and strife,
When child-like faith was forced to yield.
I struggled to the end of life,
Alas! I did not gain the field.)

II. During this controversy, the theological schools of Schleiermacher and Neander, and the philosophical systems of Schelling and Hegel arose, all striving to rise superior to the antagonism of reason and revelation, of faith and science, to reconcile the claims of both, and to point out in different ways the harmony of divine and human truth. They kept the German mind in a ferment of profound agitation for more than twenty years, (1820 to 1848.)

Of Schleiermacher and Neander we had occasion to speak already, and shall have more to say in the third part of this book. They gathered around them the noblest minds and led them to the path of evangelical faith and piety, while a number of their younger cotemporaries, as Tholuck, Olshausen, Hengstenberg, Stier, Beck, Harless, Guericke, Rudelbach, were only distantly connected with them, and occupied, from the start, a more strictly scriptural or churchly position.

The Hegelian philosophy, in its first application to theology, and in the hands of a Daub, Marheineke, and Göschel, treated rationalism with the utmost contempt, and promised to be a strong support of Christian orthodoxy. But with the appearance of the famous "Life of

Jesus," by Dr. Strauss of Tübingen, in 1835, four years after the death of Hegel, it broke asunder into two hostile branches, named after the divisions in the French Chambers, the right hand and the left hand, the centre being occupied by the deceased master.

The left wing represented theologically, by the so-called Tübingen School of Baur, Strauss, Zeller, Schwegler, developed, in a series of separate works, and in a Quarterly Review, the *Theologische Jahrbücher*, of Tübingen, the pantheistic elements of Hegelianism, and applied them to a critical dissection of the history of Christ and the apostles. According to their view, the absolute cannot be personal,—personality necessarily implying limitation, and an absolute personality being a contradiction in terms—but becomes, or is perpetually becoming personal in the endless series of human beings. Consequently Christ also, being an individual, cannot be the bearer of the fulness of the Godhead, although he was the first in whom the essential or metaphysical unity of divinity and humanity, i. e. the entire human race, became conscious. Add to this pantheistic principle the rationalistic denial of the possibility of miracles as contradicting the divinely established order of nature, and you have the clew to the understanding of the destructive criticism to which all the supernatural facts of the New Testament were subjected by the Tübingen School of pseudo-divines.

In the meantime, the chief philosophical champion of the left wing Hegelianism, Feuerbach, carried this logico-metaphysical pantheism into downright atheism, which explodes the idea of God as an objective existence, and resolves it into a sort of double vision and optical illusion of the subjective mind. Religion, therefore, according to this infernal gospel, is in fact the relation of man to himself considered as another, the growth of a morbid reflection, a grand hallucination, and that which man worships as God, is really his own soul projected on the outward screen, or his own gigantic shadow.

We have seen, in another place, how powerfully this development of pantheism and hyper-criticism acted upon the better class of German divines, like the dreams of the ancient Gnostics upon the early Fathers, and how many able and valuable works it called forth in defence of the historical basis of primitive Christianity.

The political storms of 1848 brought this second act of the drama of modern Teutonic theology to a close, and the third act commenced, of which we shall treat in the next chapter.

CHAPTER XXIV.

THEOLOGICAL SCHOOLS AND CHURCH PARTIES, CONCLUDED.

The Age of Unionism and Confessionalism—The Unionists with their three Subdivisions, the Centre, the Right Wing, and the Left Wing—The Lutherans—The Reformed.

III. FROM the revolutions of 1848, or rather the reactions which followed in rapid succession, we may date the third phase of German theology, in which the church question under its theoretical and practical aspects occupies most attention. The conflict of faith with unbelief, of Christ with anti-Christ, of theism with deism and pantheism, has given way to the controversies between Romanism and Protestantism, Lutheranism and Reform, Unionism and Confessionalism. Many who started as enthusiastic followers of Hegel, like Göschel, Martensen, Kliefoth and Kahnis, are now high church Lutherans; and others who formerly labored for the union of the Lutheran and Reformed Churches, as Hengstenberg, use their influence for its dissolution.

This shows that German theology made rapid progress, within the last few years, in the direction of orthodoxy and churchliness. But whether it has equally advanced in freshness, vigor and piety, is doubtful.

There was something great and sublime in the severe, but victorious struggle of Christian science against the most subtle forms of infidelity, that reminded one of the days of the ancient apologists and church fathers; but the bitter denominational strifes, which now fill the periodical press of Germany, especially in Prussia, the internal wars of brethren against brethren, who should be united against the common foes of Romanism and infidelity, are rather unrefreshing and humiliating. There has been, however, during the rationalistic period, and there is still such a want of discipline and so much practical disregard of the symbolical books in the German State-churches, that the reactionary zeal of a stricter school can easily be accounted for. The confessional strifes of the day may be regarded as a necessary transition to a better state of things.

If we would classify the theological schools of German Protestantism, as they now stand, we must make the denominational controversies, especially the absorbing question of Unionism and Confessionalism, of which we spoke at length in Chapters XIX. and XX., the principle of division. For the theological schools have, since 1848, descended from their former speculative heights and become identical with church parties, as in England. The Tübingen School, although not dead yet, is fast approaching its dissolution, and if infidelity is to come up again, it must likewise descend from Olympus to the plains, and assume a more popular and practical shape.

Leaving out of sight then the pantheistic infidelity described above, we may arrange the living divines of

Germany under three schools and parties, the Unionists, the exclusive Lutherans, and the Reformed. Some might be tempted to draw a parallel between them and the high-church, low-church, and broad-church parties of Anglicanism. But the points of difference far outnumber the points of resemblance. The most plausible comparison would be that between symbolical Lutheranism and Puseyism. But the former is perfectly independent of the latter, a genuine German growth, and differs materially from it in the question of episcopacy, which the Puseyites regard as the indispensable mark of the church, and in the doctrine of justification by faith *alone*, which the high Lutherans maintain as the *articulus stantis et cadentis ecclesiæ.*

1. The UNIONISTS, or UNIONS-THEOLOGEN, in the general sense of the term, agree in rejecting an exclusive confessionalism or denominationalism, and assert the principle of the fundamental agreement and fraternal communion of the Lutheran and Reformed Churches. They are by far the most numerous, especially in Prussia and Baden, and wherever the Union has been introduced. But we must distinguish among them three subdivisions, which we will arrange after the analogy of political assemblies.

(*a.*) The *Centre*, i. e., those who hold to the *consensus* of the Lutheran and Reformed symbols as the doctrinal basis of the Union, and defend at the same time the claims of a free progressive theological science. Here belong the orthodox section of the Schleiermacher-Neander School, and the majority of distinguished evangelical divines, especially in Prussia, Baden, and Würtemberg.

We mention Nitzsch, Twesten, and Hoffmann, of Berlin; Tholuck, Müller, Hupfeld, Moll, and Jacobi, of Halle; Dorner, Ehrenfeuchter, Schöberlein, and Köstlin, of Göttingen; Bleek, Hasse, and Lange, of Bonn; Liebner, of Dresden; Landerer, and Palmer, of Tübingen; Kurtz, of Dorpat; Stier, of Skeuditz; Baumgarten, of Rostock; Ullmann, and Bähr, of Carlsruhe; Ebrard, of Speyer; Herzog, of Erlangen; Umbreit, Hundeshagen, Schenkel, and Rothe, of Heidelberg. The last, however, is an altogether original genius, to whom may be applied, what Cardinal Cajetanus said of Luther: "*Habet profundos oculos et mirabiles speculationes in capite suo.*"

The chief literary organs of this school are the "*Studien und Kritiken*," a high-toned scientific quarterly, edited since 1828 by Ullmann and Umbreit, and containing valuable original investigations in all departments of theology; the "*Protestantiche Monatsblätter*," edited by Gelzer, of Basel, and devoted to the inner history of the times, and the defence of sound Protestantism against Ultramontane Romanism; the "*Deutsche Zeitschrift für Christliche Wissenschaft und Christliches Leben*," a solid and dignified weekly periodical, founded by Neander, Nitzsch and Müller, edited by Dr. Schneider, at Berlin, and keeping the medium between a theological review and a practical Church paper; the "*Allgemeine Kirchenzeitung*," of Darmstadt, established by Zimmermann and Bretschneider, and once the organ of deistic Rationalism, but now edited with more ability and faith, by Palmer and Schenkel, and defending weekly the cause of Evangelical Protestantism against Rationalism on the one hand, and exclusive Lutheranism, and especially also Romanism on the other.

Herzog's large Theological Encyclopædia, now in the course of publication, receives contributions from nearly all the divines mentioned under this head, and may therefore be regarded as a depository of the positive Evangelical Union-Theology of Germany.

Our esteemed friend, Dr. Bomberger, of Philadelphia, is doing a good service to Anglo-American Theology, in preparing, with a number of assistants, mostly of the German Reformed communion of this country, a condensed, yet faithful and reliable translation of this important and valuable work.

(*b.*) The *Right Wing* of the Unionists embraces those who still hold to the governmental union and mutual sacramental communion (*Abendmahlsgemeinschaft*) of the two churches as proclaimed by the Prussian declarations of 1834 and 1852, and take part in the Church Diet, (Stahl is one of its presiding officers,) but who maintain within these limits the right of the Confessions, especially the Lutheran symbols. Inasmuch as they resolve the Union into a mere confederation under one ecclesiastical government, presided over by the king, his minister of worship, and the Oberkirchenrath, they may be styled *Confederalists*, and inasmuch as they adhere to the distinctive tenets of the Lutheran creed, they are also called *New Lutherans*. This party stands in close connection with the political reaction which set in since 1849, in opposition to the revolutionary and liberal tendencies of the age, and is at present very influential in Prussia, being protected by the minister of public worship, Herr von Raumer, and the eminent leaders of the extreme conservative section in the Prussian Chambers, Stahl, Ludwig von Gerlach, and others.

Among the divines, Sartorius, of Königsberg, is the mildest, Hengstenberg, of Berlin, the most fearless and vigorous champion of this Confessional Lutheran Unionism. Its principal organ is the "*Evangelische Kirchenzeitung*," a weekly church paper, edited by Hengstenberg since 1827. Some of its strongest contributors are laymen, as Stahl and Göschel, of Berlin, and the genial, but Romanizing historian, Leo, of Halle, who is called sometimes the bulldog of Hengstenberg's Church Gazette.

(*c.*) The *Left Wing* is made up of the liberal and latitudinarian Unionists, who hold to the Bible as the only rule of faith and practice, but resist the binding authority of symbolical books as another form of Popery (papiernes Papstthum) incompatible with the principle of Protestant freedom and arresting the progress of theological science. Here belong Jonas, Sydow, Pischon, ministers at Berlin, Eltester, of Potsdam, and others who, in the famous Protest of 1845, broke for ever with Hengstenberg's Gazette, and represent what may be called the Left or Radical Wing of the School of Schleiermacher. They adhere more to the letter, than to the spirit of this great divine, and refuse to proceed beyond his general position in that more orthodox path, which he himself had opened, and which Twesten, Nitzsch and Müller have followed out. They are, like their admired master, liberal in politics, and cherish a bitter feeling of hostility to the reactionary and high toned monarchical tendencies which now rule the highest counsels of Prussia. Some of them, as Krause, venture occasionally upon the defence of an entire separation of Church and State, and absolute freedom of worship, after the American model, while others wait patiently for the death of the present king, hoping that the Prince of Prussia or his son will pursue a more liberal policy, and call them to the seats of power. One of their political friends, Count Schwerin, Schleiermacher's son-in-law, and one of the ablest and most respectable leaders of the liberal party in the Prussian Chambers, occupied in the revolutionary year 1848, the important post of minister of public worship, but was soon removed by the reaction.

The chief organ of this party is the "*Protestantische Kirchenzeitung für das evangelische Deutschland*," (since 1854,) ably edited by Krause, of Berlin, in connection with Eltester, Jonas, Sydow, of Prussia, and a number of preachers and divines from other German States, as Hase, Schwarz, Rückert, and Hilgenfeld, of Jena, Dittenberger, of Weimar, Credner, of Giessen, Zittel, of Baden, who can hardly be classed with the Schleiermacher School, in any sense, and are only held together temporarily by a negative opposition to the symbolical high church, hierarchical and reactionary tendencies of the New Lutheran party.

2. The LUTHERANS, i. e., the strictly symbolical Lutherans, who have no connection at all with the Prussian Establishment, and reject every kind of union and confederation with the Reformed Church, as a compromise of truth. They take no part in the Evangelical Church Diet, and still less in the Evangelical Alliance. In this, they are more consistent than the Hengstenberg-Stahl party, who still remain in the Union. As the Puseyites confine the true Church to the Episcopal organizations, and what they call the Apostolical Succession, so these

high church Lutherans would fain confine it to a certain system of doctrine as embodied in the unaltered Augsburg Confession, Luther's Catechisms, and the Form of Concord. *Reine Lehre* and *reines Bekenntniss* is their motto. To this, every other department of church-life is made subordinate, as if religion was identical with orthodoxy or correct belief, whilst it is life and power, affecting the heart and will even more than the head and intellect.

It is especially the Lutheran tenet of the eucharist, commonly called consubstantiation, (although they disown the term,) i. e., the view that Christ's body and blood are really present *in*, *with* and *under* the visible elements, which they make the touchstone of true orthodoxy. They conscientiously refuse to commune with those who hold to a merely symbolical, or dynamic, or spiritual real presence, and who confine the reception of the *res sacramenti* to the believing communicants. Some of them, I am certain, would at any time rather commune with Roman Catholics than with Zwinglians or Calvinists.

The late excellent Claus Harms, a thoroughly original and truly pious Lutheran minister, winds up his ninety-five theses, which did a very good work in 1817, with the proposition :—"The Catholic Church is a glorious Church, for it is built upon the Sacrament; the Reformed Church is a glorious Church, for it is built upon the Word; but more glorious than either, is the Lutheran Church, for it is built both upon the Word and the Sacrament, inseparably united." But many of the modern champions of Lutheranism would deny even this virtne to the Reformed Church, and charge it with rationalism, false subjectivism and spiritualism. Their excuse is that their views of the world are confined to certain sections of Germany. Were they properly acquainted with France, Holland, England, Scotland and the United States, they would probably form a very different opinion of the most active and energetic sections of Protestant Christendom. But much as they dislike the Reformed Church, they hate still more heartily the Union, which they regard as the work of religious indifferentism and even downright treason to Lutheranism, tending to poison and to destroy it.

The most learned and worthy champions of this Lutheran theology are Harless, of Munich; Löhe, of Anspach; the whole theological faculty of Erlangen, (except Herzog,) especially Thomasius, and Delitzsch; Kahnis, of Leipzic; Kliefoth, and Philippi, of Mecklenburg; Vilmar, of Marburg (who was originally Reformed;) Petri, of Hanover; Rudelbach, a Dane, and Guericke, of Halle.

Their principal theological organs are the "*Zeitschrift für Protestantismus und Kirche*," founded by Harless, and now issued monthly by the theological faculty of Erlangen; the "*Zeitscrift für die gesammte Lutherische Theologie und Kirche*," a quarterly review under the editorial supervision of Rudelbach and Guericke; and the "*Kirchliche Zeitschrift*," of Kliefoth and Mejer in Mecklenberg.

As much as these admirers of the Form of Concord unite in the opposition to the Union and the Reformed Confession, they are by no means agreed among themselves.

Some years ago a heated controversy broke out in their ranks concerning the nature of the ministerial office, which was carried on also by two old Lutheran Synods in the United States, (the Synod of Missouri, and the Synod of Buffalo,) with disgraceful violence and passion. More recently, Philippi, of Rostock attacked Hofmann, of Erlangen, and charges him with denying the true Lutheran doctrine of justification and of the atonement. The Lutheran conference which assembled at Dresden, in the summer of 1856, resolved to reintroduce private confession and absolution, and the Consistory of Munich issued an order to the churches of Bavaria to that effect. But it was answered by a number of protests from Nuremberg, and other strongholds of Lutheranism, which goes to show, that this hierarchical movement meets with no response from the heart of the people. In Mecklenburg, where this party is especially zealous, the churches, I am told, are nearly empty, and the statistics of illegitimate births are so awfully humiliating, that it would be far more important to revive general Christianity and good morals, than to denounce the Union, and to persecute Baptists and Methodists.

3. The Reformed divines in Germany are not strict Calvinists, especially as regards the doctrine of predestination; but stand in close affinity with the moderate or Melanthonian School of the Lutheran Church. Hence they fell heartily in with the Union-movement, which originated with a Reformed prince, and are mostly identified with what we have called the Centre of the Evangelical Union. So Ebrard, for several years Reformed Professor in Zürich, and in Erlangen—now President of the Consistory in the United Church of the Bavarian

Palatinate; Herzog, his successor in the Reformed Professorship at Erlangen, a native of Basel and formerly member of the United Faculty of Halle; Sack, of Magdeburg; Hundeshagen and Schenkel, who were called from Swiss Universities—the one from Berne, the other from Basel—to Heidelberg in Baden, where the two denominations are likewise united; Hagenbach, the excellent Professor of church history in Basel, and editor of the *Reformed Church Gazette* for German Switzerland, but not differing in his theological position from the former; Lange, formerly of Zürich, now laboring in Bonn. These are the most distinguished Reformed divines, who may just as well be enumerated under the first subdivision of our first class.

Schweizer, of Zürich, on the other side, the able but unsound historian of the theology of the Reformed Church, sympathizes most with the left or anti-symbolical wing of the school of Schleiermacher, and contributes to the *Protestant Church Gazette*, of Krause.

The recent revival of Confessional Lutheranism, and its attacks upon the Reformed Church, have roused the Reformed Confessionalism, especially in Hesse, and called forth a series of controversial works of Heppe in Marburg, and a denominational Reformed Church Gazette, (*Reform. Kirchenzeitung*,) published by Göbel, in Erlangen.

For some years past, an annual Reformed Conference was held in connection with the sessions of the Evangelical Church Diet, in which Hundeshagen, Schenkel, Lange, Sack, Ebrard, Sudhoff, Heppe, Göbel, Herzog, Krummacher, Mallet, Ball, and other distinguished Reformed divines and pulpit orators take part. The last one was held at Lübeck, in September 1856, and resolved to call a general conference of German Reformed ministers and laymen at Bremen, in 1857. It would be desirable to give these scattered churches of the Reformed communion a regular organization and compact unity, which would increase their efficiency. At present, however, the main forces of the German Reformed Church are flowing in the channel of the evangelical Union. If exclusive Lutheranism should succeed in breaking up the Union, it would call forth, as in the latter part of the sixteenth century, a powerful reaction and revive the spirit of Reformed denominationalism. But even in this case, the Reformed Church would hold on to the evangelical Catholic theology of Germany, and carry it forward in friendly co-operation with the moderate section of the Lutheran Church.

Even in Switzerland, the theology is altogether German; and German Evangelical divines are frequently called to the Reformed universities of Basel, Zürich, and Berne.

THIRD PART.

SKETCHES OF GERMAN DIVINES.

CHAPTER XXV.

NEANDER.

His Jewish Descent—His Conversion and Baptism—His theological Studies—Relation to Schleiermacher—His Academic Labors at Heidelberg and Berlin—Last Illness and Death—His Sister Hannchen—Neander's Personal Appearance and Eccentricities—His Moral and Religious Character—Social Habits—Lectures—His theological Works, and Merits for Church History.

ALTHOUGH the great and good Dr. Neander reposes now with the mighty dead, whose lives and labors he reproduced for the benefit of the present and coming ages, he is too fresh in the recollection of the living generation, and has exerted too much influence upon the revival of Christian faith and science in his native land, to be left out in a gallery of the Evangelical Divines of Germany, most of whom cherish his memory with the gratitude and affection of pupils or friends.

If any one of the modern divines realized the idea of a church father, equally distinguished for piety and learning, a giant in knowledge and a child in simplicity of heart, perfectly unconcerned about the things of the visible world, and exclusively devoted to the interests of the spiritual world, living more in the past than in the present, and yet laboring for the rising generation and leading it to the fountain of truth and wisdom, universally revered and beloved as a scholar, a man, and a Christian, it was Neander. Krummacher said at his grave, "One of the noblest of the noble in the kingdom of God, a prince in Zion, the youngest of the church fathers, has departed from us."

Neander was of Jewish descent, a true Nathanael, one of the noblest shoots of that wonderful people which gave birth to the Saviour of the world, and his apostles, the greatest teachers and benefactors of mankind. The dark, oriental cast of his countenance betrayed his national origin, while his mind and heart were perfectly free from the sordid traits of the modern Jew, especially from avarice. He knew nothing of the value of money, and was so liberal and generous, that his sister had to manage his purse for his own good.

His father, Emmanuel Mendel, was a common Jewish pedler; his mother, a relative of the celebrated philosopher, Mendelssohn, is said to have been a God-fearing and agreeable woman, and a tender mother. She had five children, two of whom died in insanity. Neander was the youngest, born at Göttingen, in 1789, the year of that terrible social earthquake which shook France and all Europe to the very base. At the circumcision, he received the name David. The mother removed subsequently with her children from Göttingen to Hamburg, and lived separated from her husband.

In the college of this commercial metropolis of Northern Germany, David Mendel received his classical training, and soon attracted the notice of his teachers by a rare degree of talent and industry, in connection with great oddity of appearance. He looked like a simpleton, and was the object of much ridicule, which made him angry when he observed it; but his mind was generally abstracted from the surrounding world. All who became acquainted with him, respected his talents and character, and many of them foresaw his future greatness. He associated principally with some Christian youths, Varnhagen von Ense, Wilhelm Neumann, and the poet Chamisso, who were carried away by the enthusiasm of the Romantic School of Tieck and Schlegel, and published a literary periodical.

Deeply religious by nature, Neander connected all his studies, especially the classics of Greece and Rome, with the eternal interests and destiny of man. The philosophy of Plato as well as the law of Moses proved to him a schoolmaster to Christ. Neumann wrote of him in 1806: "Plato is his idol, and his constant watchword. He sits over him day and night, and there are few who receive him so fully and with such purity of heart. Upon the world round about him he looks with profound contempt." He passed in his mind through the historical process of the Jewish and Gentile preparation of the only true and perfect religion, and was in this way specially prepared for the great mission of his life—to be the historian of Christianity. The Romantic School also, which revived the poetry and religion of the Middle Ages in opposition to the cold and dreary Rationalism of the times, had considerable effect upon him. Still more important was the influence of Schleiermacher, the German Plato, whose "Discourses on Religion," first published in 1799, conducted him to the threshhold of the Christian Revelation.

Thus fully convinced from every direction, as far as a youth of his age could be, of the divine origin and absolute truth of the Christian religion, as the fulfillment of the law and the prophets, and the desire of all nations, he resolved upon the important step to pass from the outer court into the sanctuary. Accordingly, he was baptized in 1806, in the seventeenth year of his age, his teacher, John Gurlitt, and his friends, Augustus Varnhagen, and William Neumann, assisting in the solemn ceremony as sponsors. From them he adopted the name John Augustus William Neander, (Newman.)

There still exists an essay on religion from his pen, written just before his baptism, and published by Dr. Kling in the "Studien und Kritiken" for 1851, p. 524. Although unripe, vague and mixed with error, it is characteristic of his internal history, and future stand-point, and reveals the ferment of his mind, which was even then agitated by the highest problems. A few quotations may suffice: "All religion proceeds from a desire after the infinite. It is itself the reflection of the infinite. The prophets of Judaism, and the divine Plato, especially in his Republic, proclaimed and prophesied the holy religion which should regenerate every thing, and realize the living representation of the infinite. The Word became flesh; the union and re-union of the divine and human nature took place. From faith in Christ all salvation proceeds. The object of man's life is annihilation of selfishness, and union with God and the infinite. Humility is the most sacred attribute of this divine religion, the absolute synthesis of freedom and necessity. Its social form is the church, an ideal commonwealth, distinct from the temporal state, the most perfect product of divine love and desire, an association of souls for the contemplation and enjoyment of the infinite and eternal. The Christian religion is the restoration of child-like innocence, but with the addition of clear consciousness. Its spirit is ever fresh and young, and can never die, though its temporal forms change and improve, until the absolute form be found, which will remain unshaken and unchangeable forever."

The brothers and sisters of Neander gradually followed his example. Some years afterwards his mother likewise became a convert to the Christian faith, removed to Berlin and lived with him until her death in 1817.

The baptism of David Mendel was at the same time his consecration to the holy ministry. He pursued his theological studies at Halle and Göttingen, supported in part by an uncle, Dr. Stieglitz, of Hanover.

In the former University he heard Schleiermacher, in 1806, from whom he dates a new epoch in the history of theology. He speaks, in his letters of that period, with much enthusiasm of the rare union of thorough learning and creative genius, in this extraordinary man, whose colleague he became afterwards in Berlin. To him he stood indebted, as he always acknowledged, for manifold quickening impulses, although he had no sympathy with the pantheistic and deterministic elements of his system, and was more positive and realistic in his religious convictions, laying great stress upon the doctrine of sin as a free act, or rather abuse of freedom, and upon the personality of God. He did not write much, but by means of an extraordinary memory he could dictate Schleiermacher's lectures almost sentence by sentence.

He had the misfortune, with many other students, to be robbed by the French soldiers after the battle of Jena, and as Napoleon suspended the University of Halle, he left for Göttingen, where he arrived penniless, with a ragged coat and hat. Here he continued his study of Plato and Plutarch, and plunged now deeper into history as taught by Planck and Heeren, into the New Testament, and the oldest church fathers, who soon became his favorite studies. His room-mate, Noodt, had great difficulty to keep him from studying all night. He became conscious at that time that church history was his peculiar field of future labor.

Having completed his academical course, he spent some time in Hamburg, and stood a brilliant examination as candidate for the ministry. But as he was poorly qualified for the pulpit, and felt himself called to an academic career, he readily followed the advice of his friend Noodt, to commence lecturing at the University of Heidelberg, where just two vacancies had been created in the theological faculty by the call of Marheineke and De Wette to the University of Berlin, in 1810. He wrote a *curriculum vitæ* and a Latin dissertation on the relation of faith and knowledge, (*de fidei gnoseosque idea secundum Clementem Alex. Heidelb.* 1811,) and was soon promoted to an extraordinary professorship.

In 1812, he published his work on Julian, the Apostate, which at once decided his qualifications for the historiography of the Church, and procured him a call to the newly founded University of Berlin, in 1813, which, through him, Schleiermacher, Marheineke, De Wette, Fichte, Hegel, Ritter, Ranke, and many other illustrious names, rose in a short time to the dignity and influence of the scientific and literary metropolis of Germany.

Since that time he labored incessantly and most faithfully in Berlin as a lecturer and writer, by word and example, till his death, on the 14th of July, 1850; only now and then breaking the uniformity of his existence, by a vacation trip, in company with his sister, or with some student, for the benefit of his weak health, and to consult rare books and unpublished manuscripts in the libraries of Vienna, Munich, Wolfenbüttel, or elsewhere.

Neander was deprived at last of his eye-sight, which had long been weakened by incessant study. Nevertheless, he continued to read and write through the assistance of a faithful pupil. In the beginning of 1850 he even established, with Drs. Müller and Nitzsch, a new periodical, the *Deutsche Zeitschrift für Christliche Wissenschaft und Christliches Leben*, and contributed several excellent papers to it, such as a retrospect of the first half of the present century, one on the difference between Hellenic and Christian Ethics, another on practical exegesis.

Even only eight days before his death, on the occasion of a visit of Gützlaff, who was then regarded by some as "the apostle of the Chinese," he made an address with youthful freshness on the Chinese mission, and looked forward with cheerful hope to the future triumphs of the kingdom of God, the description of whose growth, under the guidance of the twin parables of the mustard seed and the leaven, was the principal business of his life.

On the following Monday, he delivered his last lecture in the University, in spite of severe pains from an attack of something like cholera, so that he was scarcely able to finish and to come down the steps of the rostrum with the help of the students. His teacher and friend, Schleiermacher, likewise died in the midst of activity and usefulness, and Daub was struck dead by apoplexy at the very desk of his lecture room at Heidelberg, after having pronounced the words of Schiller: "*Das Leben ist der Güter höchstes nicht.*"

The last words of Neander, addressed to his sister, were: "I am weary, let us go home!" Then he was put to bed, and with a scarcely audible, but deeply affectionate "Good night!" he slept the last sleep, and awoke on the morning of the Lord's day, in the blessed abodes of angels and saints in heaven, in the company of St. John, Chrysostom, Augustine, Bernard, Anselm, Melanthon, and other favorite kindred spirits, there to rest from his labors, and to adore face to face the mystery of the triune God, and his wonderful counsels of wisdom and mercy.

His sister Hannah, who took care of his household, survived him four years. She was unmarried, like himself, quite original, spirited and literary, and yet practical, and for this reason indispensable to him. I saw her once more a few weeks before her death, in the summer of 1854, in her modest lodgings in the Kochstrasse at Berlin, and was much affected by this interview, which brought vividly to mind many scenes of former years, never to be forgotten. She was then sickly, and longing to depart from this world, which had lost all attraction for her since the loss of her beloved brother. She showed me with tears his busts, one representing him in life, the other in the repose of death, also the bust of his favorite pupil, Rossel, a youth of uncommon promise, whose untimely decease he had to deplore. These and some memorials of friends and pupils were the only things dear to her, and reminded her of happy days. But she bore her grief and desolation with Christian faith, and now rests in peace at the side of her brother.

In his outward appearance, Neander was a real curiosity, especially in the lecture-room. Think of a man of middle size, slender frame, homely, but interesting and benevolent face, dark and strongly Jewish complexion, deep seated, sparkling eyes, overshadowed by an unusually strong bushy pair of eye-brows, black hair flowing in uncombed profusion over the forehead, an old-fashioned coat, a white cravat carelessly tied, as often behind or on one side of the neck, as in front, a shabby hat set aslant, jack-boots reaching above the knees; think of him thus either as sitting at home, surrounded by books on the shelves, on the table, on the few chairs and all over the floor; or as walking *unter den Linden*, and in the *Thiergarten* of Berlin, leaning on the arm of his sister Hannchen, or a faithful student, his eyes shut or looking up to heaven, talking theology in midst of the noise and fashion of the city, and presenting altogether a most singular contrast to the teeming life around him, stared at, smiled at, wondered at, yet respectfully greeted by all who knew him; or finally as standing on the rostrum, playing with a goose quill which his amanuensis had always to provide; constantly crossing and recrossing his feet, bent forward, frequently sinking his head to discharge a morbid flow of spittle, and then again suddenly throwing it on high, especially when roused to polemic zeal against pantheism and dead formalism; at times fairly threatening to overturn the desk, and yet all the while pouring forth with the greatest earnestness and enthusiasm, without any other help than that of some illegible notes, an uninterrupted flow of learning and thought from the deep and pure fountain of the inner life; and thus with all the oddity of the outside, at once commanding the veneration and confidence of every hearer;—imagine all this, and you have a picture of Neander, the most original phenomenon in the literary world of this nineteenth century.

In all this there was not the least degree of affectation; he was perfectly natural, and almost as unconscious of his eccentricities, as a child of his innocence.

He was never married, and belonged to those exceptions where celibacy is a necessity and duty, and a means for greater usefulness in the kingdom of God. But a congenial sister kept house for him, and attended to his wants with the most tender care. The childlike intercourse of this original couple had something very touching. He was almost as helpless as a child in matters of dress. The story runs, that he once started off for the lecture-room in his morning-gown and *sans culottes*, but was happily overtaken by the watchful sister; also that once in trying a new pair of pantaloons, he kept on the old ones, drew the left half over the right leg, and cut the other half off with a scissor as superfluous! *Se non e vero, e ben trovato.* His clothing was of the most simple sort, and hardly fit for a gentleman. His moderation in eating and drinking reminded one of the self-denial of old ascetics, like St. Antony of Egypt, who ate only once in three days, and then felt ashamed, as an immortal spirit, to be in need of earthly food.

Yet Neander was extremely hospitable, and invited his friends often to dinner, and while they were enjoying the provisions of the table, he talked to them theology and religion, or branched out occasionally into harmless humor and the more trifling topics of the day, as far as they came to his notice. The students he gathered around him one evening every week, to a social tea and familiar conversation. There he gave free vent to all that agitated his mind, and rejoiced or troubled his heart, concerning the state of the Church and the movements of theological science.

As a man and a Christian, he was universally esteemed, even by those who regarded him either as too orthodox, or too latitudinarian. His absolute honesty, unaffected kindness, and deep piety, were beyond all possible doubt. Much must be attributed to his nature. He had less of the ordinary temptations which surround men generally, and was constitutionally unworldly. But supernatural grace had regenerated his heart and adorned and perfected his natural virtues. Simplicity, humility and love, the noblest gifts of grace, were the most prominent traits of his character. He possessed them to a degree in which they are rarely found in this world. With him there was no contradiction between theory and practice, head and heart. All empty show and hypocrisy, all pride and vain glory he most heartily despised. He was extremely kind, liberal and charitable in his feelings, although not free from occasional outbreaks of passion and vehemence against certain theological tendencies, which he regarded as dangerous, especially the Hegelian pantheism. I remember many traits of his benevolence to the poor, particularly poor students, to whom he was a most affectionate father.

His heart was open to friendship, and his faithful memory seldom forgot one who once had made an impression upon him, though he were only a transient visitor. Every stranger with proper recommendations, was cordially welcome to his study at the fixed hour of conversation, (between five and seven in the evening,) or at his table, and he showed himself as obliging as could possibly be expected from a man so unpractical and helpless as he. Generally he plunged at once into the deepest theological discussions, opening his mind most freely with little prudential regard to men or circumstances. So he shocked many a Puritan and Presbyterian, by inviting them to dinner on Sunday, but always won their esteem and love by the ensemble of his theology and character. He spoke the English fluently, although not quite correctly, and admired the American separation of Church and State, of politics and religion, the voluntary principle and unchecked growth of religious life. I heard him speak very kindly of Drs. Hodge, Robinson, Sears, Sprague, and I am sure, they and many others who had the pleasure of making his personal acquaintance, cherish his memory with grateful esteem and affection.

As a theological teacher, he was unsurpassed for faithfulness and efficiency. He had generally several hundred hearers, who listened to him with the profoundest attention in spite of his exceedingly awkward appearance in the chair. He always taught out of the fulness of the subject and with complete mastery of the material. His method was not mechanical and traditional, but organic and reproductive. He developed the subject and made it grow before the eyes of the student, so as to enable him to understand the inner life as well as the outward form, the origin and growth as much as the result. In this respect he was only surpassed by the unrivaled Schleiermacher.

As to Neander's theology, its principal force and charm lies in the vital union of profound learning and personal piety. Not without reason had he chosen for his motto, "*Pectus est quod theologum facit*," the *heart* makes the theologian. Another favorite motto of his was the sentence which he wrote in my Album, and which is characteristic of his unworldliness and spirituality, "*Theologia crucis, non gloriæ.*" To a distinguished American divine, he wrote in Greek the beautiful words as a memorandum: "Rejoice in Christ, be nothing in yourself, be all in Christ." He pursued theology not merely as an exercise of the understanding, but always as a sacred business of the heart, which he felt to be most intimately connected with the highest and most solemn interests of man, even his eternal welfare. The living centre and heart's blood of the science was for him faith in Jesus Christ, as the highest revelation of a holy and merciful God, as the fountain of all salvation and sanctifying grace for a ruined world. Whatever he found that was really great, noble, good and true in history, he referred directly or indirectly to the fact of the incarnation, in which he humbly adored the central sun of all history and the inmost sanctuary of the moral universe.

It must be confessed that his theolgy in many respects falls short of the proper standard of orthodoxy. He did not admit the binding authority of the symbolical books even in a restricted sense. His views on inspiration, on the sanctification of the Lord's day, and on the Holy Trinity, are somewhat loose, vague and unsatisfactory. His best disciples, in this respect, have gone beyond his position and become more orthodox and churchly.

But then it must be considered—1, that he rose in an age of universal rationalism, and was one of the earliest pioneers of evangelical faith and theology in Germany; 2, that this very liberalism, and if we choose to call it, latitudinarianism, served as a bridge for many, who could not otherwise have been rescued from the bonds of skepticism; 3, that these defects did not weaken his general conviction of the divine character of Christianity, nor affect his unfeigned, deep-rooted piety. Many of his pupils and followers surpass him in orthodoxy, but few can be found in any age, in whom doctrine was to the same extent, life and power, in whom theoretic conviction had so fully passed over into flesh and blood, in whom the love of Christ and of man glowed with so warm and pure a flame, as in the truly great and good Neander.

His greatest and most lasting merit as a theologian, lies in the department of church history, which he not only enriched with material contributions, but also with a new method of treatment more satisfactory than that of his predecessors. He is therefore called the Father of Modern Church History, and marks an epoch in this field of sacred learning fully as much as Flacius did in the sixteenth, Arnold in the seventeenth, and Mosheim in the eighteenth century. As we have given a lengthy analysis of Neander as a church historian in another work, we shall confine ourselves here to a few general remarks.

We have from his pen a general church history from the death of the apostles to the Council of Basil, in 1430, which is now accessible to all English readers in the American translation of Torry, and the Edinburgh and London reprints of the same; and a number of valuable monographs on the Apostolic Age, the Gnostics, Julian the Apostate, Tertullian, St. Chrysostom, and St. Bernard, most of which are likewise translated into the English, as well as into the French and Dutch languages. Of his posthumous works, which are to embrace all of his lectures on New Testament exegesis, symbolics, dogmatics, and ethics, the doctrine-history (Dogmengeschichte) has just appeared (in two volumes, 1856 and '57) under the editorial care of one of his most faithful pupils, Dr. J. L. Jacobi of Halle.

He is by no means a model as a *writer* of church history. His style is too monotonous and diffuse, without any picturesque alternation of light and shade, and flows like a quiet stream over an unbroken plain. He was also poorly qualified to do justice to the political and æsthetic departments and connections of this science, and his chapters on church government and sacred art are therefore very defective.

But his great fort lies in a thorough mastery, independent investigation, and scrupulously conscientious use of the sources; and above all, in the extraordinary talent of bringing out, in a genetic way, the hidden life of Christianity and representing it as a leaven-like power that pervades and sanctifies the lump of society from within. He restored the religious and practical element to its due prominence, in opposition to the coldly intellectual and critical method of the rationalistic historians who immediately preceded him; yet without thereby wronging in the least the claims of science, or running into narrow sectarian extremes, like the pietistic Arnold. He everywhere follows the footsteps of the Saviour in His march through the various ages of the Church, and kisses them reverently wherever he finds them. He traces them in the writings of an Origen and a Tertullian, a Chrysostom and an Augustin, a Bernard and a Thomas Aquinas, a Luther and a Melanthon, a Calvin and a Fenelon. Christ was to him the divine harmony of all the discords of churches and sects, or as he liked to repeat after Pascal: *En Jesus Christ toutes les contradictions sont accordées.*

He no doubt went too far sometimes in his liberality. By trying to do all justice even to heretics and sectarians, he was in danger sometimes, like Arnold and Milner, although, of course, in a far less degree, of doing injustice to the champions of orthodoxy and the

Church. There is in him a want of the proper appreciation of the objective, realistic element in church history. He is more the historian of the invisible kingdom of Christ in the hearts of his individual members, than of the visible church in its great conflict and contact with a wicked world.

These and other defects, however, are less dangerous and censurable than those of the opposite extreme, and cannot blind us, of course, to the real excellences and immortal merits of his historical works. He is emphatically the evangelical regenerator of this branch of theology. He made it a running commentary on Christ's precious promise to be with his people to the end of the world, and even with two or three of his humblest disciples where they are assembled in his name. Thus church history becomes to the intelligent reader a book of devotion as well as useful and interesting information, or to use Neander's own words, in the preface to the first volume of his large work, "a living witness for the divine power of Christianity, a school of Christian experience, a voice of edification, instruction and warning, sounding through all ages, for all who are disposed to hear."

CHAPTER XXVI.

THOLUCK.

His early History and Conversion—The True Consecration of the Skeptic—Baron von Kottwitz—Tholuck's academic Career at Berlin and Halle—His Personal Character, and Love for the Students—His Lectures, and Sermons—His Scholarship, and Theological Position—His Works and Merits.

NEXT to Neander, no German divine of the present century is more extensively known in the Protestant churches of France, Holland, England and America, than Dr. Frederick Augustus Tholuck, of Halle. His disciples are scattered nearly all over the Protestant world, and gratefully remember his genial influence and personal attention. His name will always be honorably connected with the history of the revival of evangelical theology and piety in Germany.

Like the great majority of distinguished scholars, Tholuck is of poor and humble descent. He was born at Breslau in 1799. He labored for some time, if I remember right, in the office of a jeweller in Silesia. But some benevolent friends furnished him the means to satisfy his noble ambition and ardent thirst for knowledge in the gymnasium of his native city, and subsequently in the university of Berlin. He studied day and night to such an excess that he undermined his health, and contracted a chronic affection of his eyes.

He had naturally a strong inclination to skepticism and pantheism, and was filled with prejudices against the pietists and mystics, as the serious Christians were then called. "The contracted views of life," he says, "that were associated in my mind with these epithets, disposed me carefully to shun all acquaintance with them, believing that it would check all vigor of action and all freedom of thought; that it would make all the movements of the soul as monotonous as the tinkling of a hand-bell, and cast over the whole path of life, and impress on one's very countenance, the pale hues of death. Under such chilling influences, I imagined that the beauty and splendor of the wide fields of science must be exchanged for a miserable garden of pot-herbs; the rich profusion, the ever varied novelties of the Eden of nature, for a narrow cloister walk; and the immeasurable magnificence of the starry heavens, for the damp and gloom of a vaulted catacomb." He left the college of Breslau with a sophomorical speech in which he glorified Mohamedanism as a religion of equal dignity and beauty with Christianity.

The experience of sin and grace in his heart, the intercourse with Neander and other pious men, and the study of the Scriptures saved him from the whirlpool of infidelity. He was awakened in his twentieth year as a student in Berlin, contemporaneously with his friends, Julius Müller, Rothe and Olshausen, who became subsequently distinguished divines. He himself gives a spirited and interesting account of the internal conflicts through which he passed, in his youthful work, "Sin and Redemption, or the True Consecration of the

Skeptic," (first published in 1825,) which in its seven editions has done a great deal of good, especially among students of theology, and led many from the barren desert of rationalism to the green meadows and fresh fountains of the Gospel of Christ. It was translated long since by Ryland, with a commendatory introduction by Dr. John Pye Smith, and has been recently republished in this country. (Gould & Lincoln, Boston, 1854.) It was a refutation in fact, though not in original intention, of the semi-rationalistic religious novel of De Wette, "Theodore, or the Consecration of the Skeptic," 1822. It describes in a series of letters, with the fresh inspiration of the first love to the Saviour, the learned aberrations and the conversion of two young divines; Julius, who is supposed to be Dr. Julius Müller, now Tholuck's colleague, and Guido, in whom the author has portraitured himself.

From this book, as well as from private sources, we learn that the Baron von Kottwitz, a true Christian nobleman, and an exceedingly worthy member of the Moravian congregation in Berlin, was the principal human instrument in Tholuck's conversion.

I had the pleasure of frequently seeing and conversing with this John-like disciple of the Lord, in his extreme old age in the years 1840 and 1842, having been introduced to him by the kindness of Tholuck, and I never met a man who seemed so nearly to approach the ideal of an evangelical saint. He lived in very plain style on the Alexander Platz in Berlin, in an orphan asylum which he founded, or superintended, and took special delight in the company of young divines. He pointed them to the Lamb of God which taketh away the sin of the world, and to his everlasting Gospel as the only source of true theology and usefulness in the Church. Not only Tholuck, but also Neander, Olshausen, Rothe, Müller, Hengstenberg, and many others were edified and encouraged by his word and example, and he may be regarded as one of the lay-fathers of the modern evangelical theology of Germany. It was impossible to resist the influence of the purity and simplicity of his character, and his ardent love to God and man. He combined in a rare degree the finest culture of a noble man with childlike faith, true dignity with unaffected humility. He seemed to be transformed into the holy image of Jesus. His whole life was a course of unostentatious, disinterested benevolence, an imitation of Him who went about doing good and sacrificed himself for the salvation of the world. Kottwitz is the "Father Abraham," in Tholuck's book, of whom Guido writes to his friend Julius: "This venerable saint has been residing here for a few years, enjoying a perpetual Sabbath of the soul, akin to that of the spirits of the just above, uniting a blissful repose with an equally blissful activity of love. To a very advanced age he was incessantly occupied, both in his journeys and in his fixed abode, with works of philanthropy and piety. The dwellings of misery and sorrow have seen him most frequently; for his highest gratification has been to dry up the tears of the afflicted. He has travelled far and wide. Where his influence and power have been the greatest, he has improved the hospitals and jails; where his effort for doing good on a larger scale met with opposition, he betook himself to the relief of solitary wretchedness. . . He seemed to be a special representative of heaven, and to impart to all consolation and relief. It is true, I had daily held intercourse with the spirits of Augustin, Melanthon, Luther, Francke and Spangenberg, by means of their writings; but to see such a discipline! Be assured, Julius, that what I have learnt from this 'living epistle of Christ,' goes far beyond books and systems." The writer then gives an affecting account of an interview with the patriarch, and relates his almost prophetical views on the great revival which should soon revolutionize the theological world of Germany, and the dangers connected with it.

"The greater the crisis," said the patriarch, "the more needful is it to unite the wisdom of the serpent with the simplicity of the dove. I therefore address you as such an one who, perhaps, will soon be engaged at the university as one of the instruments employed by God in that important period. The work of God's Spirit is greater than either you or the majority can estimate. A great resurrection morning has dawned. Hundreds of youths, on all sides, have been awakened by the Spirit of God. Everywhere, true believers are coming into closer union. Science herself is becoming again the handmaid and friend of the Crucified. Civil governments also, though in part still hostile to this great moral revolution, from a dread of its producing political commotions, are many of them favorable, and where they are not, the conflicting energy of the light is so much the stronger. Many enlightened preachers already proclaim the Gospel in its power; many who are still in obscurity will come forward. I see the dawn; the day itself I shall behold, not here, but from a higher place. You will live to witness it below. Despise not the words of a grey-headed old man, who would give you, with true affection, a few hints relative to this great day. The more divine a power is, the more to be deprecated is its perversion. When those last times are spoken of in Scripture, in which the Gospel shall be spread over the whole world, it is declared that the truth will not only have to contend with the proportionably more violent counterworking of the enemy, but also with a great measure of delusion and error within the kingdom of light. Such is the course of things, that every truth has its shadow; and the greatest truth is attended by the greatest shadow. Above all things take care that the tempter do not introduce his craft into the congregation of the faithful. There will be those for whom the simple Gospel will not suffice. When a man has experienced the forgiveness of his sins, and has for a little while enjoyed the happiness of that mercy, it not unfrequently appears to his evil and inconstant heart too humiliating a condition to be constantly receiving grace for grace. There is no other radical cure for a proud, self-willed heart, than every day and every hour to repeat that act by which we first come to Christ. Pray that you may have more of that childlike spirit that regards the grace of your Lord as a perennial fountain of life. Especially avoid the error of those who seek life for the sake of light, who would make religion a mere stepping stone to intellectual superiority. Such persons will never attain to a vital apprehension of divine things; for our God is a jealous God, and will be loved by us for his own sake. The intellectual power, the mental enlargement, arising from converse with the great objects of faith, is always to be regarded as a secondary and supplementary benefit to that which it is the immediate object of the Gospel to bestow. Despise not human greatness or talent, or ability of any kind, but beware lest you overvalue it. I see a time coming—indeed it is already at hand—in which gifted men will lift up their voice for the truth; but woe to the times in which admiration and applause of the speaker shall be substituted for laying to heart the truth which he delivers! Perhaps in the next generation there will be no one in some parts of Germany who will not wish to be called a Christian. Learn to distinguish the spirits. * * * The sum of my exhortation is 'humility and love.'"

The conversion of Tholuck determined his call to the science of theology. As a young man of extraordinary talents and attainments, he was soon promoted to a professorship of Old Testament exegesis in Berlin, in the place of De Wette, who was deposed on account of his extenuation of the guilt of Sand's murder of Kotzebue, in a letter of consolation to his mother. He devoted himself at first with special zeal to the study of oriental languages and literature, and wrote, when quite a youth, from Arabic, Persic and Turkish manuscripts, a learned volume, *De Suffismo Persarum*, or the mystic theosophy of the Persians, (1821,) which was followed afterwards by an interesting collection of translations from the mystic poets of the East, (*Blüthensammlung orientalischer Mystik.*)

After the death of the venerable Dr. Knapp, professor of dogmatics and exegesis at Halle, Tholuck was appointed his successor in 1826, and has remained in this post ever since, with the exception of a short residence at Rome, in the capacity of a chaplain of the Prussian embassy.

The University of Halle was at that time in a most deplorable condition as regards orthodoxy and piety. Knapp had been for years the only evangelical teacher in the place, and although his learning and piety, working on quietly, were not without a blessing, he was thrown into the shade by the celebrity of Gesenius and Wegscheider, who continued almost to the end of their lives, to be the guides of the theological students, and systematically disqualified them for the office of the Christian ministry. The great influence of Gesenius can easily be accounted for by his distinguished talent for teaching, his entertaining wit, and his abiding merits in the department of Hebrew grammar and lexicography; but that Wegscheider, the good natured and morally estimable, but intolerably dull, dry and tedious Wegscheider, could gather at one time round his lectures, hundreds of admiring students, is hardly conceivable at this time of day. He was doomed, however, to experience the mortification of outliving his own reputation, and to see his audience sink down from five hundred to half a dozen. For this was the number, when I once, from curiosity, attended one of his insipid lectures on dogmatics in 1840, a few years before his death.

Tholuck's position was at first exceedingly difficult in this reign of rationalism. He was scouted, hated, and ridiculed as a pietist, mystic, fanatic, pharisee, etc. But he persevered, and God most richly blessed his labors. A radical revolution has been wrought in Halle, as far as theology is concerned. Rationalism has entirely disappeared from the theological faculty, and there is not one among its present members (I mean the ordinary professors, Tholuck, Müller, Moll, Hupfeld, Jacobi,) who may not be regarded in all essential points as orthodox, and evangelical in sentiment.

Dr. Tholuck is now nearly sixty years of age. His outward appearance is as modest and unprepossessing, although not so original and startling, as that of the late Dr. Neander. He pays no attention to dress, has a sickly frame, is of middle size, strongly bent forward, meagre and emaciated, extremely nervous and irritable, and at times almost blind in consequence of excessive study. Hence he needs always the assistance of an amanuensis in reading and writing. But the formation of his noble forehead and the expression of his face are highly intellectual and spiritual, and his voice is clear, deep and solemn. It is only by severe abstinence, strict regularity, daily promenades and annual excursions to watering places, or the Swiss mountains, that he can keep up his physical existence. But he possesses great mastery over his condition. His bodily infirmities rarely interfere with the discharge of his duties. He hardly ever speaks of his health, and dislikes to be questioned about it. When I unexpectedly met him on my way to Halle, in 1854, on the fortifications of Magdeburg, where he was just attending theological examinations, I inquired first, in true American style, after the state of his health;

but he said, "If good friends meet after ten years of separation, they must first stare at each other in speechless wonderment," and then he embraced me. His abrupt manner and eccentric habits may repel many at the first acquaintance. But when in good humor, he can be exceedingly agreeable and entertaining; for he is naturally sociable and genial in a high degree, and has an extraordinary freshness and vivacity of mind.

Tholuck never had any children. His first wife died of consumption soon after her marriage. He then was a widower for nearly ten years, and nobody supposed that he ever would marry again. But by some romantic incident he became acquainted with the daughter of Baron von Gemmingen, an esteemed nobleman of Stuttgart, (originally of Mühlhausen in Baden,) who with his whole family had become a convert from Romanism to the Protestant faith; and found in her an accomplished, amiable, childlike and pious companion, who proves a comforting angel to him in his declining years.

One of the most striking and lovely traits of his character is his warm attachment to students. He loves them like a father. He cannot live without them. He not only invites them freely to his house and table, but is almost invariably surrounded by two or three of them on the promenades which he is obliged to take for the benefit of his health, twice a day—before dinner and supper—in spite of rain and mud in muddy Halle. His free conversations in this peripatetic style are often more interesting and stirring than his lectures. I know no teacher who can deal better with active young minds. He makes liberal allowance for their difference of constitution and temper, and likes a collision of opinions, if they proceed alike from an honest search after truth. His object is not to make disciples and convert them to a particular system—for he himself can hardly be said to have a system—but to rouse their slumbering faculties and to put them on the track of independent research. He instructs them by his extensive information, he entertains them by his wit, he wins by his affections, and edifies by his piety. Not unfrequently he exercises the students by odd and startling questions on remote and curious topics, in German, French, English, Latin, Greek, Hebrew, or any other language which they may understand. If it was the proper place, I could tell, from a six months' residence in Tholuck's house, some amusing anecdotes of most original questions and most spicy answers, which will not so easily be forgotten by those who heard them. But there is always salt in his conversation, and his humor rests on a serious basis, as true humor always does, viz.: on the conviction of the folly of human wisdom, the weakness of mortal strength, and the vanity of all earthly things.

Tholuck is a personal favorite also with students and scholars from foreign countries, especially from England, Scotland and the United States. By his perfect mastery over the modern languages of Europe, the natural quickness and versatility of his mind, his extensive personal acquaintances, and his frequent vacation trips to England, Switzerland and France, he is admirably qualified to introduce strangers to a correct knowledge and appreciation of the state of science and religion in Germany. He is very fond of bringing scholars from different parts of the world together and trying experiments on their conflicting national views and tastes. Thus, for instance, he would ask a German Lutheran: "Does this tree in some sense belong to the Deity?" After receiving a qualified affirmative, he would turn to a Scotch Presbyterian or a New England Puritan, with the question: "Does this not strike you as inexpressibly absurd?" Which is, of course, assented to in the most unqualified manner. After a hearty laugh, he would then make some interesting remarks on the natural leaning of the German mind and the Lutheran speculation to pantheism, or a mixture of God and the world, church and state, scripture and tradition, the regenerate and the unregenerate, and the constitutional inclination of the English mind and the Reformed theology to the opposite extreme of a dualistic separation of the divine and human, the spiritual and temporal.

Tholuck is an admirable teacher and lecturer, fresh, interesting and suggestive, and free from that tiresome pedantry and endless "Gründlichkeit," which characterizes so many German scholars. He uses notes and frequently dictates, but branches out into explanatory remarks and happy illustrations from all departments of knowledge and experience.

He is also one of the most eloquent pulpit orators of Germany. He preaches every other week to the members of the University of Halle, and occasionally as guest on his vacation trips. His sickly, but spiritual and solemn appearance, the earnestness of his manner, the lightning flashes of his genius, his striking rhetorical transitions and his deep religious experience, impart to his sermons, of which several volumes have been published, a high degree of impressiveness. His "Hours of Christian Devotion," wherein he opposes a pure evangelical piety to the rationalistic sentimentality of Zschocke's widely circulated "Stunden der Andacht," are among the best devotional works of modern times.

As a scholar, Tholuck is distinguished not so much by depth and thoroughness of knowledge in any single department, as by the astonishing extent and variety of erudition. He is at home in theology, philology, philosophy, history, poetry; in ancient and modern, oriental and occidental, heathen, Jewish, Mohamedan, and Christian literature.

His facility in acquiring languages is truly amazing. He speaks probably more languages, ancient and modern, than any man living; and was only surpassed in this respect by the late Cardinal Mezzofanti, who is said to have spoken over fifty languages and dialects with more or less ease.

In most of his writings he surprises the reader with a mass of quotations gathered from the remotest sources; although they have at times, it must be confessed, little connection with and shed no new light upon the subject in hand, and make the impression of a superfluous display of learning. "*Ne quid nimis.*" Still they are almost always interesting and suggestive.

With this comprehensive erudition he combines great quickness, originality, and freshness of mind, and a lively imagination almost sufficient to make the fortune of a poet. In this respect he has a certain affinity with Hase, the Church historian. He has no compact, logically defined system of thought—a want which is owing partly to the vivacity and impulsiveness of his genius. But he abounds in ingenious and striking views and profound hints, which stimulate to further inquiry.

As a theological writer, Tholuck has devoted his best powers to Biblical exegesis. Here he achieved his most enduring merits. He was one of the first to redeem this important branch of theology from the icy grasp of Rationalism, to imbue it with a believing spirit, and to re-open the rich exegetical resources of the Fathers and the Reformers, especially John Calvin, whose invaluable Latin commentaries on all the books of the New Testament excepting the Apocalypse, he republished in a cheap and convenient form. The first edition of his own Exposition of the Epistle to the Romans, which appeared in 1824, although very imperfect and unsatisfactory, struck out a new path, and marks an epoch in the history of the exegetical literature of Germany. His name will therefore always be mentioned in connection with that of his friend Olshausen, amongst the chief regenerators of the true interpretation of the Holy Word of God.

He frequently fails to satisfy the reader on the precise meaning of the most difficult passages, and after raising his expectation to a high degree, breaks off abruptly with some piquant remarks or a dazzling firework of rare quotations in poetry and prose, which are better calculated to shed lustre upon his own learning than upon the hidden meaning of the sacred author. He has not the same genial and harmonious flow of a profoundly pious and speculative spirit, which constitutes the peculiar charm of Olshausen's volumes on the Gospels; but he excels him in learning. He lacks the elegant polish and finish of Lücke's exposition of the writings of St. John; but he enters more deeply into the religious element of the holy authors. His views on inspiration are not so orthodox as those of Hengstenberg and Stier; yet he bows with equal reverence and humility before the inexhaustible depth and wisdom of the Word of God, whose living power he feels in his heart.

We have from Tholuck's pen Commentaries on the Epistles to the Romans, the Hebrews, the Sermon on the Mount, the Gospel of St. John, and the Psalms, several of which have been translated into the English, although not from the latest and best editions. They are of very unequal merit. Some are intended for ripe scholars and permanent use; others for students only, and will be superseded. The most solid, accurate, and thorough of his exegetical works, is the Explanation of Christ's Sermon on the Mount, (third edition, 1845,) which throws a flood of light—philological, historical, and dogmatical—on the fifth, sixth, and seventh chapters of St. Matthew, and labors to exhaust the subject as far as possible. It will therefore always be resorted to as one of the richest mines on this portion of the Scriptures. Next to it comes his Commentary on the Romans, in its newly elaborated form, (sixth edition, 1856,) which throws the first editions altogether into the shade. His work on the Hebrews is not near as thorough and exhaustive as that of Dr. Bleek, who spent twenty years of indefatigable study on this wonderful epistle, but is far better adapted for the use of students.

In close connection with his exegetical labors stands his critical and apologetical work on the "Credibility of the Gospel History," which is one of the most learned and triumphant answers to the notorious "Leben Jesu" of Strauss, and abounds in pointed remarks, sparkling wit, and brilliant erudition.

Tholuck published for several years a journal under the title "Literarischer Anzeiger," which was principally devoted to reviews of new theological works. With many other periodicals, it was buried in the flood of the Revolution of 1848. He now contributes occasional papers to the "Deutsche Zeitschrift" of Berlin, with whose theological position he best agrees.

He is a decided friend of the Evangelical Union, and deplores the confessional and denominational quarrels which have broken out anew in Germany. He has grown old in the successful conflict against infidelity, and dislikes to see the war with the foreign enemy changed into an internal war of brothers. He is convinced, however, as I heard from his own mouth, that the now prevailing high church Lutheranism is merely on the surface and has no roots in the heart of German Protestantism.

In his most recent productions, on the "Spirit of the Lutheran Divines of Wittenberg in the Seventeenth Century," 1852, and on "The Academic Life of the Seventeenth Century, with special regard to the Protestant Theological Faculties of Germany," in two parts, 1853 and 1854, he gives, mostly from manuscript sources, a very interesting and graphic, but by no means favorable picture of the palmy days of orthodox Lutheranism, for the instruction and warning of those cotemporaries who would so zealously revive it as the best state of the Church, without considering that it was followed by the terrible apostacy of Rationalism. What in the name of common decency, shall we think, for instance, of such a redoubted and invincible champion of Lutheran orthodoxy and implacable enemy of Calvinists, Zwinglians, Syncretists, &c., as Abraham Calov, of Wittenberg, who, Tholuck tells us, piously buried not less than five wives and thirteen children, and yet in the seventy-second year of his age, four months after the death of his fifth wife, carried to the altar the daughter of his equally orthodox colleague, Quenstedt!

The works just mentioned, are forerunners simply of an extensive History of Rationalism, in which the indefatigable and ever youthful author has been engaged for some years. This, when completed, will be a most valuable contribution to the history of German Protestantism, if we are to judge from the extent of his preparations, and from the animated sketch of the same subject, which is found in the second volume of his Miscellaneous Essays.

CHAPTER XXVII.

OLSHAUSEN.

Notice of his Life—His Commentary on the New Testament—Character of his Exegesis—The Doctrine of Inspiration—Continuation, and English Translation of Olshausen.

THE late Dr. Hermann Olshausen was born in 1796, at Oldesloe, in the duchy of Holstein, about twenty-four miles from Hamburg. He studied theology in the Universities of Kiel and Berlin, and was elected professor at Königsberg, in 1821, where he taught till 1834. He then followed a call to a theological professorship at Erlangen, Bavaria, and died in 1839, in the prime of life. From all accounts he was a truly lovely man, and combined with profound scholarship the graces of social refinement and devout piety. I never saw him, but occasionally met his widow at Giebichenstein and at Berlin, and found her a highly accomplished and estimable Christian lady, who holds her lamented husband in sacred remembrance. She belongs to the Moravian community. A brother of Olshausen lives at St. Louis, and is the author of a work on Missouri, and a history of the Mormons.

Olshausen is one of the most illustrious modern reformers of Biblical Exegesis. His Commentary on the

New Testament, on which his immortality rests, is a work of real genius; it made a decided impression when it first appeared, and will exert no doubt, for many ages to come, a silent, but deep and lasting influence far beyond the circle of readers, for which it was originally intended. Like Neander's church history, it has become already, we may say, a standard work of English and American, as well as German literature, and will soon enjoy a wider circulation in Great Britain and the United States, than in the land of its birth.

To write a commentary that would be interesting as well as instructive, and invite the reader not merely to occasional reference, but to connected study, is a most difficult task. Olshausen succeeded in it better than most of the commentators, and ranks in this respect with Chrysostom, Calvin, Tholuck, and Lücke. His work is eminently readable, free from learned pedantry, and moves on in easy, graceful dignity.

But the principal merit and greatest charm of Olshausen's exegesis, lies in its spirit. He excels beyond most commentators, in what we may call the art of organic reproduction of the sacred text, and the explanation of Scripture by Scripture. The philological portions are often too brief and unsatisfactory for the advanced scholar; but he pays the more careful attention to the theological exposition, enters into the marrow of religious ideas, and introduces the student to the spirit and inward unity of the divine revelation in its various stages of development under the old and new dispensation. He has an instinctive power of seizing, as if by a sacred sympathy, the true meaning of the inspired writer, and bringing to light the hidden connections and transitions, the remote allusions and far reaching bearing of the text.

There is nothing mechanical and superficial about him. He is always working in the mines, and digging at the roots. Sometimes his mysticism carries him beyond the limits of sound and sober criticism. But there is a peculiar charm in his mysticism, and even its occasional mistakes are far preferable to that cold, dry and lifeless exegesis which weighs the spiritual and eternal truths of God in the scales of Aristotle's logic, Kühner's grammar, and Wahl's dictionary. A Fritzsche and Strauss may sneer at some expositions of Olshausen; but the pious student will read him with delight and profit, and regard the spiritual depth and the warm glow of a profoundly pious heart, as the sweetest charm and highest recommendation of his work. He approaches the Bible, with devout reverence, as the Word of the living God, leads the reader into the sanctissimum, and makes him feel that here is the gate of heaven.

It is true, Olshausen is no believer in a literal, mechanical inspiration as taught by the Protestant divines of the seventeenth century, and as held to this day by most of the popular English commentators. We readily admit that he may have made now and then an unnecessary concession to neology, which was still in power when he commenced the publication of his commentary.

But such cases are only of trifling moment and never touch the substance of a fact, or any article of faith and practice. And then, with all respect for the theory of literal inspiration, it seems to us that it leaves out of sight, and cannot account for, the human element in the origin, preservation, and propagation of the Holy Scriptures, which stares the critic in the face from every direction. The error of rationalism does not lie in calling attention to the human form of the Bible, but in denying its divine contents, and in ignoring the glory of the only begotten of the Father, which shines through the veil of the flesh full of grace and of truth. "The Word became flesh." This may be applied to the written as well as the personal Word. The Holy Scriptures are strictly divine, and strictly human, from beginning to end. The two natures are here united in one organic whole. The Holy Spirit lived, thought, moved in, and spoke through, the prophets and apostles, but as conscious, intelligent, free agents, not as blind and passive machines.

The interpreter, then, must bring to light the real humanity, as well as the real divinity of the Bible; he must let the several books grow out of the twofold source, and view them in their organic connection with the historical relations, the peculiar temper and spirit of the writer. Such exegesis instead of diminishing our faith in the Scriptures, is calculated to strengthen it and to put it on a firmer basis against which the attacks of infidelity can have no force. In this way the Gospels and Epistles become living productions to our generation; and although they had in every case, specific wants and well defined objects in view, they will be found to be at the same time, the most universal books in the world, Even the most minute references to concrete circumstances of the time of composition are applicable to the general wants and conditions of the human heart. We do not assert that Olshausen or any other German commentator, does full justice to both sides of the Bible, but we must maintain, that this is the true aim of every interpreter who would satisfy both the wants of faith, and of theological science.

It is to be regretted that Olshausen did not live to complete his commentary on the New Testament. We would have been especially pleased to see an exposition of the Epistle to the Hebrews, the Epistles of John, and the Revelation, from his pen. After a long interruption, one of his ablest and most learned disciples, Ebrard, in connection with Wiesinger, has undertaken the completion of the work. But I know of no living divine who could infuse that mystic depth and flow of soul, which constitutes the peculiar attraction of Olshausen's volumes, especially the first two, on the Gospels.

The Edinburgh translation of this commentary, which forms a part of Clark's Foreign Theological Library, is now in course of republication at New York, under the editorial care of Professor Kendrick, of Rochester, who revised the translation, embodied Ebrard's improvements from the last edition of the original, with occasional notes of his own, where he thought it necessary to dissent from the author, and added Olshausen's valuable tract on the Genuineness of the Writings of the New Testament (translated by Fosdick,) as an appropriate introduction. The first two volumes which appeared in 1856 and '57, were welcomed with great favor by our leading theological organs, and we have reason to believe that Olshausen will become more and more a favorite guide for American students of the Word of God.

CHAPTER XXVIII.

HENGSTENBERG.

His Position and Influence—His Moral Courage and Independence—His Education and Conversion—Hengstenberg as a Lecturer—His theological Stand-point, and uncompromising Hostility to Rationalism—His Relation to English and American Orthodoxy—His Critical and Exegetical Works on the Old Testament—Commentary on the Apocalypse—His Evangelical Church Gazette, the leading Organ of the Orthodox Party in the Prussian Church—His Correspondents—His recent Progress in High Church Confessionalism—Present Relation to the Union and the Church Question.

Dr. Ernst Wilhelm Hengstenberg, Professor of Old Testament Exegesis in the University of Berlin, is one of the most unpopular and yet one of the most important and influential men in the kingdom of Prussia. He leads the extreme right wing of the orthodox party in the Established Church, and is the uncompromising opponent of all rationalists and semi-rationalists, all latitudinarians and liberals. He is simply professor, author and editor of a semi-weekly church gazette, and holds no seat in the *Consistorium* and *Oberkirchenrath*, like his colleagues, Nitzsch, Twesten and Strauss; nor does he ever preach. But in an unofficial way his power has been widely felt for the last few years in the administration of ecclesiastical affairs. He is the confidential adviser of Herr von Raumer, the present minister of public worship and instruction in that kingdom, who rarely makes an important appointment without his consent. It has been said that Hengstenberg, Ludwig von Gerlach and Stahl, are the three popes, who, since the Revolution of 1848, rule the Church and State of Prussia. At all events they have much more real power and deeper influence than Herr von Manteuffel and the other ministers of the Crown.

This position Hengstenberg owes to his learning, and above all to his character and principles. Being married into a noble family and living in comfortable circumstances, he associates freely with the highest classes of society in Berlin. But he never courts the favor, or flatters the pride of the men in power. Even his bitterest enemies must acknowledge his manly independence and consistency. He is, in the proper sense of the term, a theological *character*, ruled by principle, and subordinating all temporal considerations to his conscientious convictions of truth.

He shrinks from no opposition, no matter from what quarter it may arise, and hesitates not to attack corruption in the highest places, whenever he feels it his duty to do so. Thus for instance he wrote a series of severe articles against the order of the Freemasons, and denounced it as unchurchly, deistic and infidel in its tendency, although the Prince of Prussia, heir presumptive to the crown, is one of its chief patrons. Still more recently he came out in the same spirit of fearless independence, against duelling, with reference to the unfortunate Hinkeldey-Rochow affair, which created a great stir in the nobility and aristocracy. He wants kings of

God's grace like David, but also court preachers and professors like Nathan and Elijah.

As a lecturer he generally disappoints the expectations of those who hear him for the first time. For instead of seeing an athletic figure, looking like a lion, and speaking in a voice of thunder, they will find a middle sized, thin, delicately built, refined looking, neat and well dressed gentleman, reading slavishly from his manuscript, in a half-singing, high silvery, monotonous tone. But what he says, and the manner in which he says it, is exceedingly positive and dogmatical. He knows also, how, by private intercourse, to attract students to his person, and still more to his views. He is an excellent judge of character, far better than the good natured Neander was, who suffered himself so often to be deceived. He seldom recommends a young man, who does not afterwards realize his expectations. In his friendships he is perfectly reliable.

Hengstenberg is, I believe, a Westphalian by birth, and the son of a Reformed clergyman. He was born in 1802, and studied philology, especially the oriental languages, in the University of Bonn. His first appearance before the public was as a translator of the metaphysics of Aristotle. After the completion of his university course, he spent a short time at Basel as the private tutor of Dr. Stähelin, now professor of oriental literature and Old Testament Exegesis in the university of that city. In 1824 he graduated as licentiate of theology at Berlin, and settled as *Privatdocent* in the university. In 1826 he was already promoted to an extraordinary, and some years afterwards to an ordinary professorship of Old

Testament exegesis and to a seat in the theological faculty. He soon acquired a commanding influence in the Church at large by the publication of the "Evangelische Kirchenzeitung," which he commenced in 1827, and continues to edit to this day.

I am not acquainted with the particulars of his change of views, which seems to have been very sudden, as in the case of Calvin. The study of the Bible was probably the chief means. It is said that while at Bonn, he belonged to the liberal and progressive class of students. But in Berlin he took at once his place amongst the most evangelical and orthodox divines of the younger generation. When he arrived there, a revival of Christian theology and piety had already commenced in the higher classes. He associated at that time with Neander, Tholuck, Olshausen, Baron von Kottwitz, Count Voss, von Bethmann Hollweg, the Gerlach family, and other leaders of the rising evangelical party, who no doubt contributed to shape his views, although he is too much their contemporary, and too independent in character to be called the pupil of any of them.

With Schleiermacher's system he seems never to have had the least sympathy, and he permitted one of his correspondents (Steiger) to assail it in his journal as semi-rationalistic and pantheistic. This attack against an older colleague, together with the somewhat indelicate but well deserved exposure of the frivolities of Gesenius' lectures at Halle, so offended Neander, that he publicly broke off his former (merely nominal) connection with the "Evangelische Kirchenzeitung," in 1830, and ever afterwards occupied a somewhat antagonistic position to Hengstenberg, who was altogether too sharp and uncompromising for his mild and conciliatory temper. But personally, the colleagues always esteemed each other as scholars and Christians, and after Neander's death, Hengstenberg, in the preface to the Kirchenzeitung of 1851, gave a grateful testimony to his excellent character and immortal merits. He correctly remarks there, that the theological differences between them arose from the fact that Neander started from Schleiermacher, while he being younger, had the advantage to commence with the more advanced position of Neander, from which he then proceeded to a still more decidedly Scriptural and churchly stand-point.

Dr. Hengstenberg's theology has throughout a polemical and apologetical character. Of all the modern German divines he is the most orthodox champion of the genuineness, integrity, inspiration and divine authority of the Bible, especially the Old Testament, against the attacks of modern skepticism. In some respects he reminds us of the early Fathers in their conflict with the heathen persecution and heretical perversion of Christianity. But while Justin Martyr, Irenaeus, Tertullian, etc., were mostly and directly concerned with doctrines, Hengstenberg's proper field is Biblical literature; and while the former appealed to Catholic tradition as much as to the Scripture, as a bulwark against heretics, the latter stands on decidedly Protestant ground, i. e., the absolute supremacy of the Bible; although, of course, he makes due account of the patristic testimonies and the faith of the Church concerning the canonical books. He has, indeed, been charged recently with a Romanizing tendency. But this is certainly an error as regards the rule of faith, and all the positive articles of the Protestant creed. It is true, however, that he always regarded the Catholic Church as a confederate of the Evangelical Church in opposition to rationalism and pantheism, and hence he subordinates the Romish controversy to the more fundamental controversy between faith and infidelity, Christ and Anti-Christ.

Hengstenberg is not a philosophical and systematic divine, but an eminent critic and controversialist. He is not an originator of new ideas, but a skillful advocate of old ones. He is not a man of brilliant genius, but of very solid talent, profound learning, strong reasoning power, and clear direct common sense. He has little imagination and artistic taste, but a keen understanding and unbending will. His theology rests on practical experience as well as scientific investigation, and is pervaded throughout by a serious and energetic piety. Although he professes now the distinctive Lutheran tenets, he has unquestionably a striking constitutional resemblance to Calvin, more so at least, than any other German divine, and owes a great deal to the study of his works, especially his incomparable Commentaries, of which he republished the one on Genesis (1838.) Had he been born and raised in Scotland or New England, he would no doubt be a most rigorous Calvinist.

The Calvinistic features of his mind and moral character, in connection with his high views on inspiration and the divine authority of the Scriptures, account for the fact that Hengstenberg is better understood and more generally appreciated in England and America, than almost any other German theologian. Most of his exegetical and critical works are now translated and embodied in Clark's Foreign Library. He would be a decided favorite and standard writer among Presbyterians and Puritans, if it was not for his high-church views on the sacraments and on church authority, which he developed more recently—although not in his commentaries—and which diminished his popularity in this direction, while they may perhaps have increased it among Episcopalians. To this must be added his views on the Sabbath, the middle state, and the Romish question, in which he differs considerably from Puritanism.

His political or high-state principles harmonize still less with those generally entertained by Christians of the English tongue, or even in France and in Switzerland. Although he cannot help respecting England and America for the sake of their religion, yet he evidently dislikes liberal, especially republican institutions. His sympathies are altogether with an absolute jure-divino monarchy. He opposed the liberal movements of 1848 and 1849, without the least qualification, as a diabolical outbreak, and contributed as much as any man to restore the old order of things in Prussia.

Thus we may say, he is in some respects the most Puritanic and Americanizing, and in other respects the most un-Puritanic and anti-American divine of Germany.

To do justice to Hengstenberg as a scientific divine, we must go back thirty years, to a time when rationalism was at the zenith of its power and influence, and sapped the very foundations of evangelical Protestantism, the authority and inspiration of the holy Scriptures. His theological career begun in an inexorable antagonism to this great and powerful modern heresy. He stood up for the divine origin and authority of the Bible, and the faith of the Church against the destructive criticism of its most learned modern assailants. He met them not only with all the weapons of logic and learning, but traced also their views to the moral depravity of the heart and its secret hostility to truth and righteousness, as the deepest source of all forms of heresy and infidelity. Thus, without divesting the controversy of its scientific and literary character, he gave it at the same time a moral and practical aspect, and mixed with his arguments the prophetical threats of God's wrath upon his enemies and lukewarm friends.

This is the principal reason why he exposed himself to more bitter hatred, calumny, and slander, than any other divine of the present century. The Rationalists regard him as a Protestant Torquemada, who in another age and under similar circumstances would have sent as many heretics to the auto-da-fe's, as the first Inquisitor-General of Spain. Even Hase, who has too much spirit and taste to sympathize with the ordinary rationalism of a Röhr and Schulz, forgets his usual candor and impartiality, when he comes, in his Church History, to Hengstenberg, whose Kirchenzeitung he characterizes, as embracing "the greatest variety of religious elements, from the genuine piety of a Luther or Spener, full of joyful faith in a God born of a virgin, down through the gradations of mere party zeal, pride, and mental imbecility, till we reach the hypocrisy which abuses the language of ardent piety as a means to selfish ends, or even as a cloak of crimes." All this is highly exaggerated. We are firmly convinced, from long and close observation, of the purity and integrity of Hengstenberg's character; at the same time we have not a particle of doubt, that had he lived in the sixteenth century, or even in the seventeenth, he would have approved in the most unqualified terms of the burning of Servetus.

This unyielding firmness and severity of character, which reminds one at times of the zeal of the Old Testament prophets, was no doubt necessary and of essential service to German theology in the revolutionary crisis through which it had to pass. There must be Lutheran as well as Melanthonian, Pauline as well as Johannean characters in the church. His moral courage in view of the fiercest literary persecution is worthy of all praise, and will alone secure for him the admiration and esteem of posterity. He stood like a rock in the midst of the fluctuations of ever changing opinions and heresies, and we have no doubt, that, if circumstances required it, he would not shrink a moment from sealing his faith with his blood.

At the same time, we must admit that rationalism assumes with Hengstenberg a very wide range, and embraces also the various forms of undecided and inconsistent supernaturalism, and all the medium positions which have their mission and relative importance as well as his unyielding orthodoxy. He is constitutionally opposed to all compromises; he knows no middle course between faith and unbelief, orthodoxy and heresy. He attacks as enemies of Christ, all who are not openly his friends. He even denounced the Gustavus Adolphus Society, and prophesied its speedy dissolution, because it did not start at once with a strictly confessional basis. But it succeeded after all, and does a good work—his opposition notwithstanding. He makes great account of the word: "He that is not with me, is against me, and he that gathereth not with me, scattereth abroad." But he forgets that the same Saviour says on another occasion what is equally true, and equally worthy to be kept in mind when we judge of others: "He that is not against us, is on our part." His zeal often degenerates into harshness and injustice. His theology breathes more the spirit of the Old, than of the New Testament. His polemics, although always clothed in earnest and decent language, often assume an unnecessary degree of bitterness and wield too freely the weapons of sarcastic scorn. No wonder, that he alienated from him not only the whole school of Schleiermacher, but also that of Neander.

Hengstenberg's writings extend more or less over the whole field of Biblical literature. He lectures also on theological encyclopedia and several books of the New Testament, and his Kirchenzeitung touches upon all the important ecclesiastical questions of the day.

But his main strength and most lasting merits lie in the critical defence and explanation of the Old Testament as the revelation of the only true and living God. It is well known that rationalism aimed its most unsparing blows at this portion of the canon. Eichhorn, Bertholdt, De Wette, in his earlier period, Gesenius, Bohlen, Lengerke, Vatke, and others, vied with each other in cutting to pieces the venerable writings of Moses and the prophets, with the knife of learned and acute, but arbitrary and irreverent criticism, and in thus representing them as productions of a later age, unworthy of credit. This destructive process was soon afterwards applied to the gospels and epistles of the New Testament. Strauss resolved the whole history of the God-man as recorded by St. Matthew, Mark, Luke and John, into a mythical dream, and Baur went so far as to deny the apostolical origin of all the books of the New Testament, with the exception of four epistles of Paul and the Revelation of John. It is easy to see that such criticism struck at the root of Christianity, which must stand or fall with the divine inspiration and authority of its original records. The question then here raised was one of life and death, especially for Protestantism which regards the canonical Scriptures as its bulwark, as the only infallible and sufficient rule of faith and practice.

It was against these assaults of modern scientific infidelity that Hengstenberg, in the three volumes of *Beiträge*, or "Contributions to the Introduction to the Old Testament," (1831, &c.) defended the genuineness and integrity of some of the most important books of the Jewish canon, the prophecies of Daniel, (given up even by Bleek as *vaticinia post eventum*,) Zechariah, and the Pentateuch. It must be admitted, that he disposes of many difficulties rather by dogmatic assertion and sophistic evasion, than by satisfactory, solid argument. But upon the whole, these "Contributions" are a triumphant vindication of the orthodox view, and the most learned and acute investigations ever made in this field. The opponents were at first disposed proudly to ignore them as vain attempts to restore obsolete absurdities; but with all the affectation of contempt they felt the destruction which his learning and arguments caused amongst their ranks, and lived to see most of their own critical novelties growing obsolete, to be assigned at last to the history of the aberrations of the human mind.

Still more important than his Beiträge, which were originally designed to extend over all the assailed portions of the Jewish canon, is the "Christology of the Old Testament," commenced in 1829, in three volumes, and now re-published since 1854 in a second thoroughly revised edition, and translated by Dr. Meyer of Edinburgh, for Clark's Foreign Library. It contains a full exposition of all the Messianic prophecies from the first promise after the fall to the extinction of prophecy, with constant polemical reference to the modern rationalistic literature.

At first his view of prophecy was very external and mechanical. But in the progress of the work, and especially in the new edition, it underwent considerable modifications, and became more spiritual and organic. He now recognizes the idea of a gradual development of the Messianic promise in keeping with the wants and capacities of the people to whom it was given. It seems impossible that most English divines should still shut their eyes to this law, which pervades all created life, all the works of God. We need only examine impartially the respective passages of Genesis, to see that there is a gradual progress of the Messianic prophecy as regards clearness and distinctness from the general promise of a victory of the woman's seed over the serpent, to the patriarchal hope of a blessing that should proceed from Abraham's, and more particularly from Isaac's posterity to the nations of the earth; and from this, to the promise of the Lawgiver and Shiloh from the tribe of Judah. In the first case we have simply the assurance of the fact of a future victory, without any hint as to the manner of its accomplishment; in the second, we are pointed to the particular nation, and in the third to the tribe, from which it should proceed, with the additional declaration that salvation thus promised would be comprehended not in a nation, or an abstract power, but in an individual. In David's time, we learn the family of the future Messiah; and the later prophets, Isaiah especially, reveal to us his character and the form and circumstances, even the sufferings through which he would accomplish the redemption of Israel not only, but of the whole world.

With all his unrelenting opposition to the neological theories, Hengstenberg does not entirely concur with the old Protestant orthodoxy, which overlooks the gradual progress of the revelation from its incipient stages to its culmination point in the incarnation of the eternal Word. A still stronger proof of the difference is furnished by his little book on the prophecies of Balaam (1842.) For here he gives up the literal interpretation altogether, and resolves the speaking of the ass and the appearance of the angel into a *vision* which occurred to Balaam. Also in his Commentary on the Song of Solomon, (1853,) while he revives and defends the allegorical interpretation, he yet modifies the old view, which regarded it as a direct representation of the union of Christ with his Church, and conceives it to be a prophetic picture of the relation of the literal Israel, the bride, to the Messiah before and after his coming.

The most valuable exegetical work of Hengstenberg next to his Old Testament Christology, is an extended Commentary on the Psalms, in four volumes, which has been translated into English, and furnished the groundwork besides for the more popular and condensed work of Dr. A. Alexander, of Princeton, on the same subject. Here the polemical character recedes more into the background, and gives place to a considerable amount of practical and edifying observations.

More recently this learned divine has also entered the domain of New Testament exegesis, but with far less success. His commentary on the Revelation of St. John, which might as well have been left untranslated for the author's popularity in England and America, contains a great deal indeed that is permanently valuable, and has in many respects shed new light upon its prophetic mysteries. But he permitted the political and social convulsions of the years 1848 and '49, during which the work was written, to have too much influence upon the interpretation. His own view of the millennium is, to say the least, fully as unsatisfactory as the theories of Herder, Eichhorn, Ewald, Lücke, Züllig, etc., which he treats with so much contempt. For he regards it as something past, and dates it from the downfall of German heathenism, to the infidelity and the revolutions of our age, thus identifying it substantially with the reign of popery and the duration of the German empire!

He may be right in rejecting the anti-popery scheme of interpretation, which identifies the beast with *Christian* Rome. But to commence the millennial reign of Christ and the captivity of Satan with the rise of the papal power in the eighth century, to extend it through the darkest ages without making any distinction between them and the period of the Reformation, and to terminate it with the revolutions of 1848, when we are told Satan was let loose again, is too absurd a notion to commend itself to the good sense of the Christian community. It is also already sufficiently refuted by subsequent events, so that we doubt whether Hengstenberg himself would be willing still to call the present period of reaction and growing confessionalism the age of Gog and Magog.

Upon the whole, we are far from regarding Hengstenberg as a model interpreter. He is somewhat external and mechanical in his conceptions, bitter in his polemics, categorical and dogmatic in tone, diffuse and careless in style. But with all these defects he stands first amongst the restorers of a believing exegesis of the Old Testament.

Since he broke the ice, a number of younger men, some his direct pupils, as Hävernick, (who died, alas! too early,) and others, more independent co-laborers, as Ranke, the brother of the celebrated historian, Delitzsch and Hofmann in Erlangen, Baumgarten in Rostock, Oehler in Tübingen, Keil and Kurtz in Dorpat, and Bähr in Carlsruhe, have followed and created a rich and valuable literature relating to the elucidation of the Old Testament as a genuine revelation of the only true God and a preparation of the New Testament, which is concealed in the Old, while the Old is revealed in the New.

In conclusion we must add a few remarks on Hengstenberg as editor of the "Evangelische Kirchenzeitung," and leader of the orthodox party in the established Church of Prussia. This practical part of his activity, though less known in America, is fully as important and influential for Germany as the one we have more fully considered.

He founded this semi-weekly organ in 1827, so that it has already reached the fifty-eighth volume. It can hardly be called a Church Gazette, for it has given very little news during the last ten or twenty years. Sometimes, indeed, we read in it extended accounts of the condition of the church in Hesse, or Baden, or Saxony; but they have nearly always a polemical object in view, and are calculated to give offence and create a sensation. Some of these reports make capital out of scandal, and assume a revolutionary attitude against the church authorities, e. g., in Baden, which is quite inconsistent with Hengstenberg's doctrine on the duty of absolute submission to the powers that be.

The chief object of the Kirchenzeitung is to discuss, in an earnest and thorough, yet popular style, the leading religious and ecclesiastical questions of the day for the benefit of ministers and educated laymen. This is generally done with a very high degree of ability and power. Many articles belong to the best order of polemical and ascetic writing. The editor gives his own views in full in the "*Vorwort*," which occupies the greater part of the January numbers, and which is called by his admirers Hengstenberg's *Thronrede*. He generally commences it with the solemn application of some prophetic portion of Scripture to the times; then he reviews the principal ecclesiastical events of the preceding year, and gives his deliberate judgment on the pending questions.

But the journal owes its reputation fully as much, if not more, to a most able corps of anonymous, yet well known correspondents. Amongst these we mention the late Otto von Gerlach, and Steiger, who assisted in founding it; Tholuck, and Lange, who contributed many of the most spicy and interesting articles, but had no connection with it for several years past; Huber, the author of Sketches of Spain, and Ireland, and a History of the English Universities; Stahl, the eloquent lawyer and advocate of Lutheranism; Ludwig von Gerlach, a statesman of brilliant genius, who can defend the oddest propositions with the greatest plausibility; Göschel, the speculative New Lutheran, who, in his former days, labored with more ingenuity than truth to prove Hegel and Göthe to have been orthodox Christians; Vilmar, the eloquent champion of Hessian Puseyism; Leo, the genial historian and fierce polemic, who fully comes up to his name. For the last two or three years, however, Hengstenberg's paper has declined considerably in vivacity, freshness and interest.

The "Kirchenzeitung" started from the pietistic school, and had at first the support and good wishes of all who labored and prayed for the revival of piety and vital Christianity in Germany. It also stood decidedly on the basis of the evangelical Union, as established in Prussia since 1817, and made little or no account of the differences between the Lutheran and the Reformed confessions. It regarded both as essentially agreed in all the fundamental articles of Christianity, and equally opposed to the rationalistic and infidel spirit of the age, which it felt itself called upon to combat.

But in the course of time the journal assumed a more exclusive confessional tone. The *Vorwort* of 1844 marked a turn in this respect. Since the revolutions of 1848 it became still more decided in this direction, so that it should now be called the organ of the Lutheran party in the Evangelical Church of Prussia, instead of Evangelical Church Gazette. He himself admits the change, and remarks in the *Vorwort* to the year 1856, p. 48: "The editor of the Evangelical Church Gazette has often been charged with inconsistency in his relation to the Union. In reply to this we have to say that retractations were never considered a disgrace in the Church. On the contrary, it is a gift of God to be pliable and capable of learning in advanced years."

The change consists principally in two points, the conversion from the Calvinistic to the Lutheran view of the Lord's Supper, and the conviction that the Lutheran Confession must be guarded in all its rights within the United Church of Prussia. With this understanding he professes still to adhere to the Union as explained in the royal declaration of March 6, 1852. The whole tendency of his journal, however, whether it be his intention or not, looks evidently towards a dissolution of the Union and the restoration of confessional Lutheranism.

His opposition, it is true, is not so much directed

against the Reformed church, as against those Unionists who seek to amalgamate the two churches, and to absorb the old Confessions in a more liberal creed, or no-creed. This loose latitudinarianism and semi-rationalistic liberalism injures the cause of the Union more than its enemies do; and against it Hengstenberg defends the good right of the reformatory confessions which should never be given up until we have something better and more perfect in their place, which our distracted age seems to be unable to produce. The Reformed church he still professes highly to esteem in its proper character, especially for its energetic piety and self-denying zeal for Christ's kingdom at home and abroad. But he thinks it has no proper national root in Germany, except on the frontiers, and has not developed there its peculiar excellences as in Scotland. He goes with the Lutheran party because it defends, in his view, a higher degree of orthodoxy, and promises to be a stronger national bulwark against infidelity.

We readily admit that the Prussian Union labors under very serious defects, and is any thing but completed. As a State-Church measure, especially, it is simply an experiment of doubtful success. But the resuscitation of Old Lutheranism or any other system, which has been tried in a former age, and been found wanting, will certainly not heal the defects or better satisfy the wants of the age. No, Germany and the Church generally need a plentiful effusion of the Holy Spirit, which will bring about a new reformation and open a new chapter in history.

Hengstenberg's power and influence has never been

greater than at the present time. But after all, the high church confessionalism, or Lutheran exclusivism, has no deep root in the people, and makes itself exceedingly obnoxious to all the friends of liberty by its close alliance with the political reaction that has set in since 1849. He has not only denounced in most unsparing terms the recent revolutionary movements, without any qualification, but even frequently and bitterly attacked the worthy Lutheran pastors in Holstein, because they opposed, not from revolutionary propensity, but simply for conscience sake, and on the ground of ancient rights, the anti-German regulations of despotic Denmark, and in consequence of it forfeited their offices and emoluments. It is evident that Dr. Hengstenberg has no sympathy whatever with religious and political freedom, which must necessarily result from Protestantism, wherever it is fully and consistently developed. By opposing all liberal movements, he opposes the spirit of the age, the tendency of history, and helps to provoke a new and more fearful revolution, which will sweep away all the artificial restorations of by-gone forms of life.

And here is the defect in the high-churchism of Hengstenberg and his school. The churchly tendencies which are indeed needed, should not flow in the narrow channel of Lutheran denominationalism, or any ism or sect, but be as broad and comprehensive as the kingdom of Christ, and in harmony with the deepest wants and movements of the age that hates despotism and loves freedom in Church and State.

CHAPTER XXIX.

TWESTEN.

The Progress of German Theology in the Direction of Orthodoxy—Schleiermacher, Neander, Tholuck, and Hengstenberg in their mutual Relations—The Systematic Divines of the Evangelical Union-School—Dr. Twesten—His Personal Character and Social Habits—His Work on Dogmatics—His Standpoint and Merits—His View of Religion—His Relation to Schleiermacher and the Union.

SCHLEIERMACHER, Neander, Tholuck, and Hengstenberg represent as many steps in the scale of rapid progress, which the evangelical theology of Germany has made within the first half of the nineteenth century. It was a steady movement from an ideal Christianity of religious speculation to the Scriptural faith, and from the Scriptural faith to churchly orthodoxy, yet all within the strict limits of the Protestant principle.

Schleiermacher first built a bridge over the abyss that divides the dismal swamp of skepticism from the sunny hills of faith, and kindled again the flame of religion and of the Christian consciousness. Neander enriched this new theology with the experience of a pious heart, and the treasures of church history of all ages and nations. Tholuck and his friend Olshausen refreshed and invigorated it at the fountain of the New Testament as the word of truth and life. All felt the importance and revived the feeling of Christian union and communion, but they remained comparatively indifferent to the "pilgrim-dress" of particular confessions and symbols, and greatly preferred the life of Christianity to the forms of the Church. Hengstenberg took his firm stand from the start on the sure word of prophecy as an external testimony and authority, defended especially the claims of the Old Testament, so utterly disregarded or neglected by Schleiermacher and his school, and drew around the interpretation of the Bible and the life of Christianity more and more closely the wall of the Lutheran creed. Theology soared at first so high into the airy regions as to lose sight of the terra firma of the Bible and the Church, but has now exchanged the wings for the strait-jacket of denominational orthodoxy, and is in danger of suffering from want of breath and fresh air. Thus we have here a retrogression rather than a progression, a contraction instead of an expansion. But it must not be forgotten, on the other hand, that the restraints of law and authority are necessary to the proper enjoyment of freedom, and that every healthy progress in the Church is conditioned by a revival of the faith of the past, especially by a return to the ever fresh fountain of the holy Scriptures, as the Reformation of the sixteenth century amply proves.

We now proceed to consider another succession of divines, whose force lies in systematic divinity, especially in dogmatics. Twesten, Nitzsch, and Müller started from Schleiermacher, even more so than this can be said of Tholuck and Olshausen, but went likewise far beyond his standpoint to a more positive and orthodox position. Yet they still adhere to the principle of the

Union, and are its chief doctrinal representatives. A younger generation of didactic divines, Martensen, Thomasius, Hofmann, Kahnis, and Philippi went beyond this standpoint into what they regard as the unconquerable tower of symbolical Lutheranism, although they themselves cannot deny altogether the effect of the stages of development which lie between the composition of the *Formula Concordiae* and Hofmann's *Schriftbeweis*, and which never can be entirely undone.

Dr. August Detlev Christian Twesten is a native of Glückstadt, the capital of the Duchy of Holstein, a thoroughly German Province—which belongs to Denmark in body only, not in soul. Born in 1789, and for some time professor of languages in one of the colleges of Berlin, he was one of the earliest followers, and an intimate personal friend of Schleiermacher. After his death in 1834, he was called from the University of Kiel, where he had been professor since 1814, to succeed him in the chair of systematic divinity. He is also *Oberconsistorialrath* and member of the *Oberkirchenrath*, where he displays considerable administrative capacities.

Coming after the greatest theological genius of modern times, his position was a very difficult one, as in the more recent case of Lehnerdt, who succeeded Neander as professor of church history. If Twesten failed to satisfy the expectations of the theological public at large—before which he very rarely appears in the shape of books—he has proved a faithful and conscientious teacher in his immediate field of labor. If he falls far behind his predecessor in natural endowments and commanding influence, he certainly has greatly the advantage of him in soundness and orthodoxy of views.

Dr. Twesten is a gentleman of courteous manners, kindly disposition, and fine social qualities. Although a close student, he mixes freely with the world in his leisure hours. He resembles in this respect Schleiermacher, and has none of the awkward eccentricities and unpractical traits of Neander. Every Thursday evening, and on special occasions, he gathers a large class of the very best literary society of Berlin around his hospitable board in the Commandanten Strasse, on the Dönhofs-Platz. I gratefully remember many an instructive and delightful hour I spent there in conversation with some of the most learned men and most accomplished ladies of Europe. He does not confine himself to his profession at all; ministers, philosophers, historians, naturalists, philologists, antiquarians, travellers, general scholars, and artists are equally welcome on these social gatherings. There are few men who have a more extensive, and at the same time more solid and accurate information, than Twesten. He converses well on almost any topic. He does not speak English himself, but takes much interest in English affairs; and when I saw him last, his daughter was engaged, and is married I suppose by this time, to the Prussian Correspondent of the *London Times*.

As a writer, he is one of the least prolific of all the more eminent German divines. This is owing partly to a certain timidity and conscientiousness. He is unwilling to publish anything, which he has not first thoroughly searched and mastered, and for which there seems to him no urgent need. He wrote an analytical logic, a critical edition of the three oecumenical creeds and the unaltered Augsburg Confession, essays on Flacius Illyricus, on Schleiermacher's Ethics, &c.

But his only theological work of any size are the Lectures on the Dogmatics of the Evangelical Lutheran Church, and even they are not completed. The first volume, containing the introductory chapters on religion, revelation, inspiration, the authority and inspiration of the Scriptures, the use of reason, the history of dogmatic literature, appeared in 1826, and went through several editions since. The second volume, dedicated to his friend and colleague, Dr. Neander, was delayed till 1837, and embraces only the doctrine of God, the Holy Trinity, the creation and preservation of the world, and angelology. The remaining volumes, with the anthropology, christology, ecclesiology, soteriology and eschatology, have not made their appearance yet, and as caution, solidity and conscientiousness are wont to grow with years and experience, they will perhaps never be finished. The author must feel, too, that the times have left the work in its original plan behind, and that he himself could not complete it in the spirit and form in which he commenced it. Schleiermacher's system is now a matter of history, and De Wette's compend, which he followed, as to order and arrangement, is thrown out of sight by Hase's *Hutterus Redivivus*, and similar manuals. Nevertheless, even in their unfinished condition, the dogmatics of Twesten have great and abiding excellences.

For he is perhaps the clearest thinker and writer

amongst all the systematic divines of Germany. He possesses the gift of didactic exposition and analysis in an eminent degree. His learning is always accurate, minute and thoroughly digested; his style transparent, smooth and polished. The English reader, to whom the original is not accessible, may form a conception from the translation of his chapter on the Trinity, which Professor H. B. Smith, of Union Theological Seminary, New York, furnished a few years ago for the pages of the *Bibliotheca Sacra.*

His standpoint may be briefly indicated thus—Schleiermacher's system passing over into Lutheran orthodoxy, under a modernized form; or the Lutheran scholasticism of the seventeenth century revived, enlarged and liberalized by the scientific influence of Schleiermacher and the tolerant spirit of the Evangelical Union.

In the first volume Twesten starts from, and ably defends, Schleiermacher's view of the nature of religion, namely, that it is primarily neither knowledge, nor action, neither theory, nor practice, but *feeling*, the feeling of absolute dependence upon God operating afterwards, it is true, upon both the other mental powers of thought and volition. This definition views religion merely under its subjective aspect, and is liable besides to the very same objection of one-sidedness, which Schleiermacher urges with irresistible force against the other two, which place the peculiar essence of religion, either exclusively in the intellect, (*modus Deum cognoscendi,*) or as one-sidedly in the will. The former or intellectual theory identifies it with knowledge, and thus makes the degree of piety to depend upon the amount of theoretical insight and theological scholarship, which is evidently contradicted by everyday experience. Even the modification of this view, which lays the main stress not upon religious knowledge as such, but upon the correctness and soundness of knowledge, (orthodoxy,) is false, since orthodoxy has often been united with ungodliness, and heresy and ignorance with piety. The exclusively practical view on the other hand, would resolve religion into mere morality, as was done in fact by the Stoics, by Kant, and many of the modern Unitarians, and thus destroys its specific character and mission altogether. Religion properly understood and carried out, must needs lead to virtue and holiness, but there is a great deal of morality in the world, which has no connection with piety whatever. Schleiermacher's ingenious theory of feeling avoids these extremes, it is true, but falls into the error of confining religion too much to the emotions and affections, or rather to an immediate consciousness of the heart, the degree of which is as uncertain an index of true piety as the amount of knowledge of divine things, or a correct moral deportment.

T. D. Morell, who thinks that "no man has ever pursued with greater penetration of mind and earnestness of spirit the pathway of a divine philosophy," than Schleiermacher, has recently endeavored in his "Philosophy of Religion," to naturalize his conception of religion in England. But in doing so, he made a serious mistake by translating Schleiermacher's *schlechthiniges Abhängigkeits-Gefühl*, "the absolute feeling of dependence," instead of "the feeling of absolute dependence," thus misplacing the absolute and connecting it with feeling, which is always relative and conditioned.

We hold that religion in the subjective sense, especially under its most complete, i. e., the Christian form, lies back of the three psychological faculties, thought, volition, and feeling, in the deepest centre of man's personality, and is as comprehensive as life itself. It is the higher, spiritual life of man, the life of Christ in us, the union and communion of the whole soul and all its faculties with God, the fountain of life and peace, and tends to penetrate and to sanctify equally all the parts and powers of the natural man, head, heart, and will, and eventually even the body itself. It is moreover not only a life of dependence upon God, as Schleiermacher has it, who shows here his connection with Calvin's supralapsarianism, but fully as much a life of freedom in God, according to the Augustinian maxim, *Deo servire vera libertas est*, or as some ancient liturgies beautifully express it, "Thy service, O God, is perfect freedom."

But Twesten, while agreeing in the main with Schleiermacher's theory of feeling, lays more stress than his master, on the element of knowledge, especially correct and sound knowledge of religion, or agreement with the faith of the church as expressed in her doctrinal standards. This is the point which connects him with the older Protestant theology.

This appears more fully in the second volume of his Dogmatics, which succeeded the first after an interval of eleven years. Here he falls back upon the Lutheran scholasticism of the seventeenth century, whose principal champions were Gerhard, Hutter, Calov, Quenstedt, and Baier. But he surrounds its skeleton of acute logical definitions and distinctions with the flesh and blood of modern culture and taste, and inspires into it a new life. In the place of Schleiermacher's pantheistic tendency, his Sabellian view of the Trinity, his skepticism concerning the existence of good and bad angels, his denial of the devil, we have here the orthodox views on these subjects, clearly stated and ably defended. The same improvements, and such they certainly are in a material point of view, may be expected from the remaining volumes, should they ever be published. The fact is that the peculiar heresies of Schleiermacher have been long thrown aside by his ablest disciples, and there is no doubt that he would do the same, could he lead his life over again in our own age.

The predominance of the Lutheran element is very natural in Twesten. For in Holstein, his native province, Lutheranism enters without a rival into the life-blood of the people. There labored his friend, the celebrated preacher Harms, than whom no man of modern times bore a stronger constitutional resemblance to the great Reformer of Wittenberg, and whose 95 Theses were a timely and successful translation of the famous Protestant Manifesto of 1517.

But with all his conviction of the essential truth of Lutheranism in its catholic and denominational doctrines, Twesten is perfectly free from sectarian bigotry and exclusiveness. This is implied already in his relation to Schleiermacher who never denied his Reformed origin; and in his position as theological teacher in a Church and University, where the Lutheran Confession is united with the Reformed. We quote here from his preface to the second volume, which clearly defines his position to Lutheranism and the Union:—

"It was the great error of the older Lutheran theologians—but not of the Lutheran alone, but more or less of all alike—that they would only suffer trees of one kind to grow within the enclosure of the Church, at least of the Lutheran Church. No one can more deeply regret than I do that the two evangelical churches separated from each other; that the Melanthonian type was excluded; that a Calixtus, an Arndt, a Spener, were so bitterly and so violently persecuted. No one can more heartily rejoice than I do, that in this respect a new era has arrived; that in a large part of Germany the Lutherans and the Reformed have come to a mutual understanding, (I assume from real conviction, and not from any compulsion of conscience,) to regard their confessional differences as no hinderance to church-fellowship; that, where people are assured of agreement in the fundamental articles of the gospel, they do not stand upon the letter of symbolical forms, in order to recognize each other as brethren of one mind and spirit. Only it should not be forgotten that the old Lutheran doctrine has a right to be properly recognized and represented; and that when men claim liberty for every other view, but grudge it to this one, they show the same partiality and intolerance, which they charge upon Lutheranism. The didactic theology here presented, it is true, is by no means a mere reiteration of the old; but while, according to Schleiermacher, a sound and vigorous life of the Church requires that two tendencies should be represented in it—both the conservative tendency which insists upon the permanent importance and reality of the old, so often too lightly set aside, and the progressive tendency which labors to cast everything into a new shape—yet is it more the first of these tendencies than the second, to which this work adheres."

This position Twesten still occupies. Both as an academic teacher and as a member of the highest ecclesiastical tribunal of Prussia, he defends, in a mild and conciliatory way, the conservative Lutheran interests in the bosom of the United Evangelical Church of Prussia.

CHAPTER XXX.

NITZSCH.

His general Character and Position—His Peculiarities as a Writer—Sketch of his Life and sphere of Activity—His System of Christian Doctrine, and theological Standpoint—His other Works—His character as Lecturer, Preacher to the University, and Member of the highest Church Council in Prussia—Lehnerdt—Strauss.

Of all the German divines still living there is none who carries with him so much moral weight in his personal appearance as Dr. Nitzsch, formerly of Bonn, now of Berlin. Hengstenberg surpasses him in energy and decision of will, as well as in clearly defined and settled views. But Nitzsch has greater dignity of character, as he is more venerable by age, and more winning by mildness and charity. He is emphatically *a homo gravis*, and yet very unassuming and plain in address and manner, both in the lecture room, in the pulpit, and at home. The words, *conscientia fundamentum est scientiæ*, which he wrote once in my Album, may be regarded as his motto. He moves like a patriarch, combining the present generation with the age of Schleiermacher and Neander, among the professors, ministers and students of Berlin. The concluding remarks of his beautiful oration on the death of the latter in 1850, will be fully applicable to himself, when he shall be called to his rest: "Still he (Neander) stands before us like the man who, from one watch of the night to the other, looks out for the breaking of the day. Still do we see him verifying before our eyes the words, 'Seek that which is above, not that which is on the earth.' And who is there among us, what youth, what man, what individual called to noble aims, who would not need to set true greatness before his eyes, and to see the truth confirmed that the root of greatness is simplicity and humility? Well! He who gave him, hath taken him away. The Lord's name be praised! *Have pia anima!* I add no more."

The personal weight of a character thoroughly imbued with the moral element of Christianity, must be taken into account, if we would form a proper estimate of this divine. His published productions give no just idea of the man, especially to one not fully master of the German. The English edition of his System of Christian Doctrine, the only one of his books, I believe, which has been translated, is said to be almost unreadable. His style, though nervous, pregnant and pointed, is heavy, abrupt and not unfrequently obscure, and offers unsurmountable difficulties to a translator. He has not the gift of clear analysis and transparent development of ideas which Twesten possesses in so eminent a degree; but he is more original and profound; more stimulating and suggestive. He abounds in brief, aphoristic and often enigmatical hints, like Bengel in his Gnomon. He scatters around him pregnant seeds of thought. He is a metaphysician who digs at the root of religious truth, or a miner who brings forth the precious metal in its primitive state for the elaboration of others.

Carl Immanuel Nitzsch was born in 1787, two years before Neander and Twesten. His father, Carl Ludwig, was General Superintendent and the first Director of the Theological Seminary at Wittenberg, the birth-place of the Lutheran Reformation, and published several Latin dissertations, to which the son occasionally refers with filial regard and affection. He received the thorough classical training for which the schools of Saxony and Prussia are distinguished. His principal theological teacher was probably Reinhard, one of the last and most respectable representatives of the supernaturalistic school. But he must have been early influenced by the new theological system of Schleiermacher, and the development of philosophy since Kant, and more particularly since Schelling. His first literary efforts were two Latin dissertations on the apocryphal gospels and on the Testament of the Twelve Patriarchs, (1810.)

He commenced public life in 1812, as deacon of that venerable castle-church at whose gates Luther affixed the famous ninety-five theses againt the indulgences of the Dominican mountebank Tetzel. Subsequently he became superintendent and theological professor of the Seminary at Wittenberg. Here he moved altogether on Lutheran ground, but fell heartily in with the Union as soon as it was introduced in 1817.

In 1822, he was elected professor of theology and preacher to the newly founded University of Bonn. Here he spent the years of his manhood as the acknowledged head of the theological faculty, and the chief attraction to students who came from various parts of

Germany and Switzerland to be benefited by his lectures, sermons and exemplary life. He took, at the same time, an active interest in all the practical questions and affairs of the Church in the Western provinces of Prussia, and acquired a love for the peculiar institutions and the practical spirit of the Reformed Confession which prevails on the banks of the Rhine, from its fountain-head in Graubündten to its mouth in Holland. He prefers the Presbyterial and Synodical constitution to every other form of church government.

In 1846, he was one of the leaders of the General Synod which convened at Berlin, and drew up the new formula of ordination, with a view to give a doctrinal expression to the Union. In 1847 he accepted a call to Berlin to fill the vacancy created in the theological faculty by the death of Dr. Marheineke. He is now the oldest divine of that University, but as active and useful as ever. In addition to his lectures, he preaches once in two weeks to the professors and students, and attends the sessions of the *Oberkirchenrath*, of which he is a regular member. Quite recently he was elected Propst (provost) of St. Nicolai. These are certainly as many important offices as any man in the vigor of life can well attend to.

As a theological author, Nitzsch is best known by his *System der Christlichen Lehre*, which appeared first in 1828, and often since, (6th edition, 1851.) It struck out a new path in the line of didactic theology. It gives, with compressed brevity, an exhibition of Christian dogmatics and ethics, as an undivided system of life, without, however, intending to dispute the right of the separate treatment of these two departments which has been usual since Danaeus and Calixtus. He thus brings out at every point the organic connection of doctrine and practice, of truth and holiness. He shows the moral bearing of all the articles of faith, and the doctrinal root of all the Christian virtues. This we take to be the most characteristic feature and the principal merit of his work. To English taste the ethical sections will appear more valuable than the dogmatic expositions, several of which, as the one on the atonement, differ considerably from the commonly received forms of statement. But his views are certainly genial and profound. He draws the material directly from the Holy Scriptures and the Christian consciousness, but in a number of learned exegetical, critical, historical and philosophical notes added to the sections, he refers to more recent systems and opinions, particularly those of a speculative kind, in the way of opposition or approval. He bows before the Scriptures with a reverential mind as the unerring word of the living God, and brings to light many precious pearls from its secret treasures. He thus represents the progress of the Schleiermacherian system to Biblical theology, while Twesten proceeded from the same school to the churchly orthodoxy of Lutheranism.

As regards the confessional differences, Nitzsch is more decidedly a man of the Union than his colleague just named. For although of strictly Lutheran descent, he spent, as already remarked, more than twenty years in the atmosphere of the Reformed church, and took an active part, from the start, in the Union, which he regards as the beginning simply of a movement that must comprehend ultimately, all the sections of Christendom. In his theology, the Lutheran and Reformed features are so intimately interwoven, that it would be a vain attempt to separate them. He esteems the Augsburg Confession as the fundamental and most national symbol of German Protestantism, and defended its public recognition under this character before the Church Diet of Berlin in 1853. But he equally admires the Heidelberg Catechism. In questions of worship he sympathizes more with the Lutheran principle, but in questions of government and discipline he stands on the Reformed side.

The same unionism pervades his Practical Theology, a very instructive and suggestive, but as yet unfinished work, and his numerous periodical writings.

Nitzsch is regarded as one of the ablest champions of Protestantism against the powerful attack of Möhler's Symbolik. His articles on the subject, first published in the "*Studien und Kritiken*," and then in separate book form in 1835, enriched by 100 Protestant Theses, are certainly more orthodox than the able and learned work of Baur against the same author, and commend themselves by their dignified, gentlemanly and truly Christian tone of polemics. Möhler himself expressed great respect for Nitzsch, and had formed the design of a lengthy reply, which, however, he never executed. But they can hardly be considered a full and satisfactory refutation of the most earnest, philosophical and eloquent controversial work of modern Romanism. The Protestant Möhler has not yet made his appearance.

He prepared a similar series of articles against the infidel Dogmatics of Strauss, a work which, like his notorious "Leben Jesu," ends in absolute negation, not only of all revealed truth, but even of the immortality of the soul, and thus refutes itself most effectually. He wrote also a number of Latin dissertations, and is one of the founders of, and frequent contributors to, three theological journals, the "Studien und Kritiken," the "Bonner Monatschrift," and the "Deutsche Zeitschrift für Christl. Wissenschaft und Christl. Leben."

As a lecturer, Nitzsch has the singular habit of half buttoning and unbuttoning his coat, and taking snuff at regular intervals. But the sense of ridicule is kept down by his dignified and venerable appearance, and the excellent matter of his lectures on the various branches of systematic and practical theology. He has probably more personal influence upon the students than any of his colleagues.

His sermons, of which several volumes were published, are not popular, but well calculated to instruct and edify an intellectual and literary audience. They abound in rich thought, taken from the fresh fountain of truth, presented without the drapery of eloquence, but with deep feeling and unction, and pervaded by a vein of earnestness that appeals to the inmost moral sensibilities of the heart. I recollect more particularly a most sublime and impressive discourse of his, delivered in March, 1854, in the Dorotheen Kirche, on the moral dignity and grandeur of Christ under his sufferings, and the duty of sacrificing his honor before men in order to receive it under a higher form from God. Professors

Ritter, Ranke, and other distinguished scholars listened to it with profound attention, and I heard them speak of him afterwards in high terms of admiration.

Nitzsch presides over a theological conference of the ministers of Berlin, and generally opens its monthly meetings with an expository lecture on some passage of Scripture, which is followed by a free discussion, and closed by a social meal. I heard once from his lips, on such an occasion, a truly sublime exposition of the seventeenth chapter of St. John, the sanctissimum of the Gospel history, which filled the audience with a thrilling sense of the awful majesty and depth of the Saviour's intercessory prayer, the grandest prayer ever uttered on earth.

As a member of the Prussian Oberkirchenrath, Nitzsch represents the confessional union of the Lutheran and Reformed church, or the consensus-party. His position in this respect is a very important and difficult one in view of the growing denominationalism around him. He defines his Unionism at length in his "Urkundenbuch der Evangelischen Union," (1853,) and in his more recent reply to Dr. Kahnis.

Finally, we must add that he is one of the founders and managers of the German Evangelical Church Diet, and took an active part in its leading reports and debates at most of its annual meetings since 1848.

Nitzsch, Hengstenberg and Twesten are the most prominent divines of Berlin. The other members of the theological faculty are Dr. Lehnerdt, the successor of Neander in the chair of Church History, an excellent teacher, of decidedly evangelical character, but hardly known as a writer; and Dr. F. Strauss, professor of practical theology, the author of a very instructive and interesting work on the Church Year, and several popular religious works, of which the "Glockentöne" have gone through a number of editions. He is at the same time one of the four court and cathedral preachers, and was in his younger years a very spirited and animated pulpit orator. He did a great deal of good among the higher classes of Berlin, and exerted much influence on the king, who admitted him to intimate personal intercourse before he ascended the throne. His son, Frederick Strauss, is *Privatdocent* of theology in Berlin, and the author of a popular work of travels to the holy land. Of the extraordinary professors, Vatke and Piper are best known; the first as a Hegelian, the other as an independent disciple of Neander, and a very learned ecclesiastical antiquarian.

CHAPTER XXXI.

JULIUS MULLER.

Personal Notice—Muller's Character as a Divine—His Work on Sin—His attempt to show the Doctrinal Unity of Protestantism—The Formula Consensus—The other Divines of Halle, Hupfeld, Jacobi, and Guericke.

Dr. Julius Muller is a contemporary, intimate friend and colleague of Dr. Tholuck, who gave him, under the name of Julius, a permanent place in his early work on Sin and Redemption, by lending him the beautiful letters to Guido, on the intellectual and moral conflict of a noble youth, winding his way through the dreary labyrinths of skepticism to the clear light of faith in the Redeemer. He is a brother of Ottfried Müller, one of the seven protesting professors of Göttingen, and an eminent Greek scholar and antiquarian, who died at Athens in 1840. Contrary to the rule of German divines, he labored first in the practical sphere before he entered the academic career. He was a number of years pastor at Schönbrunn in Silesia, his native province, then University preacher at Göttingen. In 1835 he received a call to Marburg as professor. From thence he removed to Halle in 1839, where he has labored ever since as teacher of the various branches of systematic and practical theology, and as a member of the Consistory for the province of Magdeburg. The students call him humorously the "Sünden-Müller," with reference to his great work on Sin, and to distinguish him from the legion of Müllers who are quite as common in Germany as the Millers and Smiths in England and America. But this is no mark of disrespect; on the contrary, he enjoys their unbounded regard and confidence, as a teacher, man and Christian.

Next to Tholuck, he forms undoubtedly the chief attraction of the University of Halle, and attaches young men, not so quickly, but more deeply and permanently to his person. He is a tall, dignified, fine looking, earnest, courteous and amiable Christian gentleman, whom it is impossible not to love and esteem. By some misfortune he lost one eye long since, and quite recently, we are sorry to learn, was struck with apoplexy, which injured his memory and threatens to interfere materially with the prosecution of his labors. His loss would be deeply felt, not only in Halle, but in Germany at large, as he combines much moral weight and practical wisdom with his learning, and stands as a sort of umpire amidst the ecclesiastical conflicts of the day.

Müller takes also a leading part in the movement to restore the matrimonial legislation of Prussia, which facilitates divorce for trifling reasons, to Scriptural and evangelical principles, and delivered a masterly essay on the sanctity and indissolubleness of marriage before the Church Diet at Frankfort, 1854, and a year afterwards before the Conference of Gnadau.

He is unquestionably one of the deepest and most

pious speculative divines of the present age, and at the same time a very polished and tasteful writer, which is quite a recommendation. For to write a good style was till more recently the exception rather than the rule among German theologians.

His largest work, and a lasting monument of his philosophical and theological scholarship, is "The Christian Doctrine of Sin," third edition, 1849, in two volumes. The English translation by the Rev. W. Pulsford, which forms volumes 27 and 29 of the excellent series of Clark's Foreign Library, is too literal and slavish, and for this reason frequently awkward and unintelligible. Nevertheless it was received favorably by the better organs of the English press. The *British Quarterly Review* speaks of the book as "the most weighty and important contribution to the cause of dogmatic theology which Germany has recently produced. It unites, in a high degree, depth and comprehensiveness with practical earnestness and clearness. It is profound even to the contentment of a German mind, yet rarely obscure and uninstructive; the author evinces his thorough metaphysical training, and his work is pervaded by the presence of a shining and disciplined intellect, and the rare mastery of a large and skillful argumentative grasp. He has in no sense taken up his subject as so much mere theological task-work by which to gain a reputation—but it has plainly been with him long a favorite sphere of reflection, the haunt and main region of his spirit during many years of silent and meditative preparation; he has felt its surpassing interest, its grand significancy, its solemn importance."

The true knowledge of sin lies at the foundation of Christian theology and experience. Without it we cannot understand the mystery of divine grace and the redemption through Christ. Schleiermacher, owing to the pantheistic leaning of his philosophy, is very unsatisfactory on this cardinal article. It was therefore a happy choice that Müller, one of his early disciples and admirers, should make it the subject of a profound investigation in the light of the Holy Scriptures, of Christian experience and an enlightened philosophy. He approaches his task with deep seriousness, and the feeling of its great difficulty. With all due respect for the different attempts to solve the problem of sin, he keeps constantly in mind the imperfection of all earthly knowledge, and the unsearchable background of the divine mysteries. This humility becomes a theologian and a Christian, infinitely better than that pride of science which characterizes so many writings of the Hegelian school. The method is for the most part speculative and dialectic, yet there is interwoven with it a large amount of carefully sifted exegetical and historical matter, touching the origin, nature and effect of sin, and its relation to human freedom. The author subjects the principles of the various philosophical systems from Plato to Hegel, as far as they have a bearing upon these questions and promise to answer them, to a careful and penetrating criticism. The order and arrangement of the material is perhaps not sufficiently clear and simple. Nor are the results always satisfactory; the origin of sin especially is a mystery still, and not cleared up by the theory of a transcendental, *pre-*

adamitic fall. But no one can lay aside the book, the study of which indeed requires close and earnest thought, without high esteem for the learning and character of the writer, and gratitude for much intellectual and spiritual benefit.

Should the author's life be spared, we may expect from him in due time a complete exhibition of the system of Christian dogmatics and ethics.

Passing by the solid and instructive reviews and essays which Dr. Müller furnishes occasionally for the pages of the *Deutsche Zeitschrift* of Berlin, of which he is one of the founders, and for Ullmann's *Studien und Kritiken*, we must mention another work which, though more immediately designed for the present conflict of unionism and confessionalism in Prussia, deserves, nevertheless, the attention of all who feel an interest in the doctrinal unity and difference of evangelical Protestantism.

We mean the book on the "Evangelical Union, its nature and divine right," 1854. It is written with tender regard to the orthodox Lutherans who have conscientious scruples about the Union, regarding it as a sacrifice of truth and compromise with error and indifferentism. It rests on a deep sense of the evil of schism in Protestantism, and an anxious desire to promote the harmony of the body of Christ. "To unite," he says, "what is internally divided, is an unprofitable work; but to divide what belongs together, is still more unprofitable." He discusses with much learning and depth, yet clearly, the unity and variety of the church in general, and the doctrinal differences of the Lutheran and German Reformed confessions in particular, especially the controversies on predestination and the Lord's Supper, with the view to show that the latter do not necessarily contradict and exclude each other, but represent different aspects of the same truth, and may and should be reconciled by going back to their religious root, and beyond them to a more scientific statement. The most important part, perhaps, is the draught of a *formula consensus*, as a doctrinal basis for the evangelical church of Prussia, which professes to be based upon the symbolical books of both churches as far as they agree, but which never yet has defined this agreement in a formal way. Müller's sketch is altogether based upon, and stated in the spirit, and often in the very words of the œcumenical, and the oldest Protestant symbols, especially the Augsburg, and Helvetic Confessions, the Articles of Smalkald, and the Heidelberg Catechism, and covers all the vital doctrines of the gospel.

Time must reveal whether this *formula* will remain a mere proposition, or be adopted as it is, or made at least the basis of a formal confession of the united Church. The author hopes it may yet be used for such a practical purpose at some future day; but he is modest enough to regard it merely as a preparatory work which admits of great improvements, and may require material changes. During the session of the Church Diet at Frankfort, a special conference was held for the purpose of discussing the subject of this doctrinal *consensus*, and a Committee consisting of Dr. Müller, and a few others, was appointed with the direction to draw up such a formula. But I am unable to say whether they have arrived at a definite result.

Besides Tholuck and Müller, the theological faculty of Halle includes Hupfeld, Moll and Jacobi, to whom must be added the extraordinary professors, Dähne, Guericke, Franke and Dietlein. Hupfeld is the successor of Gesenius, and not inferior to him in Hebrew and oriental learning, while far excelling him in a sound theological and Christian spirit. Moll is an able teacher and writer on the different branches of practical theology. Jacobi, who was recently called there from Königsberg, is one of the most faithful disciples of Neander, and lectures on church history. Of the extraordinary professors, Guericke, although very unpopular as a teacher, on account of his repulsive style of delivery, is best known abroad as a champion of Lutheran orthodoxy, and author of useful compilations and manuals on Church History, Archæology, and Introduction to the New Testament.

CHAPTER XXXII.

ULLMANN.

Ullmann's Academic Career—His Present Position and Labors as Prelate at Carlsruhe—The Character of his Theology—His Apologetic and Christological Works—The Sinlessness of Jesus—Essay on the Distinctive Character of Christianity—His Historical Works—The Reformers before the Reformation—Arguments for Protestantism—Gregory of Nazianzen—The Studien und Kritiken.

DR. CARL ULLMANN was born toward the end of the last century at Epfenbach in the Palatinate, studied partly at the University of Tübingen, where he formed the intimate friendship with the distinguished Swabian poet, Gustav Schwab, and commenced his professorial career at Heidelberg. In 1829 he accepted a call to the University of Halle, but in 1836 he returned to Heidelberg as Professor of ecclesiastical history and Church counsellor, (Kirchenrath,) and spent there the best years of his manhood.

In 1853 he was elected to the prelacy, or the highest ecclesiastical dignity of the evangelical Church in the grand duchy of Baden. He now resides at Carlsruhe, the capital of that country, and his time is principally taken up with matters of church government.

However much his withdrawal from the academic

chair may be regretted in the interest of theological science and literature, his services in the equally if not more influential position he now occupies, are very important. In connection with his like-minded colleague, the learned Dr. Bähr, the author of a very valuable work on the Symbolism of the Mosaic worship, he faithfully endeavors to build up the Protestant Church of Baden, which was deeply undermined by theological rationalism and political red-republicanism.

A General Synod met for this purpose at Carlsruhe in 1855, and its labors were crowned with as much success as could be expected under the circumstances. The rationalistic Catechism heretofore in use, is to be replaced by a far better one constructed on the basis of the small Lutheran and the Heidelberg Catechisms. Similar reforms are contemplated in regard to the liturgy, and the common school books. Both Ullmann and Bähr, although originally Reformed, stand on the Union of the two Confessions, which was introduced in Baden in 1819, at a period of prevailing religious indifferentism, but which is assuming now more and more, under the influence of these men and the excellent theological faculty of Heidelberg, a positive evangelical character. We only regret that the *Oberkirchenrath* of Baden in its zeal for the Union, saw fit to depose two restless old Lutheran ministers hostile to the Union, (Eichhorn and Haag,) by which act it exposed itself to the charge of intolerance.

Ullmann started from the school of Schleiermacher and Neander, and was at first somewhat latitudinarian in doctrine and too compromising in disposition; but he grew with the better spirit of the age, in orthodoxy and evangelical sentiment. He is of small stature, has a modest, but gentlemanly air, and a smiling pleasant countenance. His mind is not so strong and original as that of Schleiermacher, Rothe, Baur, and others, but remarkably clear, orderly, well balanced and stored with theological and general learning. His temper is quiet, mild and amiable, and yet, we should think, rather sensitive and irritable. He is none of the bold, war-like and commanding characters of the type of St. Paul and Luther, but belongs to the moderate, peaceful, conciliatory order of St. John and Melanthon. Of him may be said, what Luther remarked of "Master Philippus: "Er fährt säuberlich stille daher, säet und begeusst mit Lust, nach dem ihm Gott gegeben hat seine Gaben reichlich." He is also one of the best writers amongst the German divines. His style is transparent, easy and elegant, and gives evidence of fine classical culture and artistic taste.

Ullmann has acquired a lasting reputation by a number of works, equally distinguished for solid and well digested historical information, comprehensive views, calm and clear reflection, dignified and conciliatory tone, and masterly power of exhibition. They relate partly to apologetical, partly to historical subjects, partly to the religious questions of the day.

We mention first his beautiful little book on the *Sinlessness of Jesus.* It appeared originally as an essay in the "*Studien und Kritiken*" for 1828, was then printed separately, and increased, in the sixth edition of 1853, to 299 pages. In its present improved form, it must certainly be numbered among the most valuable contributions to the apologetic literature of the Church, and is better calculated, in our judgment, to satisfy an inquiring and well cultivated mind on the claims of our holy religion, than many large volumes on the Evidences of Christianity. It shows the way by which the author himself found the truth, and by which many a theological student of Germany has since escaped the whirlpool of rationalism and pantheism.

What think ye of Christ? This is the fundamental question on which our theology, religion and salvation depend. Nothing makes so deep and lasting an impression upon our mind and heart, and settles so firmly in us the conviction of the divine origin of Christianity, as a proper view of the person of its founder. Ullmann attempts no full Christology, but takes up simply an essential part of it and treats it, both under its exegetical, dogmatical and ethical aspects, more fully and satisfactorily than was ever done before. Starting with an exposition of the nature of sin and sinlessness, he proves, from the testimony of Christ and the apostles, from the whole character of the Saviour as exhibited in the gospels, and from the redeeming and sanctifying effects of his religion upon every man who submits to its power, that he was not only free from sin, but that He realized in his person the ideal of moral and religious perfection. In the third section he refutes the objections which are raised against the reality of the sinlessness from the development of the person of Christ, and of the plan of his kingdom, from his temptation and several other facts in his life, and also the philosophical and empirical arguments against the possibility of such moral perfection in a human being. In the fourth section he draws from these premises the conclusions as to the character of Christ as the God-man, and his position in the history of the world as the Saviour of the world, and author of eternal life. An Appendix treats of the different interpretations of the temptation of Christ in the wilderness.

It is impossible to read this book attentively without being edified as well as instructed, and overwhelmed with the glory of the only begotten of the Father that shines through the veil of his flesh upon the eye of faith and enlightened reason. It would be desirable to present a full translation of Ullmann's *Sündlosigkeit Jesu* in its last newly elaborated and greatly enlarged edition, to the English reader. To it might be added his essay, *Historisch oder Mythisch;* where he brings out the significance of Christ's personality under a historical point of view, as an unanswerable argument to the infidel work of Strauss on the Life of Jesus.

In this connection we may direct attention to a somewhat similar work of a promising English divine, John Young, entitled "The Christ of History," (London and New York,) which endeavors to prove, on a different plan and with less learning, but with considerable reasoning power and great effect, the godhead of Christ, not from miracles or prophecy, but simply from the peculiar character and the particular outer conditions of his *manhood*. Its leading idea is, that Jesus was the one wonderful personality, the only one, of all that ever dwelt on this earth, who had more immediate, constant and perfect access to the infinite fountain of being than was possible to the constitution of a mere creature.

Closely connected with the subject of the work on the sinless perfection of Christ's person, and equally interesting and instructive, is Ullmann's tract on the distinctive character and essence of the Christian Religion, or, *Das Wesen des Christenthums.* It is free from learned apparatus, and treated in a manner that makes it accessible to the educated layman as well as the professional theologian. Soon after its first appearance in the *Studien und Kritiken* for 1845, Dr. Nevin furnished a free and spirited translation of it, as an introduction to his "Mystical Presence." But it was subsequently much enlarged and includes in its third edition (Hamburg, 1849,) several additional chapters on the nature of Christian faith, love and the Church, also a valuable critical appendix on Feuerbach's infamous book on the Essence of Christianity. We would greatly prefer, if the author had entered also into the Scriptural part of the investigation, and made it the basis, instead of confining himself to a philosophico-dogmatical exposition.

Ullmann derives the whole meaning and significance of the Christian religion from the person of its founder as representing the true and abiding union of God and man. The ancient Greek Church, which produced the dogmas, and styled itself emphatically the Orthodox, viewed it mainly as doctrine. The Latin Church in the middle ages, which had to civilize and regulate the life of the Northern barbarians, and called itself the Catholic in an exclusive sense of the term, regarded it as a system of moral law and a disciplinary institute with the claim of universal authority. The Evangelical Churches, which sprang up with the Reformation of the sixteenth century in the bosom of the Germanic nations, find the essence of Christianity in its character, as gospel and redemption, by which the sinner is justified before God through faith, and is made truly free.

These three historical conceptions of Christianity, as doctrine, as moral law, and as a source of redemption and spiritual freedom, are true as far as they go, but they do not exhaust the whole truth. They must be comprehended in a fourth view, which regards it as the absolutely perfect religion, because it unites God and man, not in a pantheistic sense, however, but with the full recognition of a personal God, and his positive revelation to sinful, fallen man. This view unfolded itself from an early period, especially in the mysticism of the middle ages, and appears more fully in the philosophical and theological speculations of modern times, although frequently distorted into pantheism. We may expect that this conception of Christianity, like the former three, will be actualized in a corresponding form of organization, in the Church of the future, that shall join in harmony the highest spirituality, catholicity, and freedom, and reflect the fullness of the divine-human life of the Saviour's person in his people.

This historical progress through which the apprehension of Christianity passed in the actual life of church history, was reproduced by modern theology in the way of reflection. It has been described successively as doctrine by the older orthodox and supernaturalistic divines, as a moral law by the Kantian school, as a system of redemption by Schleiermacher, and as a real union of the divine and human in the Hegelian philosophy. Ullmann carefully points out the truth in these various conceptions, and at the same time their defects and errors, as they appear in the modern schools, especially the Kantian, which is essentially rationalistic, and the Hegelian, which is essentially pantheistic.

Christ is indeed the teacher of all saving truth, the law-giver and king of his people, the redeemer and Saviour of the world. But if we ask what constituted him all this, we must reply, his own person, at once human and divine; his life filled with all the attributes of God, and representing at the same time the highest conception of nature and man; complete and self-sufficient in its own fullness, and yet by this fullness itself the principle of a new corresponding life-process, in the way of self-communication, for the human world. Religion in its very nature is love. It starts in this character from God as redeeming love to man, and returns again in the form of human love to its source; a circling stream from God to God. Its highest manifestation on both sides, must constitute the utmost summit of the religious life. This we find in Christ as the living fountain, which sends its streams over to the community of believers, without ever being exhausted, or even diminished, so that the very last and highest development of the Church will only be a reflection of his glory and forever centre around his theanthropic mediatorial person.

But we must proceed to Ullmann's "*Reformers before the Reformation*," in two volumes, 1841–42, which form now a part of the new series of Clark's Foreign Theological Library. This work assigns to the author a rank among the first church historians of the present century, and justified the expectation that he would be elected the successor of Neander in Berlin. It is certainly one of the strongest historical arguments for the Reformation which has yet been presented, and under this view mainly we here direct attention to it.

The first and principal justification of Protestantism lies in its essential agreement with the New Testament, especially the epistles of St. Paul. Hence a certain Protestant, when asked by a Romanist, "Where was your religion before Luther?" promptly replied, "Where yours never was, in the Bible." If this argument be well founded, it cannot be neutralized by any amount of tradition. We are far from undervaluing the testimony of ecclesiastical antiquity. But of what avail are all quotations from the school-men and the fathers, great and good, yet erring men as they were, in favor of this or that Romish dogma or usage, as long as we have the inspired and unerring word of God on our side, and as long as we can point to the epistles of the Romans and Galatians, as the grand charter of our evangelical liberty and direct communion with the Saviour!

The second great argument for evangelical Protestantism may be found in the effects which it produced in the religious, moral and intellectual life of those nations which embraced it, and which compare favorably, to say the least, with all the doings of Romanism since the sixteenth century. All the philosophical discussions about the defects of the Protestant principle will fail to carry ultimate conviction, if it can be proved by the testimony of three hundred years, that it bore good fruit, by which, the Saviour himself tells us, we should judge the character of the tree. We do not mean, of course, that Protestantism in any of its forms is perfect; on the contrary, we look for still higher and better manifestations of Christianity in time to come. But we do maintain that it has done as much good in proportion to its means and the comparatively short time of its operation, as any other form of Christianity, and need not be ashamed of a comparison in this respect with either the Greek or the Roman Church.

But Protestantism needs another kind of historical argument in addition to this, in order to be fully justified as a link in the unbroken chain of Christ's kingdom on earth. It must be shown that it was not an arbitrary outbreak and radical revolution, as Romanists would make us believe, but a necessary product of the preceding life of the church, and a real reformation with a positive Christian principle that carried the previous life of the Church to a higher position.

This argument again has a negative and a positive aspect. It can be made to appear, first, that the Reformation was called forth as an inevitable reaction of the better life of the Church itself against the many abuses and corruptions that had crept into it during the middle ages. Under this view the Protestant was right, when he answered the question of the Romanist, "Where was Protestantism before the Reformation?" by the other question, "Where was your face this morning before it was washed?" But then, it must be shown at the same time, that the distinctive principles of the Reformers were not absolutely new, but were proclaimed already in previous centuries, not only by sectaries, but more clearly and fully by some of the best men within the bosom of mediæval Catholicism, so that we may speak in some sense of a history of Protestantism before the Reformation as well as after it.

This is precisely the position and object of the work before us. The first attempt of the kind was made by Flacius, the chief author of the Magdeburg Centuries, in his learned book on the *Testes Veritatis*, or Witnesses of the Evangelical Truth in Catholic Times. But what Flacius attempted in a crude form in the infancy of Protestant historiography, and with an unmeasured polemical zeal against the Romanists of his age, Ullmann has carried out with all the help of modern erudition, in the calm, truth-loving spirit of an impartial historian, and with full acknowledgment of the great and abiding merits of Catholicism as the Christianizer and civilizer of the barbarian nations of the dark ages. With him, the Reformation is not so much a rebellion, as the flower and fruit rather of the better and deeper life of Christianity, that slumbered in the maternal bosom of mediæval Catholicism. And this, it seems to us, is the noblest and strongest historical vindication of it.

Ullmann pays special attention to the German and Dutch forerunners of the Reformation, from the thirteenth to the fifteenth century, and treats them with exhaustive minuteness of detail. We find here reliable and carefully sifted information on the life and theology of John von Goch, John von Wesel, the Brethren of the Common Life, and the various schools of the mystics,

Ruysbroek, Suso, Tauler, Thomas a Kempis, (to whom Ullmann vindicates, with triumphant success, the inimitable book on the Imitation of Christ,) the anonymous author of the curious tract on German Theology, (recently translated into English by Susanna Winkworth, with prefaces from Chevalier Bunsen, and Rector Kingsley,) and Staupitz, the patron and early friend of Luther. The latter and principal part of the second volume is taken up with the author's former monograph on John Wessel, in an improved form which leaves but little to be added.

But the work of Ullmann, although very satisfactory as far as it goes, does not exhaust the general subject, which would require two or three additional volumes. He leaves out of view the important preparatory movements of Wicliffe and the Lollards, in England; of Huss and the Hussites, in Bohemia; of Savonarola, in Italy, and of what is generally called the Revival of Letters and classical learning by such men as Erasmus, Reuchlin, Agricola, not to speak of the more negative preparation of the Reformation by the anti-Catholic sects of the middle ages, especially the Waldenses and Albigenses. A complete work on this whole subject in a condensed and popular form for the general reader, would do good service to the cause of sound conservative Protestantism.

We can only allude to Ullmann's monograph on Gregory of Nazianzen, (1825,) as the most complete work on the life and doctrines of this eminent divine of the ancient Greek church, who, for his able defence of the Nicene faith, and the divinity of Christ, was emphatically styled the "Theologian."

Finally, Ullmann is well known as the chief founder and editor of the "*Studien und Kritiken*," which has been before the public since the year 1828, as one of the ablest and most learned theological journals of Germany. It contains many contributions of more than passing interest from his own pen, and that of his friend and co-editor, Prof. Umbreit, of Heidelberg, the author of valuable commentaries on several books of the Old Testament, also from Schleiermacher, who suggested the establishment of such a periodical, Lücke, Nitzsch, Gieseler, Tholuck, Müller, Bleek, Hundeshagen, and other distinguished divines.

CHAPTER XXXIII.

ROTHE.

Rothe's Position and Genius—His Theological Ethics—Views on Speculative Theology, or Theosophy—His Work on the Primitive Church—Views on the Origin of Episcopacy—Comparison with Isaac Taylor and Nevin, on Early Christianity—Rothe's Theory of the Church as related to the State, and its final dissolution into a new Theocracy—Critical Remarks.

Dr. Richard Rothe, a cotemporary and early friend of Tholuck, Müller, and Olshausen, was formerly Director of the Theological Seminary at Wittenberg; for a short time, like Tholuck, chaplain of the Prussian embassy at Rome, at the time when Bunsen occupied the legation; then Professor and Seminary Director in Heidelberg. In 1849, he succeeded Dr. Nitzsch in Bonn; but in 1853 or '54, he returned to Heidelberg to take the place of Ullmann, and will probably spend there the rest of his days. He is exceedingly popular as a teacher, and enjoys the respect and admiration of all who know him personally as a most excellent man and humble Christian. But out of Germany he is little known, and will only be read and appreciated by those who take a very special interest in the more remote speculations and researches of German theology.

We must assign to Rothe the very first place among

the *speculative* divines of the present day. He surpasses even Nitzsch, Müller, Dorner, Martensen, and Baur in vigorous grasp and independence of thought, and is hardly inferior in this respect to Schleiermacher. But like him, he is too original in his views to form a school in the strict sense of the term. He will always occupy an isolated position, and be a pilgrim and stranger in the surrounding world. Of this he is himself painfully conscious, but cannot help it. His province is rather to stir up and stimulate the youthful mind, and to open new paths for theological speculation.

His principal production is the System of Theological Ethics, or Moral Theology, in three volumes, 1845–'48. We regard it as the greatest work on speculative divinity which has appeared since Schleiermacher's Dogmatics—full of power, boldness, and originality. It is truly a work of art as well as of science, and the several stones of the ethical system are reared up here into a magnificent Gothic cathedral by the skill of a master architect. Those who formed their idea of this important science from such books as Dr. Wayland's popular Moral Philosophy, will lose both sight and hearing before they have read two pages of the work before us. But those who are accustomed to go beneath the shallow surface of things to the fundamental principles and general laws of the moral universe, will feel amply repaid by a careful study of it, however often they may be compelled to differ *toto cœlo* from the author's views.

Rothe's Ethics are in some sense a complete system of speculative theology, or theosophy. He defines ethics to be the science of the moral; but he understands the moral (das Sittliche) in the widest sense of the word, so as to include in it the whole life of the human mind, viewed as a mastery of the material nature by the rational personality, or a process of transformation of nature into the spirit; and this life not only in its individual form, but also in all the social relations of the family, science and art, Church and State. He then handles his subject under the threefold aspect of the doctrine of the good, (*Güterlehre,*) the doctrine of virtue, (*Tugendlehre,*) and the doctrine of duties, (*Pflichtenlehre.*) In the introduction and in the first part he discusses profoundly and yet clearly the fundamental questions and general principles, and leads the reader through the abstrusest regions of thought up to the giddy height of speculation, until in spirit he attains to the complete realization of the idea of morality, viz., the absolute dominion of mind over matter, or of reason over nature, or the perfect kingdom of Christ upon the new earth wherein dwelleth righteousness. He is, however, well aware that science and life are by no means commensurate, and that speculation of the widest grasp and the keenest insight can only afford a relative degree of satisfaction. "Woe's me!" he says as modestly as beautifully, "if God and the world do not continue beyond all measure greater to me than my own idea of them." In the two following parts, especially the third, he descends gradually into the more familiar regions of the concrete moral life, and unfolds some of the most exalted and noble views respecting the different virtues and duties of a Christian man, such as one seeks in vain for in most of the popular manuals of moral philosophy.

Dr. Rothe professes to know nothing of philosophy and the wisdom of this world. Like Schleiermacher, he wishes to keep it entirely distinct and separate from theology. And yet an English and American reader would find the theological writings of both these eminent authors replete with philosophy.

To solve this apparent contradiction, we must remember, in the first place, that Rothe is no follower of any other man's philosophy. He has evidently learnt much from Hegel and Schleiermacher, but their ideas undergo a process of transformation in his brain, and come out as something altogether new and original.

In the next place, we must make a *distinction* between philosophical and theological speculation. The first starts from self-consciousness, the Cartesian principle *cogito, ergo sum*, and proceeds according to the laws of natural reasoning. The second begins with the consciousness of God in the human soul, rests on religious experience, and finds its objective contents provided ready to its hand in divine revelation.

Rothe's speculation is altogether of the latter kind. As already intimated, he is a theosopher rather than a philosopher—like Clemens of Alexandria, Jacob Böhm, Oetinger, Baader, von Schaden. The consciousness of the Divine is to him the primary datum, the starting point for speculation. This consciousness he regards as an immediately certain fact, more certain and undeniable even than self-consciousness. We may quote here in further illustration some characteristic sentences from the introductory sections of Rothe's Theological Ethics, which will give the reader a pretty clear idea of his whole speculative stand-point and method.

"Piety," he says, "has already essentially ceased to be piety, so soon as it needs for its certitude a *proof* either of its own reality, or that of its object. The confession of the pious is this: God is as immediately certain to me as myself, because I cannot feel or conceive of the consciousness and the thought of myself in any other way, than as immediately connected with the feeling and the thought of God; self-consciousness cannot complete itself within me without the Divine consciousness; or, rather, God is to me more immediately certain than myself; for in the light of my Divine consciousness my self-consciousness first truly realizes itself: God is to me the absolutely and immediately certain, and I become first truly certain of myself by means of my certainty of God." Then, speaking of the difference of philosophical and theological speculation, he remarks: "However nearly they may be related to each other, yet, in form, they must always be distinct; for though proceeding by one and the same law, yet they go two different roads, because they start from two different points. Both construe the universe *a priori:* philosophical speculation thinks and comprehends it by virtue of the idea of self, theological speculation by virtue of the idea of God, on which account it is called theosophy. Theological speculation can only begin with the idea of God; philosophical speculation, which apparently cannot begin with it, will be obliged to end by it, when everything else is brought into order and harmony."

This religious or theological speculation, he goes on to show, is not at all necessary to piety as the condition of its inward certitude, which is primary, absolute, and altogether independent upon any demonstration of the logical understanding; but it is necessary, in order that piety might truly comprehend itself. "Piety (and that of a Christian character) is essentially an affair of the whole man: he only is truly pious who is so, or wishes to be so with his whole being; not only with all his feelings and impulses, but also with all the faculties of the understanding and powers of the will. On the side of the self-consciousness piety is, primitively speaking, an affair of feeling, as on the side of activity an affair of impulse; but by virtue of an inward necessity it cannot remain so. Without destroying itself, as religious feeling, it marches onwards, by virtue of its own inward vital energy, to religious thinking; first of all, to mere reflection, but then afterwards to religious speculation. In this way it makes good to the understanding its original, immediate, and (on the side of feeling) absolute certitude; and, however superfluously, furnishes a proof for its own truth. But piety adduces this proof, not in order to demonstrate to itself its own certitude, but in order formally to expound the foundation of the same. Theological speculation thus springs out of an immediate religious life; out of the immediate desire of piety itself clearly to understand all it possesses, to know what infinite riches lie hidden in its spontaneous fullness, while yet in its immediate and unreflective form. (Comp. 1 Cor. ii. 12.) Thinking, and that speculative thinking, is, therefore, to it an absolute necessity, in exactly the same proportion in which the function of thought generally is developed in the religious individual. Religious speculation has, therefore, its motive and occasion, not by any means in religious skepticism, but, on the contrary, in an unconditioned religious vitality. In the plenitude of its absolute certainty, it is bold enough to consider even speculation as a province springing out of itself, and to venture on its conquest. In the inspiration of this most joyous self-confidence, it trusts itself fearlessly upon the ocean of thought, well assured that it will not be overwhelmed in it. That it must be ultimately successful in speculating upon itself, it is well assured from the immediate unconditioned certainty of its own absolute reality; but even in the feeling of its own exuberance, it says freely to itself that it can only succeed by a slow process, and by the concentration of all its powers."

As to the creed of the Church, Rothe occupies a very independent relation to it. This follows very naturally from his views of the Church, which he does by no means identify with Christianity, as we shall see more fully hereafter. He boldly asserts that speculative theology must be heterodox, in a good sense of the term; for it rises from the fact, that reason no longer finds in the dogmas of the Church a satisfactory expression of Christian truth, and seeks to elevate them to a higher form, and to present them under new aspects. Accordingly, his views on the Trinity, his Christology and Soteriology agree neither with the Lutheran, nor the Reformed, nor any other existing orthodoxy. They stand alone as ingenious attempts to give these doctrines a new scientific shape and form. Quite different, however, is the relation of speculative theology to the Holy

Scriptures in the Evangelical Church. As the authentic expression of Christianity in its original freshness and purity, they are, according to Rothe, the indispensable Canon and rule for all branches of theology. Whenever theological speculation contradicts the Scriptures, it must be in error, and must confess its results to be abortive. Its highest aim should be rather to furnish a key for opening the full sense of the Bible beyond the past and present state of knowledge in the various denominations. In its procedure, speculative theology must, indeed, be guided, says Rothe, by the requisitions of thought, and the authority of logic and dialectics. But at the end of its independent labor, it approaches the tribunal of the Scriptures, and, conscious of its own weakness, it submits itself unconditionally to their infallible judgment. He does not inform us, however, who is to decide the true meaning of the Scriptures in the case of dissent.

Rothe's theology or theosophy, then, while it is independent of, and partly at war with, the particular systems of Church orthodoxy as expressed in the symbolical books, professes and sincerely wishes to be agreed with Christianity as contained in the Bible. In a beautiful passage of the preface, he solemnly declares that, "unconditional faith in Christ as the real and only Redeemer, and love to him, is the animating principle of his theological speculation," that Christ is to him "the sanctissimum of humanity, the highest which ever entered the consciousness of man, a sunrise in history, which alone sheds light over all the objects that fall under our observation."

But here the question arises, Is it right and safe to

make such a distinction between Christianity and the Church?

This leads us to speak of another remarkable book of this eminent scholar, which made great sensation in its day, "*Die Anfänge der christlichen Kirche, und ihrer Verfassung*," of which the first volume appeared in 1837. The second volume, though long completed in manuscript, was never published.

This work on the Primitive Church has a historical, and a philosophical aspect. The body of it is a most learned and elaborate discussion on the organization of ancient Christianity, the rise of episcopacy, and the development of the catholic idea of the church from the days of the apostles to the age of St. Augustin. The author tries to show that the episcopal supervision grew out of the wants of the Church towards the end of the first century, under the direct sanction of the surviving apostles, especially St. John in Asia Minor, and found its way instinctively into all parts of Christendom, as a substitute for the apostolical office, and the only form of government which promised to secure the unity and to maintain the identity of the Church during those times of bloody persecution from without, and heretical perversion from within.

Under this view, Rothe's *Anfänge* are a real masterpiece of critical research on one of the most difficult and obscure topics of ancient Church history. I know of no Anglican work that could at all compare with it in well digested learning, penetrating sagacity and power of combination, and make out so strong a case for the apostolical origin and historical necessity of episcopacy. But he lays too much stress upon many vague and unreliable traditions, and his very ingenuity and talent of critical combination leads him astray to hasty conclusions. Hence there is not a single German historian, (Thiersch may be mentioned as an exception, but he is an Irvingite,) who has adopted his view.

The standpoint of Rothe, however, is very different from that of high church Anglican divines, on the same subject. He has no intention to defend the Episcopal hierarchy in itself against Presbyterianism, or Congregationalism, or any other ecclesiastical constitution of the present time. On the contrary, he regards it as a merely temporary institution, which was destined to pass away and to make room for other forms of organization. His only design is to illustrate Episcopacy in its natural rise out of the needs of the Church when she had become widowed, so to speak, by the departure of the apostles, and in its historical necessity for the earliest centuries,—and this in organic connection with the whole ancient idea of the Church as the body of Christ, as a visible unity, that connects itself with the apostles by an outward, tangible and unbroken succession in doctrine and discipline. His book would prove too much for the Anglicans, inasmuch as they detach the Episcopal forms from those catholic ideas which produced, at a later period, under the same historical necessity and monarchical impulse, the Metropolitan, Patriarchal, and Papal constitutions, and thus carried up the hierarchical organization to a pyramidical apex, until this was broken at the time of the Reformation, and gave way to the various forms of Protestantism. Rothe has shown beyond successful contradiction, we think, that the animus and tendency of the second and third centuries, as regards the idea of the Church and its attributes of unity, catholicity, holiness and apostolicity, was not Protestant, but strongly Catholic, and found its natural completion in the Roman primacy as the visible centre of unity.

In this respect, his "*Anfänge*" form an interesting parallel to Isaac Taylor's "Ancient Christianity," a very learned and able work, which was intended originally to be an indirect refutation of Puseyism. It makes out a strong case indeed against it on its own historical ground. For it proves successfully that the Nicene age which the Oxford school holds up, with pedantic zeal, as the true type of primitive Catholicity, in opposition to Romanism as well as Protestantism, was already decidedly Romanizing in doctrine, discipline and mode of piety, and that the later Romanism, instead of being an apostacy from the Christianity of Basil and Ambrose, of Cyril and Jerome, was its natural development, and in many respects even an improvement upon it. He makes large use of Salvianus, who, although himself a Catholic, gives an appalling picture of the moral corruptions of the Christians of his age, as contrasted with the heathen barbarians. Taylor shows also, by ample quotations, that some of the most distinguished champions of the Church of the fourth and fifth centuries carried the fondness for miracles, the idolatrous veneration of saints and relics, and the glorification of human works, of monastic and ascetic piety, voluntary poverty and celibacy, etc., fully as far, if not farther, than the divines of the fully grown Papacy.

Dr. Nevin, in his famous articles on Early Christianity, and on Cyprian, in the *Mercersburg Review*, discussed the same subject as Taylor, with equal vigor and earnestness, but with the opposite intention not to attack the error, but to defend the truth which underlies the old catholic doctrines and usages, to point out the antagonism of modern unchurchly and unsacramental Puritanism with the theology of the œcumenical creeds, and to show the necessity of some theory of historical development in order to reconcile Protestantism with the idea of an unbroken Church in the world, and with the age of martyrs and confessors.

Dr. Rothe has no polemical reference either to Puseyism, as Taylor, or to Puritanism, as Nevin. Nor is he troubled in the least by the real or apparent difference between the modern Protestant and the ancient Catholic Christianity. With all his admission of the essentially Romanizing tendency of the age of Ignatius, Cyprian and Leo, and with all his regard for this form of Christianity, as a great historical phenomenon, he is as decidedly and thoroughly Protestant in his constitution and conviction as Neander, who puts a somewhat different face upon the patristic theology, and regards it as more nearly approaching in spirit to sound evangelical Protestantism than Rothe.

This appears clearly from the philosophical portion of his work on the Primitive Church. In the First Book, (pp. 1–138,) for which he expresses more concern than for all the rest, he analyzes at length the relation of the Church to Christianity, and arrives at the startling conclusion that the Church is merely a transient form of

Christianity, and must resolve itself at last into the State. This view drew upon him sharp attacks not only from his own former friend, Hengstenberg, and other orthodox reviewers, but even from theologians of the Hegelian school, whose philosophical assumptions seem logically to lead to a similar result. Hence he never published the second volume.

To do him justice, we must remember that Rothe starts with an ideal conception of the State which has as yet nowhere been realized. He understands by it a thoroughly Christianized community of nations, a family of God embracing the whole of mankind. He has, of course, not the remotest thought, that Christianity which he regards as the absolute and perfect religion, will ever perish; on the contrary, he contemplates its complete triumph over the world. But he makes a distinction between Christianity or the Kingdom of Heaven, and the Church, and maintains that the perfect realization of the former is that of a State, or a kingdom, as the very name seems to indicate. His opinion is that the Christian religion will so interpenetrate the whole moral life of mankind, and become so naturalized in all the relations of society, that there will be no longer any room left at last for a separate and distinct religious organization, i. e., for a Church, but that the Church itself will pass over into a Divine State or theocracy including all nations.

This process of a dissolution of the Church, our author thinks, is very slow, and may require many centuries or thousands of years for its completion. But it has actually commenced with the Reformation that destroyed the outward unity, so essential to the nature of the

Church as a body. The old Protestant divines still retained the Catholic idea of the Church, while they had lost its reality, by making a distinction between the visible and invisible Church, and ascribing the attributes of unity, catholicity and holiness to the latter only, and not to the former. This whole distinction, however, he regards as untenable, since the very conception of the Church requires an organization, and consequently visibility. The fact is that the Church has since that time broken up more and more into an indefinite number of confessions, denominations and sects, and the tendency of Protestantism is, not to reconstruct the former organization of Christianity, but to prepare for it gradually a new and higher form of existence in the natural order of society, i. e., the State.

But here we must ask, Has the State advanced in Christian character in proportion as the Church lost her power? Has it not shown of late a disposition in Europe (think of the first French revolution, and the revolutions of 1848,) to emancipate itself not only from the control and influence of the Church, but from Christianity and religion altogether, and to set itself up on an atheistic and materialistic basis? And if we look to America, the land of the future, does it not present a complete separation of Church and State without the least disposition on the side of the former to resolve itself into the latter, and to entrust the care of religion to statesmen and politicians? And has not, on the other hand, the recent revival of Christianity both in Europe and America, both in Protestantism and Romanism, been at the same time a revival of the Churches and their peculiar institutions? Does not Rothe's view, if it is to be carried into practice, impose upon the ministers of the Church the suicidal duty of laboring for the dissolution of the Church, that the ideal Christian State may the more speedily appear?

These are only some of the difficulties and objections to this interesting, but singular theory. I had a long conversation with the excellent Dr. Rothe, in 1854, on this topic, and pressed upon his consideration especially the independent position of the spiritual and secular powers in our own country, which seems to indicate strongly that Church history, in the new world at least, moves in a direction the very opposite of his speculation. He denied the force of the objection, inasmuch as in the United States Christianity had ceased to be a power and organization over against the people, or outside of it, a hierarchy, a priesthood, a particular caste, or whatever you may call it, and had become, or promised to become, a truly national concern, the voluntary expression of the people's will, an inherent element of the general life, and that was the very thing he wanted.

Yet Christianity exists in the United States in the form of churches, nourished by the means of grace, and these churches are clearly determined to maintain their independence of the State government, with all due respect for the civil authority in all temporal matters. It is true the churches are divided. But can they not be united by a new reformation? It is true that none of the existing ecclesiastical organizations can be regarded as perfect and final, and hence the folly of every form of exclusive denominationalism or sectarianism. Christianity is infinitely larger, broader, richer, deeper, than any of the visible church organizations that exist at present, or have existed in times past. So far Rothe is perfectly right. We hold, also, that Christianity tends to naturalize itself more and more in the world, but not with the view to be secularized, but rather to spiritualize the world and to transform it into the heavenly kingdom. We think it very likely that the separate existence of Church and State is merely a transition to a final union of them in a theocracy, where God will be all in all.

But instead of saying that the Church shall be dissolved into the State, we would rather reverse Rothe's formula and say, that the State shall be transformed into the Church, and all the kingdoms and powers of this world shall be given to the people of God, that Christ may rule king of nations, as he now ruleth king of saints in the Church which is his body, the fulness of Him that filleth all in all.

CHAPTER XXXIV.

DORNER.

Personal Notice—Dorner's Theological Position and Early Popularity—His History of Christology—Other Literary Labors—Relation to the Practical Questions of the Age.

DR. J. A. DORNER, one of the ablest speculative divines of the age, is the son of a clergyman in Würtemberg, graduated at the University of Tübingen as the first in his class, made a literary journey to the North of Germany, Holland and England, and returned to his alma mater as *Repetent*, (fellow and tutor.) After the death of the venerable Steudel, the last of the supernaturalists of the old order, he was elected his successor as professor of systematic theolgy, in 1838, before he had attained the usual age for such an important post. I heard his first course of lectures, on apologetics and dogmatics, into which he threw the whole energy of his mind, laboring to prove the harmony of Christian theology and sound philosophy, and making the dialectics of Schleiermacher and Hegel subservient to the defence of the truths of revelation, while Dr. Baur employed his genius and learning, and the same categories of Hegel, for the opposite purpose of undermining the historical foundations of Christianity. He formed thus, in connection with the excellent Dr. Schmid, a powerful opposition to the so-called Tübingen School, which just then unfolded its greatest activity and influence. A few years afterwards, he accepted a call to the University of Kiel in Holstein, and subsequently to Königsberg; from thence to Bonn, and finally, in 1853, to Göttingen.

Dorner combines profound learning, critical penetration and power of generalization, with an earnest Christian spirit. He is thoroughly trained in the ancient and modern schools of philosophy, and gave evidence, on his first appearance before the public, of his ability to defeat the pantheistic Hegelians with their own weapons, and thus to do most important service at that particular crisis of German theology. Hence his sudden popularity, and the many calls which urged him from one university to another, to the injury perhaps of his literary labors.

He owes his early reputation to a truly valuable, and we may say, classical history of Christology, (*Entwicklungsgeschichte der Lehre von der Person Christi,*) from the close of the apostolic age down to the present time. It appeared first in 1836 and '37, in the Theological Quarterly Review of Tübingen, since discontinued, and then, somewhat enlarged, as a separate volume. Subsequently, the author re-wrote it entirely, and more than doubled its size. The first volume of the second edition, which comes down to the Œcumenical Council of Constantinople, A. D. 381, and embraces not less than 1130 pages, was published in 1845; the second and last volume, which will be equal in size, is not quite finished to this day, owing no doubt in part to the author's frequent changes of residence.

In this greatly improved form, the work before us is the most elaborate and complete history of the ecclesiastical doctrine of Christ's person, viewed in close connection with the inseparable dogmas of the Incarnation and the Holy Trinity, and will be quoted as an authority for a long time to come. The subject is of central importance to the whole system of theology. It is doubly so in view of the fact that the latest and most subtle forms of infidelity were principally directed against the Gospel history and the theanthropic foundation of the Christian Church. Shortly before the first edition of Dorner's Christology, Strauss, his fellow student, had published the famous Life of Jesus, (1835,) and soon afterwards Dr. Baur, his former teacher, and colleague, came out with three most learned volumes on the history of the Christian doctrine on the Trinity and the Incarnation of God, (1841—'43.) The second edition of Dorner's work frequently alludes to this and other productions of the Tübingen School, and it may be regarded, to a considerable extent, as a positive refutation of their mythological Christology and perversions of early doctrine history. The reader will here find full, critical, well-digested and reliable information on the Gnostic, Ebionitic, Arian, Nestorian, and Eutychian controversies, which resulted in the œcumenical decisions of the fourth and fifth centuries, concerning the constitution of Christ's person, as held to this day by the orthodox churches, Protestant as well as Catholic. This historical value is independent of the author's peculiar view on the generic character of Christ's person, and his hypothesis, already brought out by Irenaeus, that the incarnation would have taken place even without the fall, as the necessary completion of God's revelation, and the perfection of man's nature. The style of Dorner is dignified and scientific, but not free from a somewhat artificial and stiff terminology. This want of simplicity, in connection with the Hegelian method, accounts for the prejudice of Neander against his work, although it gave way somewhat after the great historian had a personal interview with the author in 1843.

As to an English translation which has been spoken of long since, both in England and in this country, it would require a hand of unusual skill and perseverance. We think it more desirable, however, that some able divine should prepare an independent Christological work, on the basis of the labors, not only of Dorner, but also of Liebner, Thomasius, Lange, Ullmann, and Wilberforce, (on the Incarnation,) and condense the biblical historical and dogmatic material into one volume. Such a book, well executed, would fill a most important place in English literature. For the solution of the Christ-question is the deepest problem of theology and the necessary condition of the settlement of the Church-question in its widest application.

Dr. Dorner is an occasional contributor to several theological periodicals, and to Herzog's Encyclopædia. In July, 1856, he commenced, in connection with Ehrenfeuchter of Göttingen, Liebner of Dresden, Landerer and Palmer of Tübingen, and Weizsäcker of Stuttgart, the publication of a new Quarterly, similar in character and tendency to the *Studien und Kritiken*, under the title *Jahrbücher für deutsche Theologie*. It is to be purely scientific, and to take no part in the confessional controversies of the day.

He is, however, by no means indifferent to the more practical questions of the Church. He assisted in founding the German Church Diet, before which he ventured, in 1850, to express his sympathy with Holstein against Denmark; he defended the liberal union principles of the Göttingen faculty against the exclusive confessionalism of the clergy of Hanover; and took up the pen recently, in a review of Bunsen's "Signs of the Times," for the cause of religious liberty against the reactionary tendencies of Stahl and Hengstenberg. His proper province, however, is systematic and speculative divinity, or dogmatics and ethics. He takes considerable interest in Anglo-American Christianity, and told me once that if German theology was to make a deep impression upon the churches of England and Scotland, it would have to be done mainly through the medium of America.

CHAPTER XXXV.

LANGE.

Lange, the Representative of Poetical Theology, and Theological Poetry,—His Excellences and Defects—His Life of Christ—His Christian Dogmatics—Origin and Education—Early Productions—The "Land of Glory"—Strauss called to Zurich—A Republican Revolution—Lange elected in his place—His Labors in Zurich and Bonn.

DR. JOHN PETER LANGE, professor of divinity in the University of Bònn, is a poetical theologian and a theological poet. His mind is genial, fresh and rich, abounding in original ideas, ingenious speculations and striking combinations, and at the same time thoroughly imbued with the spirit of vital, evangelical Christianity. He has a keen eye for, and a lively sympathy with, the beauties of the Bible. It is to him the highest poetry as well as the deepest philosophy. He could heartily subscribe to what Coleridge says of poetry, that it is "the blossom and the fragrancy of all human knowledge, human thoughts, human emotions, passions and language;" and that it carries with it "its own exceeding great reward, by giving the habit of discovering the good and beautiful in all that meets and surrounds us." He has an unbounded confidence in the absolute power of Christianity to take up all the relations of life, all sciences and arts, to transform them by its spirit and to sanctify them to the glory of God. "Nihil humani a me alienum puto," and "All is yours," may be said to be the motto of his theology and philosophy.

It is refreshing and animating, after long and close application to abstruse science and severe logic, to follow such a highly gifted and deeply pious writer as Lange, in his excursions over the green meadows, through the wild forests and to the lofty mountains of God's nature and revelation. His imagination soars at times to the region of the clouds and beyond it to the very portals of the "land of glory," where truth and beauty, theology and poetry, science and art shall forever be united in the beatific vision and angelic praise of God, the eternal fountain of all truth, beauty, and goodness.

Yet, after all, science is not art, and art is not science, at least in this sublunar world; and we should not confound their boundaries. It is well enough to infuse into scientific discussion an imaginative element sufficient to give it the charm of freshness and vivacity, as is the case for instance with the exegetical works of Olshausen, Tholuck and Lücke, and the church history of Hase; but it must be held under the strict control of reason and sober thought, and be subordinate altogether to the main object of instruction. This is not always the case with Dr. Lange. He has almost too much imagination for a theologian, and too much reflection for a poet. Many of his views and combinations, however interesting, striking and suggestive, cannot stand the test of criticism, and must be set down as mere notions and fancies.

Another fault is his excess of fertility as a writer. Even the richest genius should prudently husband his resources, and freely and closely apply the pruning knife to the luxuriant productions of his pen. Lange's style, moreover, although it rises occasionally into a high order of eloquence and beauty, is, generally speaking, too redundant and prolix, and bears marks of hasty composition. To a translator he offers unsurmountable difficulties, and it is not likely that any of his books will become familiar to English readers. This is to be regretted on account of the excellent spirit they breathe, and the many gems of pregnant, sublime and suggestive thoughts they contain.

Lange's largest works are a "Life of Jesus, according to the Gospels," in three volumes, (1844–'47;) a "History of the Apostolic Age," in two volumes, (1853–'54;) and a system of "Christian Dogmatics," (1849–'52,) in three parts, of which the first is called "Philosophical Dogmatics," the second, "Positive Dogmatics," the third, "Applied (*angewandte*) Dogmatics," or "Polemics and Irenics." The subdivisions in the third part, and the ingenious comparative delineation of religious corruptions, diseases and errors in Paganism, Judaism, Mohamedanism, and Christianity, would be especially puzzling to an English reader who is not sufficiently initiated into the deeper mysteries of German speculation. But these works, as a whole, are noble monuments of Christian research and piety.

We will select at random a few passages of the Dogmatics, and translate them as well as we can, to give the reader an idea of Lange's speculation and style.

Definition of dogma, (vol. i. p. 3.)

"Genuine dogmas are the ideal life-pictures of the race, in which divinity and humanity, the world of mind and the world of matter, heaven and earth, the realm of the idea and human society, are brought together into one. They embrace the divine and the human, the spiritual and the natural contents of his conception of the world in concentrated forms, and in so far constitute the essential wealth of his conscious spiritual life."

The Trinity as the law of all life, (i. 11.)

"The number one is plainly the number of power, of origin, and of action. God is, first of all, one as Almighty, as the Lord and Creator of the world, as the Unchangeable, the Fountain of Truth. Lowest, and furthest from this highest unity, the unity of God, stands the unity of the elementary atom.

"But unity comes only to its true manifestation in life; and polarity, or dynamic twofoldness, (*Zweifaltigkeit,*) is the law of life. The highest polarity is found in the eternal Godhead, in the relation of the Father to the Son. The lowest appears in the antagonism of positive and negative electricity. It then reveals itself in a thousand forms, in the opposite between space and matter, between centripetal and centrifugal force, between day and night, between the root and the stem, between the male and the female sex.

"But as long as life comes out only in the form of polarity, it exhibits itself as bound and limited. The one element requires and excludes, limits and conditions the other. It is only in trinity, that life first reveals itself as free intellectual life, as a life which reproduces itself, and yet remains identical, in that it loses and finds itself again in its polar opposite.

"Hence three is the completed one, the number of self-consciousness, of the Ego, of the spirit, and hence also of the Godhead as revealed. Here we have the source of the symbolism of numbers, as set forth of old in the Holy Scriptures, and the philosophy of Pythagoras."

Johann Peter Lange was born (1802) and raised in

the neighborhood of Elberfeld, Prussia, and in the bosom of the German Reformed Church. To this Church he is to this day warmly and deeply attached, but without the least bigotry and exclusiveness. For he strongly believes in, and hopefully looks to, the final solution of all the discords of church history in the perfect kingdom of Christ, that shall unite in harmony the elements of truth and beauty scattered among the various denominations of Christendom. Even the Catholic Church of the Middle Ages is to him not an apostacy, but a type and symbol rather, or a premature carnal anticipation of the future glorious reign of Christ among all the nations of the earth.

He was originally a farmer, and was seen many a time to bring butter and eggs to market. But he managed, by honorable exertion, to get an education, and to graduate at the University of Bonn. He labored then for a number of years as pastor of a Reformed church at Duisburg, and soon attracted considerable attention by several volumes of religious poetry, and beautiful essays on various theological and practical topics. Some of the finest and most interesting contributions to former volumes of Hengstenberg's "Evangelical Church Gazette," when it stood on a more liberal basis than it does now, are from Lange's pen.

I remember well the delight with which I read, when a student at Tübingen, a series of articles on the "Land of Glory," which he furnished for that periodical in 1837, with the object to show that there is somewhere in the centre of the universe, a supernatural, yet literal, *i. e.*, local heaven, to which the Saviour ascended,

—a Mount Zion, an abode of the blessed, a celestial city, the free Jerusalem, the true and eternal metropolis of Christendom; where the Triune God reveals his highest majesty, power, and love; where the saints dwell with Christ in transcendent glory and peace; and where truth, beauty, and holiness are blended in perfect harmony forever. The speculations about the locality of heaven are, of course, very controvertible; but the vein of sacred poetry, the sublime flight of sanctified imagination, the religious fervor and devotion, the aspiration after the true home of the spirit and the eternal hills of salvation, impart to those articles a peculiar charm. They partake somewhat of the character of the deservedly popular works of Rev. H. Harbaugh, on the heavenly world.

In 1839, the famous Dr. Strauss—who resolves the Gospel history of salvation into an incoherent and self-contradictory mythological poem, and denies even the existence of a personal God and the immortality of the soul—was duly elected professor of Christian dogmatics and ethics in the University of Zürich, by the radical party which was then in power, and consisted mostly of unprincipled demagogues and frivolous infidels. The Germans in their proverbial patience and political passivity, would, of course, have submitted to this as to any other measure of their paternal governments. Many a man has been elected to the highest seat of ecclesiastical power in the German States, who is almost as heterodox as Strauss, or even belongs to his pantheistic school; and yet the people quietly put up with it, and smoked their pipes as good-naturedly as ever. But the free Swiss would not acquiesce in such an act of suicidal folly, which placed in the chair of Zwingli a man who had insulted their Christianity, and could only utterly disqualify the candidates of the ministry to be committed to his instruction, for the holy office by making them either open destroyers of the Church, or consummate hypocrites. The uncommon sense of the Germans may not exactly see this glaring inconsistency; but to the common sense of Englishmen and Americans it is as plain as day-light. Accordingly, the people of the Canton of Zürich rose in their republican majesty, like the recent Vigilance Committee of California; marched to the city under the lead of an energetic country pastor; and with what weapons they could hastily collect, scared the radical clique away, who very courageously took to their heels; then they placed the government into the hands of conservative, trustworthy Christian men, and quietly retired to their mountain homes without shedding a drop of blood. The revolution was the work of a few hours. But as Strauss had been legally elected, and accepted the appointment, he, being a high-minded and independent philosopher—claimed at least the half of the salary and enjoys it, I believe, to this day.

The new government elected Mr. Lange in the place claimed, but never occupied by Strauss. They could not have made a better and more significant choice at that time. For Lange had already written one of the ablest replies to the "*Leben Jesu*" of the former, in defence especially of the infant history of the Saviour; and a few years afterwards, he met the arguments of the Tübingen critic more at length and triumphantly in his own work on the Life of Jesus. And yet with all his uncompromising hostility to this modern infidelity, he is personally a modest, amiable, and lovely Christian gentleman, who could satisfy the wishes of the party that called him, without giving just cause of offence to the opposition.

For nearly fourteen years, he labored faithfully and conscientiously on the classical soil of the Swiss Reformation, and took part in every enterprise which was calculated to revive evangelical life and activity. His usefulness was unfortunately neutralized to some extent by the counteracting influence of his own colleagues—Schweizer and Hitzig—who are men of an altogether different spirit. Yet his labors were not without a lasting blessing, and will be held in grateful remembrance by a devoted circle of his friends among the clergy and the people of Zurich, who manifested their affection for him in a very touching manner, when, in 1854, he left the charming city of Zwingli in obedience to a call from his alma mater, the University of Bonn.

CHAPTER XXXVI.

EBRARD.

Sketch of his Life—His Literary Fertility—Excellences and Defects of his Writings—His Defence of the Gospel-history against the destructive Criticism of the Tubingen School—His Dogmatic Works and Relation to the German Reformed Church—His Views on Predestination and the Eucharist—His Lectures on Practical Theology.

Dr. Johannes Heinrich August Ebrard is a Bavarian by birth and education, but a Huguenot by descent, and combines with German depth and learning the boldness and energy of those French Calvinists who, under the persecution of Louis XIV., sacrificed home and country for their faith. He studied at Erlangen, and commenced there his academic career as *Privatdocent.* His favorite teachers who exerted most influence over his mind, were Olshausen, the distinguished commentator, whose work he has now completed, and Krafft, the former incumbent of the only Reformed professorship in that University, which was established for the benefit of the few Reformed congregations in the predominantly Catholic and Lutheran Kingdom of Bavaria, especially for the Rhenish province. Dr. Krafft, though little known as a scholar and writer, stood for a long time alone among his colleagues in the defence of pure Scriptural truth from the chair and the pulpit, and was the chief instrument in the hands of God to revive evangelical theology and piety in that part of Germany. This is admitted even by high-toned Lutherans, and I remember to have heard Dr. Harless, now of Munich, and Professor Stahl, of Berlin, who taught formerly in Erlangen, express themselves much indebted to the spiritual influence and edifying sermons of this venerable servant of Christ.

After the decease of Dr. Krafft, Ebrard was elected in his place, and returned again to his alma mater, after he had labored for several years (from 1844 to '49) as theological professor in Zürich with considerable success. In the midst of a strictly Lutheran faculty, he boldly defended Reformed doctrines and usages. For, with the exception of this one Reformed professorship, Erlangen is now the most flourishing school of orthodox Lutheranism in all Germany, and its theological faculty, consisting of Thomasius, Delitzsch, Hofmann, Harnack, (Höfling died a few years ago,) enjoys great confidence for its faithful adherence to the Augsburg Confession and the Form of Concord.

In 1853, Ebrard was removed by his government, I know not for what reason, as *Consistorialrath* to Speyer, the capital of Rhenish Bavaria, once the residence of several German emperors, and the birth-place of the religious designation of *Protestants.* Here he is engaged mainly in the practical duties of church government and discipline. He is determined, too much perhaps, to keep up the Union of the Lutherans and Reformed which was introduced there in 1818, after the model of Prussia, and to put down all attempts at a revival of separate and exclusive confessionalism. This seems to be inconsistent with his love and zeal for the Reformed Church of his fathers, but it only seems so; for he never opposed the Union where it once existed, and maintains that the Reformed Confession has always been catholic and conciliatory in spirit, and favorable to a union with the Lutherans of the Melanthonian school.

We regret that he is thus withdrawn from the academic field of labor for which he seems better adapted than for the post he now occupies. Still such an active and ambitious mind, and such a hard student as he is, will never permit practical duties to occupy his time to the exclusion of theological research and literary labor. He took an active part also from the beginning in the German Church Diet, and attended the meeting of the Evangelical Alliance in London, 1851. He is a good French, and tolerably good English scholar, and has his eye upon the progress of the Reformed Church out of Germany as well as in Germany.

Dr. Ebrard is unquestionably one of the most talented, learned, energetic and zealous among the divines of the present generation. His literary fertility seems to be inexhaustible. Although hardly more than forty years of age, he has written already a large number of works on the most important and difficult topics of exegetical, historical, and systematic divinity. Among these deserve especial mention a critical history of the life of Christ, (*Wissenschaftliche Kritik der evangelischen Geschichte*, first edition 1841–'42, in 3 vols.; 2d ed., 1850, in 1 vol. of 956 pages;) a system of didactic theology, (*Christliche Dogmatik*, 1851–'52, in 2 vols.;) a history of the doctrine on the Lord's Supper from the apostles down to the present time, (1845, 2 vols. ;) a collection of Reformed liturgies, (*Reformirtes Kirchenbuch*, 1847 ;) lectures on practical theology, (1854 ;) and commentaries on the Epistle to the Hebrews, (1850 ;) and on the Revelation, (1852,) which form a part of the exegetical work of Olshausen. In addition to this, he contributes freely to the *Studien und Kritiken*, and to Herzog's *Encyclopædia*, and writes occasionally pamphlets on the theological and religious controversies of the day. He also founded and edited, while at Zürich, a spirited but short-lived periodical entitled, "The Church of the Future," helped to establish afterwards the Reformed Church Gazette of Erlangen, and edits now again a weekly ecclesiastical paper for Rhenish Bavaria.

Such excessive activity of the pen seems necessarily to imply superficiality. And yet such a charge would be unjust in the case before us. It is true, none of Ebrard's works are free from serious objections and defects. He is too quick and hasty in forming his judgment. His tone is too confident, dogmatic, and at times almost arrogant, or, in the expressive language of German students, *burschikos*. He is constitutionally pugnacious, and defies the world, the devil, and all his hosts. He treats his opponents as if they were mere school-boys, and often indulges in his ironical and sarcastic propensity at the expense of theological dignity and decorum. His style lacks careful polish, symmetry and condensation, and is disfigured by too many foreign expressions and emphatic words, or, as we would say, italics.

But with all these defects, which are most obvious in his earlier writings, he generally masters his subject, shrinks from no difficulty, however perplexing, penetrates into the heart of things, is rich and happy in illustration, often profound, always independent, fresh, vigorous and interesting. Nor must his fondness for jokes and witticisms be mistaken for levity. He is no doubt at heart an earnest man, lives in the fear of God, and devotes his fine talents to the cause of Christianity.

His large work on the evangelical history, is a valuable contribution to the apologetic literature of the present century, and may be regarded, upon the whole, as one of the most complete and triumphant refutations of the more recent attacks of German infidelity and semi-infidelity on the credibility of the canonical Gospels. He goes to the enormous trouble of exploring the labyrinth of modern criticism to its remotest corners, and exposes, without fear and favor, both by argument and ridicule, the weakness, the inconsistencies and contradictions of the endless hypotheses of Strauss, Baur, Bruno Bauer, Gfrörer, Weisse, Schweizer, and others, who either undermine the historical foundation of Christianity, and place it on a level with the ancient mythologies, or create at least an irreconcilable chasm between the synoptic and the Johannean narratives of Christ, and sacrifice the one or the other.

In his doctrinal and liturgical writings, Ebrard is, as already intimated, one of the leading champions of the Reformed theology in Germany as distinct from the Lutheran, although altogether friendly to the Union. For it is not the rigid Calvinism of the Synods of Dort, and Westminster, which he defends, but the German or Melanthonian type of the Reformed communion as embodied in the Heidelberg Catechism.

The principal difference between the two systems may be reduced to two points. First, the former makes an abstract eternal decree the source, and the incarnation and the church simply a means, of salvation; while the latter derives it from the person of Christ, who in his divine nature is older than all decrees. Secondly, Calvinism teaches a double eternal decree, a reprobation as well as an election, and thus necessarily limits the atonement to a part of the race; while the German Reformed Church passes the decree of reprobation over in silence, and extends the intrinsic power and divine intention and offer, though by no means the real acceptance, of salvation to the whole world in the sense of the passage: "He is the propitiation for our sins; and not for our's only, but also for the sins of the whole world," (1 John i. 2); and "God will have all men to be saved, and to come to the knowledge of the truth," (1 Tim. ii. 4.)

In this respect all the evangelical Reformed divines of the age (Schweizer excepted, who is not evangelical in the American sense of the term,) are fully agreed. Lange, Heppe, Hundeshagen, Schenkel, Hagenbach, Herzog, Sudhoff, F. W. Krummacher as well as Ebrard, reject the supralapsarian, and in some sense also the infralapsarian scheme of predestination, without being on that account Arminian in any sense whatever. They all seek the solution of the difficult problem of the relation of the infinite grace of God to the finite will of man in the work of conversion and sanctification, not in the denial of one of the two factors; but either in modification of the Melanthonian synergism, or in some other medium between Calvinism and semi-Pelagianism. In opposition to this view, Dr. Alexander Schweizer, of Zürich, an able follower of Schleiermacher, in two learned but one-sided works on the doctrinal history of the Reformed Church, tries to show that the Reformed system rests on the metaphysical dogma of the absolute sovereignty of God and unconditional predestination, and must end at last, by logical consequence, in a sort of modern speculative fatalism and pantheism. But Ebrard treats his former and older colleague, in occasional foot-notes, with the utmost contempt for smuggling his crypto-pantheism into the old Reformed divines, and calls his book absolutely useless. From this judgment, however, we must dissent, much as we dislike the egotistic spirit and cold dialectics of Schweizer.

As to the doctrine of the eucharist, Ebrard adopts, with some modifications, the Calvinistic theory of a spiritual real presence and actual fruition of Christ's life through faith, in opposition both to the Lutheran dogma of an oral manducation of Christ by the unworthy as well as the worthy communicant, and to the purely symbolical view of Zwingli, although he successfully defends the reformer of Zürich against the charge of rationalism and unchurchly radicalism. His view on this topic agrees substantially with that of Dr. Nevin as expounded in his "Mystical Presence," of which Ebrard gave a very favorable and interesting review in the *Studien und Kritiken* for 1850.

Finally, Dr. Ebrard comes before us as a writer on

Practical Theology. His lectures on this branch of the sacred science were published in 1854, and are quite a valuable addition to homiletical, liturgical and pastoral literature. The author tells us in the preface that he treated the subject with a considerable degree of originality, (*ziemlich originell.*) He views practical theology not as one branch simply of divinity, co-ordinate with the other three branches of exegetical, historical, and systematic or speculative theology, according to the usual division, but as the entire theology under the aspect of art, as distinct from science. Theology, he tells us, may be regarded and treated first, as science, whose object is the theoretical knowledge of the saving truth of God revealed in Christ; secondly, as art, which looks to ecclesiastical action and the practical life of religion on the basis of scientific knowledge. This latter is animated by the ethical principle, i. e., the new life of Christ in the soul which continually tends to realize itself in the congregation, and to transform the world into the kingdom of God. It forms the crown and fruit-bearing flower, which derives juice and nourishment from the root, stem and branches of scientific theology.

From this point of view the author presents a spirited and suggestive outline of catechetics, the theory of foreign and domestic missions, which he calls halieutics, the theory of worship, including liturgics and homiletics, and the theory of pastoral care or poimenics. He shows throughout an experimental acquaintance with the practical duties of the ministry and the wants of the Church at the present time. The fourth chapter of the first part, where he deals with the general diseases of ecclesiastical life, as pietism and confessionalism, separatism and episcopalism, methodism and hierarchism, puritanism and ceremonialism, sectism, Romanism and infidelity, is especially instructive and interesting, although many of his views would require considerable modification to be fully applicable to our American Church life.

CHAPTER XXXVII.

HUNDESHAGEN, SCHENKEL, HAGENBACH, HERZOG.

Modern German Reformed Theology—Schleiermacher—Hundeshagen—His Review of German Protestantism, a mirror of the Crisis before the Revolution of 1848—Schenkel—Hagenbach—Herzog—The Theological Encyclopædia.

In connection with Lange and Ebrard we must notice several other academic divines of equal distinction, who are likewise Reformed by descent, personal association and ecclesiastical sympathy, but belong, theologically, to the evangelical union-school, and more particularly to that branch of it which we have, in a previous chapter, designated as the "Centre," in distinction from the high church confessional Unionism on the one side, and the low church latitudinarian Unionism on the other. This Union tendency of the modern Reformed theology of Germany and its liberal catholic bearing towards Lutheranism is no arbitrary innovation, but hereditary, and may be traced back to the genius of the Heidelberg Catechism and the Melanthonian Calvinistic origin of the Church of the Palatinate. In its modern scientific form it dates from the introduction of the Union in Prussia and other German States, whose rulers were originally Reformed or leaning in that direction by family ties or religious sympathies, and from the powerful influence of Schleiermacher. For he was the son of a Reformed clergyman, and himself a Reformed minister, and with all his originality and independence, he had a constitutional sympathy with the Calvinistic principle of the absolute sovereignty of God, and the absolute dependence of the creature, with the Presbyterian form of church government, and with the political liberalism of Reformed countries like Holland and England; yet he fell heartily in with the Union of 1817, and adhered to it, though he strongly disapproved the government measures for its introduction. But his school, if we may speak of one—for he denied all intention to form a school—divided into two very different branches, the positive evangelical, and the anti-confessional or latitudinarian Unionists. The above named Reformed divines, of whom we are going to speak in this chapter, belong to the former, Schweizer of Zurich, to the latter branch.

Dr. Carl Bernhard Hundeshagen, a Hessian by birth, formerly professor of ecclesiastical history in Berne, Switzerland, and now member of the theological faculty of Heidelberg, the old centre of the Palatinate church, is little known beyond Germany, but must be ranked among the most interesting of the living divines of that country, and has few equals for general intelligence, freshness and vigor of mind. His position is somewhat peculiar. His natural talents would have qualified him as well for the duties of a statesman, as for a theological chair, and he would even now make an excellent minister of public worship and instruction. He is no pedantic schoolman and bookworm, none of those monkish metaphysicians who roam over the barren deserts of abstruse speculation without ever seeing the green pastures beyond, as is the case with so many German scholars; but he takes a lively and intelligent interest in the practical questions of the day, and sympathizes with the condition, wants and sufferings of the people. He views theology, not as an abstract and isolated science, but in its connections with, and bearings upon, the various ramifications of society and national life. He keeps a watchful eye upon general literature, politics, the working of governments, the social problems, the leading organs of public opinion, and studies the movements of secular history in their relation to, and probable effect, upon the kingdom of God which they must ultimately, directly or indirectly, help to promote and to carry forward to its glorious triumphs. He feels the importance of employing other means, besides the pulpit, to revive a living Christianity among the educated classes of his fatherland; and hence he delivered an excellent series of "Testimonies for Christ," in the free lecture style, to mixed audiences of Frankfort and other cities. In politics, of which he knows more than most of the German divines, he is an admirer of constitutional freedom, and of Anglo-Saxon institutions, although he never was in England, nor speaks a word of English. His long residence in Switzerland was of benefit to him in this respect. He is a fine looking gentleman, of kindly, social disposition and agreeable conversational powers, altogether, I should judge from a few short interviews, a most genial and interesting companion.

Hundeshagen, when yet residing in Switzerland and observing from its free mountains the commotions of his native land, made quite a sensation, in 1846, by an anonymous book on "German Protestantism, its past history, and present life-questions, viewed in its connection with the entire national development, by a German divine," (3d ed. 1850.) This remarkable work is a manly and bold, yet well meant and patriotic exposure of the religious, political and social diseases of modern Germany, and represents, almost prophetically, the peculiar crisis which preceded the outbreak of the political earthquake of 1848. The author develops first the nature and object of Protestantism in its original form; then he traces the rise and power of recent Anti-Christianity in Germany, its causes and effects, following it out even to the moral destitution of German emigrants in foreign countries; and finally he discusses the movements and questions which agitated that country in the last ten years before the revolution. He accounts for the development of modern infidelity in the bosom of German Protestantism, to a considerable extent, by the political reaction since the Congress of Vienna, which crippled the free motion of national life, violently suppressed all political discontent, and indirectly forced the bitter hostility to the existing order of things, to vent itself intellectually upon the Church and Christianity. He thinks that a healthy religious life of a nation can only unfold itself on the soil of rational political freedom, as the example of England and the United States prove better than all arguments. Hence his motto: "It is not good if a people which unites all the necessary conditions for a comprehensive development, is confined to an exclusively literary existence." In reading the terse and vigorous pages of Hundeshagen's Protestantism, we see the heavy clouds gathering over Germany, we hear the rolling of the approaching thunderstorm, we feel, to use a German expression, the *vormärzliche Gewitter-schwüle.* The author was right to leave the book essentially unchanged in the subsequent editions. For it deserves to retain its original character and to be handed down to history as a faithful intellectual mirror of the critical condition of German Protestantism before 1848.

That crisis is now past, but a new one has taken its place, and the clouds seem to be again gathering over the political and ecclesiastical horizon of Germany. Another book of the kind is needed, or what would be still better, an actual remedy, that should prevent a similar outbreak, and lead a great nation into the path of a free, healthy, vigorous and comprehensive development of all its mighty intellectual and moral powers.

Dr. DANIEL SCHENKEL, a native of Schaffhausen, Switzerland, and for some time preacher of that city, succeeded, in 1850, Dr. De Wette, his teacher and friend, as professor of theology in Basel, but a few years afterwards he accepted a call to the University of Heidelberg, where he still resides. He gradually progressed from the critical skepticism of De Wette, to a more positive and orthodox position. He is a learned, prolific and fluent writer on subjects connected with the history, principle and mission of Protestantism, and the Union of Lutheranism and Reform, and a ready and fearless opponent of Romanism, and exclusive Lutheranism, which he regards as the German form of Puseyism. He is one of the editors of the *General Church Gazette* of Darmstadt, formerly the organ of the rationalism of a Bretschneider, and has imparted into its pages not only more life and vigor, but also an evangelical tone. He is a very eloquent preacher, and I found that his printed sermons were among the most popular German works in Holland. He takes a leading part in the Gustavus Adolphus Society.

Dr. K. R. Hagenbach, professor of church history at Basel, his native city, where he is connected with one of the most respectable families, wrote, in addition to the manual of doctrine-history, known to the readers of Clark's Foreign Library, a useful theological Encyclopædia, and a number of volumes on the history of Protestantism, and the early church of the ante and post-Nicene age. Most of these books were originally delivered as lectures to a mixed audience, and hence are clothed in a popular dress, although by no means superficial on that account. His style is remarkably clear, simple, easy and fluent; his tone and judgment is liberal, mild, amiable and well calculated to attract outsiders, and such as are prejudiced against more decided forms of orthodoxy. His stand-point as a historian resembles that of Hase, but it is more evangelical. He is also quite a respectable poet and a gentleman of fine taste and general culture. He edits a journal for the Reformed Churches of Switzerland with much discretion and circumspection.

Dr. I. I. Herzog, a native of Basel, was first, for

several years, professor of theology in the Academy of Lausanne in French Switzerland, and was involved, with his colleagues, the distinguished Vinet, and Chappius, in the struggles which resulted in the formation of the Free Church of the Canton de Vaud. It was there that he wrote a valuable biography of Oecolampadius, the celebrated reformer of Basel, in two volumes, 1843. After a short residence in Halle, he was elected to succeed Dr. Ebrard as professor of Reformed theology in Erlangen, 1854. He is now principally known in America as well as in Germany, as the editor of the Theological Encyclopædia, now in course of publication, to which we have alluded already in a previous chapter. The divines mentioned in this chapter, are among the largest and ablest contributors to this valuable and lasting work.

CHAPTER XXXVIII.

WICHERN.

Character of Wichern—Christian Philanthropy—The Rough House—Personal Interviews—The Church Diet and the Inner Mission—The Evangelical Conference and the Diaconate—Fliedner and the Deaconesses—Wichern in Prussia—Concluding Reflections on the Prospects of Christianity in Germany.

We conclude these sketches with the most distinguished representative of *practical* Christianity in Germany, who converts the ideas of modern evangelical theology into deeds of charity, and goes forth from his study to the lanes of public life, the dens of misery, and the hells of vice, to do the work of the merciful Samaritan, and, as far as in him lies, to reclaim society to the gospel of peace.

We do not hesitate to pronounce Dr. Wichern one of the greatest and best men of the age. He stands foremost in the ranks of Christian philanthropists on the Continent of Europe, and, since the death of Chalmers, we know of no English or American divine who equals him in fervor of spirit, and incessant activity of love to God and to fallen man. His name will ever be identified with the noble work of Inner Mission and the regeneration of German Protestantism. History will assign him a place by the side of Vincent de Paul, the father of the Sisters of Charity, Augustus Hermann Francke, the founder of the Orphan House at Halle, William Wilberforce, the emancipator of slaves, and other truly great men, who, filled with the love of Christ and generous sympathy for their suffering brethren, went about doing good, and became practical reformers and benefactors of the race.

The Rev. Dr. Wichern was born at Hamburg, in 1808, and is, therefore, now in the prime of life—although his gray hair gives him already a venerable appearance. He studied at Berlin under Schleiermacher and Neander, and still holds these teachers in grateful remembrance. He is a well educated divine, of strictly evangelical, and yet truly liberal and comprehensive views, an earnest Christian, a dignified and accomplished, yet plain and unostentatious gentleman. He has an eminently practical genius, great power of organization, untiring energy, fiery and commanding eloquence. Even before he had completed his studies he felt a strong desire to devote himself to works of charity, in a free, untrammeled way. He has since amply proved to the world that this is his peculiar mission.

Destitute of worldly means, but full of faith in God, like Francke, he founded, in 1833, near the village of Horn, about three miles from Hamburg, a vagrant school, under the characteristic name of the "*Rauhe Haus.*" It was, at first, an old broken-down farm-house; but it has grown since to be one of the most important and interesting benevolent institutions in the world. An English traveller calls it the "House among the Flowers," which is true, both in a literal and spiritual sense; and an American tourist, Brace, in his "Home Life in Germany," (p. 96,) states it as his impression, on a visit in the year 1850, that "the friend of man, searching anxiously for what man has done for his suffering fellows, may look far in both Continents, before he finds an institution so benevolent, so practical, and so truly Christian as the Hamburg Rough House."

This noble establishment is a large garden full of trees, walks, flowers, vegetables, and adjoining corn-fields, with several small, but comfortable, wood-houses, and a neat, quiet chapel. It embraces various workshops for shoemaking, tailoring, spinning, baking, etc., a commercial agency (*Agentur*) for the sale of the articles made by the boys; a printing and publishing department; a lithograph and wood engraving shop, and a book-bindery—all in very energetic and successful operation. Many excellent tracts and books are annually issued from the Institution, also a monthly periodical, under the title "*Fliegende Blätter*," which is, at the same time, the organ of the central committee of the German Church Diet for Inner Mission. The children are divided into families, each about twelve in number, and controlled by an overseer, with two assistants. These overseers are generally theological students who prepare themselves here for pastoral usefulness. Many of them have already gone out to superintend similar institutions in Germany, Switzerland, and Russia, established on the plan of the Rough House. The general management is, of course, in the hands of Wichern, who is universally respected and beloved, as a spiritual father.

And who should not venerate the man who, from the

most disinterested motives, picks up the orphan, the homeless, the outcast, from the filth and squalor, the dark cellars and vicious corners of Hamburg and other cities, to rescue them from temporal and eternal ruin, to transform them into useful men and pious Christians! He succeeded in some most desperate cases, with boys of whom the very devil seemed to have taken full possession. In this work he has gathered a rare amount of psychological knowledge and spiritual experience.

How strange! Dr. Wichern is one of the purest men; and yet he has a rare familiarity with the history and statistics of vice. He knows all about the horrible mysteries of society in such cities as Hamburg—one of the most corrupt in Germany—Berlin, Paris, and London. He spent once several weeks in visiting, with the assistance of the police-officers, the ill-famed quarters of England's capital, in close neighborhood to the magnificent palaces of Regent-Street and Westminster, and he told me, he nowhere witnessed such appalling scenes of misery and wretchedness. What prompted him to acquire such knowledge, was no idle curiosity, nor a morbid taste, but the love of Christ, who came to save sinners, and to seek that which was lost. He turns his large experience to the best account in his Rough House, which, for many wicked boys and girls, has become the birth-place of a new life, devoted to the service of God and the benefit of man.

I shall not easily forget the beautiful days I spent with this servant of Christ at Frankfort-on-the-Maine, under the hospitable roof of Dr. Varrentrapp, during the sessions of the seventh Evangelical Church Diet in September, 1854; the subsequent excursion we took to the Taunus mountains; the trip on the lovely Rhine; the visit to Dr. von Bethmann Hollweg, the noble patron of every Christian work, on his mediæval castle, Rheineck; and the last hours at Bonn, where we parted at the house of his friend, professor Perthes, never to meet again, perhaps, on this earth. But I look back with equal interest, to my first interview with him at the Rough House, in 1841, when he was yet little known, and that under the modest title, "Candidate" for the holy ministry. I had then just graduated at Berlin as "Licentiate," and published a juvenile book on the "Sin against the Holy Ghost," in which he felt deeply interested on account of the subject. But I soon found out that he knew much more about it than I. We made an excursion to the worthy pastor Gurlitt in a neighboring village, who had written an essay on the same topic. We conversed on the mysteries of sin and grace. He opened to me an awful abyss of human corruption, and gave me a horrifying account of two youths under his charge, who, although not over fifteen and eighteen years of age, had reached, apparently, the extreme of wicked rebellion against God, and come nearer the blasphemy of the Holy Ghost, than any thing I ever heard before, even Spiera's case hardly excepted, whose tale does "harrow up the soul and freeze the blood." Ever since, I followed his history with lively interest, and was greatly rejoiced to hear, a few years afterwards, and in a far distant land, that "Candidat" Wichern was crowned with the highest academic honor, not for any learned work, but for his labors of love, and that he became the acknowledged leader of a powerful movement which extends almost as far as the German name.

The year 1848, the year of bright hopes and gloomy disappointments; of noble deeds and dark crimes; the year which laid open the hidden diseases of European society, in Church and State, brought Wichern on the public stage, and gave to his ideas and plans of reform a national importance. He has a heart for German unity and liberty, and laments the political and religious dissensions of his fatherland. He deeply sympathizes with the sufferings and destitutions of the people, and follows even, with an eye of compassion, the thousands of his countrymen who leave their native home in discontent, to the extreme East, and extreme West, there to perish, alas! only too often in the cities of Constantinople, Paris, London and New York, from want of the bread of life. He knows, moreover, that mere political reforms and reactions can effect no real cure of the many evils which produced, as their natural fruit, the gigantic emigration and the late revolution. He sees that a moral regeneration of society is necessary, and especially works of Christian philanthropy, which will relieve the sufferings of the poor and destitute, destroy the envy and jealousy of the lower against the higher ranks, and recommend Christianity to the great masses, now so fearfully alienated from it.

"For fifteen years,"—he said in his first speech on the subject of Inner Mission, at the first meeting of the Church Diet, on Luther's grave,—"for fifteen years past, the thought and hope has animated me with growing vigor and clearness, that our fatherland, the heart of Europe, might yet produce from its bosom, a society and confederation of faith and love, offering itself as a sacrifice to the church and the country—a society endowed with the resources of learning, the wisdom of statesmanship, the power of political and ecclesiastical government, and with the spirit of the eternal mercy of God from which alone can proceed the salvation of nations. This hope appeared to most men a mere phantom. In Germany as it then was, this seed could not take root. The cover must first be removed from the eyes of all. This the hand of God has done in 1848: the abyss lies open, the ground is plowed and ready to receive the divine seed of a faith working by love, that it may grow up and unfold its glory. A day of God, a day of salvation for our church in our dear fatherland has arisen with the revolutionary events. It will be known and felt, that the Evangelical Church can and must become a church of the people, (*Volks-Kirche,*) by penetrating the whole nation with the whole power of the gospel, and a new life-breath of God. If the church is to become the fountain of the Christian life of the nation, it must, in its confederated capacity, make the work of *Inner Mission* its own."

Our readers are already informed about the meaning of Inner Mission. It refers to domestic heathenism which has crept into German Protestantism to such a fearful extent, and it labors to reclaim it to living Christianity. It comprehends, in one organic whole, the various efforts already commenced before by separate societies—but now carried on with more system and vigor—for the temporal and spiritual benefit of the poor, the sick, the widow, the orphan, the stranger, the emigrant, the prisoner, the travelling journeyman; the distribution of good books and tracts; the supply of destitute charges with the means of the Gospel; the founding of Young Men's Christian Associations; the arrangement of courses of lectures on instructive and useful topics, to mixed audiences in large cities; the training of deacons and deaconesses; in fact, the whole field of Christian philanthropy. It has become almost co-extensive with practical Christianity. Its moving soul is that love which is as old as the Church, and whose fountain springs from the Cross. It does the work of the Church and for the Church, and with the most active members of the Church—but mostly in the form of free association. Hence the opposition of the high church Lutherans to Inner Mission; for like the Romanists and Puseyites, they virtually identify the Church with the clergy, and disown every Christian work however good and noble, which does not proceed from the clergy and has not the official seal stamped upon it. But this principle of free association and lay activity in the Church—only think of the British and American Bible, Tract, and Missionary Societies!—has become an irresistible power of the age, and opened a new chapter in church history. Even Romanism seems to be unable to suppress it altogether, if we look at the various societies formed in 1848 under the names of Bonifacius, Boromæus, Pius, and at the singular fact, that the leading and most vigorous organs of the Roman Catholic press, even those of the ultramontane party—as the *Historisch-Politische Blätter*, *L' Univers*, and *Brownson's Review*—are conducted by laymen, generally converts from Protestantism.

The inherent life of the movement of Inner Mission, in connection with the sanction of the Kirchentag, and especially the peculiar condition of affairs at that critical period, made it spread since 1848 with unusual rapidity all over Germany and Switzerland; and its popularity and vigor seems still extending and deepening, although a number of so-called evangelical societies which owed their existence to the charm of novelty and the excitement of the moment, have already gone the way of all flesh. Wichern gives the work a fresh impulse at every meeting of the Church Diet, of which he is, upon the whole, the most popular and interesting orator. He speaks without notes, with great freedom, energy, and fluency. He is perhaps somewhat too lengthy and prolix, but commands the audience nevertheless to the end. His generous zeal for a great and good cause, his noble figure, his earnest countenance, his blue eyes sparkling with the fire of genius and sanctified benevolence, never fail to make a deep impression, as he unfolds the statistics of misery and crime, and calls upon the assembly to show their faith by works, and to stem the flood of infidelity, socialism, and revolution, by leading society back to practical virtue and religion, as revealed in the person and work of Jesus Christ.

The movement of Inner Mission does not propose any alteration in the creed and constitution of the Church. It rests throughout on the basis of the Evangelical Protestant confessions of faith, and differs therefore from Romanism as well as from mere natural philanthropy. But it may be called a practical complement to the Reformation of the sixteenth century, and to the modern evangelical theology—a noble effort to rebuild what rationalism and indifferentism have destroyed, in the moral and religious life of the nation. It insists upon works of charity, but on the ground of the merit of Christ and the free grace of God.

Quite recently an important step was taken by the Evangelical Conference which assembled at Berlin in November, 1856, to embody a part of the work of Inner Mission which was carried on thus far, as already remarked, mostly in the form of voluntary agency, in the regular machinery of the Evangelical Church of Prussia, and thus to give it an official and permanent character. We mean the introduction of the deaconate as a congregational office for the care of the poor and the sick, according to the practice of the apostolic church. Wichern and Fliedner were among the fifty-eight members of that Conference, elected by the King. They may regard this action, which will no doubt receive the sanction of the projected General Synod, as a triumph of their long and self-denying labors. But it will require some time till a sufficient number of efficient deacons and presbyters, or lay helpers of the minister in the exercise of pastoral care, can be found in a state church where the majority of congregations are either spiritually dead, as in most of the Eastern provinces, or at least composed of the most heterogeneous material. In the Western provinces, where the Reformed church prevails, the office spoken of has long been established, and is in more or less successful operation.

Closely connected with the deaconate is the institution of female deacons or deaconesses, or, if you choose to call them so, Evangelical Sisters of Charity. This should likewise be made a regular ecclesiastical office. It was agitated long before 1848, by Dr. Fliedner, an eminently practical minister, who is favorably known as the founder and director of the establishment of deaconesses at Keiserswerth on the Rhine. The celebrated Miss Florence Nightingale is one of his pupils, which alone should be sufficient to commend him to the favorable notice of Great Britain and America. By indefatigable exertions he succeeded to awaken a deep interest in this matter. Similar establishments have been founded since at Berlin, (Bethania, with a magnificent building and rich endowment by the Queen,) at Jerusalem, in connection with the Anglo-Prussian bishopric, at Smyrna, and at Pittsburg, Pa., (under the care of the Rev. Mr. Passavant, an active Lutheran minister,) and have been mostly supplied with excellent and well trained female nurses from the mother institution of Keiserswerth. Fliedner brought them himself to America, and to Jerusalem. All these institutions of Christian sisterhoods have proved a great temporal and spiritual blessing to the sick placed under their care. It has been asserted recently by a number of bishops of the Protestant Episcopal church in the United States, that "the Sisters of Charity in the Romish communion are worth, perhaps, more to their cause than the combined wealth of their hierarchy, the learning of their priesthood, and the self-sacrificing zeal of their missionaries." (*Memorial Papers*, ed. by Bishop Potter, p. 61.) This may be greatly exaggerated. But it is certainly high time that the Protestant churches should begin seriously to consider the great importance of affording the large number of unmarried and unemployed females which are found everywhere, a proper opportunity to devote their peculiar talents and gifts to the service of Christ and humanity, in the discharge of the most tender and most endearing offices of charity.

To return to Dr. Wichern, we may state in conclusion that he has been called recently to Berlin as general superintendent of the prisons, (on which subject he was consulted some years ago by the Prussian government,) and been offered a seat at the same time in the *Oberkirchenrath* and *Staatsrath*, the two highest councils of the Prussian Church and State. But it seems he has declined so far to give up his connection with the Rough House, to which he devoted the labors of his first love, and in which he trained himself to general usefulness. He could hardly find a more influential, and at the same time a more independent position, than he occupies now.

If we now look over the field and prospects of practical Christianity in Germany, the question naturally rises, Is this movement of Inner Mission likely to continue much longer, either in a free, or in an official form; or will it gradually die away, especially if Wichern and Fliedner shall once have been called to their rest? Will the work of a radical regeneration of Protestantism, on its present doctrinal basis, which the movement aims at, succeed on a large scale; or must we look for a new reformation, which the Lord alone can bring about by his Spirit? Will the thirty-eight independent sovereignties, and as many State-churches of Germany which now mar its unity and divide its strength, ever be merged into one free powerful confederation, so as to become the thinking head and the beating heart of old and ever-renewing Europe? Will that noble country ever flourish like a garden of God; or has it seen its brightest days, and fulfilled its mission to the world? Are the many signs of progress and improvement the rays of the rising, or of the setting sun? Is not the new life of Christianity, after all, confined to a comparatively small number, and are not the masses of the people, in spite of all church diets, church counsels, church ordinances, church hymns, church books and church papers, fearfully alienated from the Church, and becoming more and more addicted to the degrading and disgraceful worship of Mammon? Are not the present agitations and commotions ominous of a new political and social convulsion that shall leave the revolution of 1848 far behind, and sweep away in its current church and state, priests and kings, to make room for anarchy and dissolution? Or are they the birth-throes simply of a new creation, and the final triumphs of the everlasting Gospel of love and peace?

We cannot look through the veil of the future. But we do know that the recent revival of evangelical theology and religion which we have described in this book, is not an empty dream, but a living reality, and that its conquests in the battle with error can never be lost. We know that the practical movements which resulted from it, have been an incalculable blessing to hundreds and thousands of immortal souls. Though the tree should die in the land of its birth, its fruitful seed has already taken root in other countries, full of hope and promise. The African church died away after she had produced her greatest divine and saint; but St. Augustine's theology and piety continued to live through the middle ages, and fertilized the soil of the Reformation, and are a rich source of instruction and edification to this day.

Dr. Wichern has adopted for his motto the words of the disciple who leaned on the Master's bosom: "Faith is the victory which overcometh the world." May the faith of the apostolic church, the faith which justifies and sanctifies the whole man, the faith which worketh by love, overcome all the countless and fearful foes who contend against it in the land of the Reformation. This is our concluding hope and prayer for Germany, and for the world.

FINIS.

www.ingramcontent.com/pod-product-compliance
Lightning Source LLC
LaVergne TN
LVHW011157110826
845150LV00006B/1240

9781425545512